Right in the
Old Gazoo

Right in the Old Gazoo

A Lifetime of Scrapping
with the Press

Alan K. Simpson

William Morrow and Company, Inc.

New York

It is the policy of William Morrow and Company, Inc., and its imprints and affiliates, recognizing the importance of preserving what has been written, to print the books we publish on acid-free paper, and we exert our best efforts to that end.

Library of Congress Cataloging-in-Publication Data

Simpson, Alan K.
Right in the old gazoo : a lifetime of
scrapping with the press / Alan K. Simpson.
p.   cm.
ISBN 0-688-11358-3
1. Press and politics—United States.   2. United States—Politics
and government—1981–1989.   3. United States—Politics and
government—1989–1993.   4. United States—Politics and government—1993–
I. Title.
PN4888.P6.S56   1997
071'.3'09045—dc20   96-25482
                                                                                   CIP

Printed in the United States of America

First Edition

2   3   4   5   6   7   8   9   10

BOOK DESIGN BY CAROLINE CUNNINGHAM

TO MOM AND POP
Milward and Lorna Simpson, loving parents,
who gave their two sons, Peter and Alan,
their finest gift—themselves

TO MY WIFE, ANN
All the woman there is—or ever was

ACKNOWLEDGMENTS

I very closely observed my two dear parents as they embarked upon and fulfilled a life of public service—to see whether it changed them in any way. It did not. They laid down the marker and I followed. God rest their souls.

I acknowledge the encouragement of the dearest brother a guy could ever have, Brother Pete and dear Sis-in-law Lynne. Generous, bighearted, kind, unselfish, and unfailing in their support.

The spirited "Go to it, Pop!" from three magnificent children: son Bill, his dear wife, Debbie; son Colin, "the bachelor middle child"; and daughter Susan Simpson Gallagher and her special husband, John. All anchors for us now in the wondrous town of Cody, Wyoming, where we will be returning after public life.

Dear and dazzling wife Ann, who has been painted herein in full lush brushstrokes! I ruined more than a couple of Christmas and Thanksgiving holidays for her while scratching this work together!

Mary Kay Hill, my former Senate press secretary for eight years from 1981 to 1989, who personally remembered many of the events portrayed here and jogged my memory on others. Thanks to her for helping me prepare the skeleton outline of this work and spending so many hours with the manuscript.

Senator Bill Cohen of Maine, a wonderful pal who gave me more tips than if I had been a waiter at "21"! Always there with solid advice, wise counsel, witty understanding, and always friendship.

David McCullough, while in the midst of penning another stirring and riveting book on American history took time to read the original cluttered manuscript and with the oil of friendship helped me so in filing away some of the rough edges of my first efforts!

Dick and Lynne Cheney, fellow campaigners and colleagues and dear and loyal friends who served side by side with us while representing our native state of Wyoming in this rambunctious public life we all chose.

Special thanks to Evora Williams, the most loyal of executive secretaries, who dragged my myriad dictation tapes back to her home on nights and weekends and holidays and plowed ahead— never on "company time." Some others who have done that are now languishing in durance vile! She simply could not have done more, helped more, or remembered more. A dear and unselfish woman.

To Mike Wilson who—after I had labored lonely and long over tens of thousands of words in grappling with this missive for hundreds of hours—at the request of the publisher, joined with me to "tighten" the manuscript. When he finished it was still all Simpson and a yard wide but a lot thinner! I would say, "Mike, what the hell happened to the story about Calamity Jane?" or "What about my days in Cranbrook with Templin Licklider and Ben Snyder?" or "What about that time at the White House?" His careful comment usually was "Loved it, but it won't fit!" A kind, patient, and very able journalist. There I've said it!

To all of them my deepest thanks. An adventure for me without equal and most surely rendered far less perilous by these wonderful people and so many others.

A sometimes trite, corny, hackneyed, inadequate, and overused two words—but from the heart—just *thank you*.

THE SOCIETY OF PROFESSIONAL JOURNALISTS

CODE OF ETHICS

The SOCIETY of Professional Journalists believes the duty of journalists is to serve the truth.

We BELIEVE the agencies of mass communication are carriers of public discussion and information, acting on their Constitutional mandate and freedom to learn and report the facts.

We BELIEVE in public enlightenment as the forerunner of justice, and in our Constitutional role to seek the truth as part of the public's right to know the truth.

We BELIEVE those responsibilities carry obligations that require journalists to perform with intelligence, objectivity, accuracy, and fairness.

To these ends, we declare acceptance of the standards of practice here set forth:

I. RESPONSIBILITY:

The public's right to know of events of public importance and interest is the overriding mission of the mass media. The purpose of distributing news and enlightened opinion is to serve the general welfare. Journalists who use their professional status as representatives of the public for selfish or other unworthy motives violate a high trust.

II. FREEDOM OF THE PRESS:

Freedom of the press is to be guarded as an inalienable right of people in a free society. It carries with it the freedom and the responsibility to discuss, question, and challenge actions and utterances of our government and of our public and private institutions. Journalists uphold the right to speak unpopular opinions and the privilege to agree with the majority.

III. ETHICS:

Journalists must be free of obligation to any interest other than the public's right to know the truth.

1.   Gifts, favors, free travel, special treatment, or privileges can compromise the integrity of journalists and their employers. Nothing of value should be accepted.

2.   Secondary employment, political involvement, holding public office, and service in community organizations should be avoided if it compromises the integrity of journalists and their employers. Journalists and their employers should conduct their personal lives in a manner that protects them from conflict of interest, real or apparent. Their responsibilities to the public are paramount. That is the nature of their profession.

3.   So-called news communications from private sources should not be published or broadcast without substantiation of their claims to news values.

4.   Journalists will seek news that serves the public interest, despite the obstacles. They will make constant efforts to assure that the public's business is conducted in public and that public records are open to public inspection.

5.   Journalists acknowledge the newsman's ethic of protecting confidential sources of information.

6.   Plagiarism is dishonest and unacceptable.

IV. ACCURACY AND OBJECTIVITY:

Good faith with the public is the foundation of all worthy journalism.

1.   Truth is our ultimate goal.

2.   Objectivity in reporting the news is another goal that serves as the mark of an experienced professional. It is a standard of performance toward which we strive. We honor those who achieve it.

3.   There is no excuse for inaccuracies or lack of thoroughness.

4.   Newspaper headlines should be fully warranted by the contents of the articles they accompany. Photographs and telecasts should give an accurate picture of an event and not highlight an incident out of context.

5.   Sound practice makes clear distinction between news reports and expressions of opinion. News reports should be free of opinion or bias and represent all sides of an issue.

6.   Partisanship in editorial comment that knowingly departs from the truth violates the spirit of American journalism.

7.   Journalists recognize their responsibility for offering informed analysis, comment, and editorial opinion on public events and issues. They accept the obligation to present such material by individuals whose competence, experience, and judgment qualify them for it.

8.   Special articles or presentations devoted to advocacy or the writer's own conclusions and interpretations should be labeled as such.

V. FAIR PLAY:

Journalists at all times will show respect for the dignity, privacy, rights, and well-being of people encountered in the course of gathering and presenting the news.

1.   The news media should not communicate unofficial charges affecting reputation or moral character without giving the accused a chance to reply.

2.   The news media must guard against invading a person's right to privacy.

3.   The media should not pander to morbid curiosity about details of vice and crime.

4.   It is the duty of the news media to make prompt and complete correction of their errors.

5.   Journalists should be accountable to the public for their reports and the public should be encouraged to voice its

grievances against the media. Open dialogue with our readers, viewers, and listeners should be fostered.

VI. MUTUAL TRUST:

Adherence to this code is intended to preserve and strengthen the bond of mutual trust and respect between American journalists and the American people.

The Society shall—by programs of education and other means—encourage individual journalists to adhere to these tenets, and shall encourage journalistic publications and broadcasters to recognize their responsibility to frame codes of ethics in concert with their employees to serve as guidelines in furthering these goals.

THE FAMOUS CREED

by Walter Williams

(Bronze plaque at the entrance to the National Press Club, Washington, D.C.)

I believe in the profession of journalism.

I believe that the public journal is a public trust; that all connected with it are, to the full measure of their responsibility, trustees for the public; that acceptance of lesser service than the public service is betrayal of this trust.

I believe that clear thinking and clear statement, accuracy, and fairness are fundamental to good journalism.

I believe that a journalist should write only what he holds in his heart to be true. I believe that suppression of the news, for any consideration other than the welfare of society, is indefensible.

I believe that no one should write as a journalist what he would not say as a gentleman; that bribery by one's own pocketbook is as much to be avoided as bribery by the pocketbook of another; that individual responsibility may not be escaped by pleading another's instructions or another's dividends.

I believe that advertising, news, and editorial columns should alike service the best interests of the readers; that a single standard of helpful truth and cleanness should prevail for all; that the supreme test of good journalism is the measure of its public service.

I believe that journalism which succeeds best—and best deserves success—fears God and honors man; is stoutly independent, unmoved by pride of opinion or greed of power, constructive, tolerant but never careless, self-controlled, patient, always respectful of its readers but always unafraid; is quickly indignant at injustice; is unswayed by the appeal of privilege or the clamor of the mob; seeks to give every man a chance and, as far as law and honest wage and recognition of human brotherhood can make it so, an equal chance; is profoundly patriotic while sincerely promoting international good will and cementing world-comradeship; is a journalism of humanity, and for today's world.

Contents

ga·zoo (ge-z$\overline{oo}$') *n., pl.* **os.** *Slang.* The south end of a horse going north.

CHAPTER ONE

Right in the
Old Gazoo

The morning of March 18, 1987, was a beautiful one, suffused with the powerful promise of another D.C. spring. I had no idea, as I headed to the White House for a meeting with President Ronald Reagan, that I was about to add a new word to the American vocabulary—and see a picture of my grimacing mug displayed in newspapers and on TV broadcasts from Washington to Walla Walla.

At the time I was assistant majority leader in the Senate, the party's number-two man behind Bob Dole. As such, I was among those who played a critical role in trying to push the president's agenda through Congress. That was plenty difficult work in those days because of the media's lurid fascination with the Iran-contra episode. Surely you remember that scandal. Some months earlier, it had been disclosed that our U.S. government had sold weapons to Iran—a mortal enemy—in exchange for the release of seven American hostages. What was more, U.S. officials went behind the backs of the Congress and funneled the proceeds to the contra freedom fighters in Nicaragua. It became apparent that National

Security Adviser John Poindexter and his loyal assistant, Lieutenant Colonel Oliver North, were the only ones who knew about the whole sinister plot. But the media weren't about to buy that. They were determined to prove the unprovable—that the president damn sure knew about, and signed off on, the deal. President Reagan entreated the Congress and the citizens to move ahead with other portions of his agenda, only to find the nation distracted by Iran-contra.

The media's irrational and obsessive behavior was on my mind that March morning as I ambled into the White House for the president's regularly scheduled meeting with Republican congressional leaders. Apparently I was not alone in my pique at the press. The meeting began as many had before, with the president and the leaders of the Senate and the House sitting about the great table in the Cabinet Room. As so often happens, the intrepid Washington media were then ushered in for a few questions and a brief "photo op." While the photographers were taking their shots, we took a few of our own. We began to fire jocular questions at the reporters, thus thwarting their efforts to shout questions at the president. Several Republican leaders offered pungent comments on what they perceived as the press's mishandling and manipulation of the Iran-contra story. Then the press excitedly exited and we plowed through the agenda.

After the meeting, we all filed out the driveway door of the west wing. As usual, there was a good gathering of reporters off to the right. They began to hail us to come on over and share our thoughts with them. One zealous, grim-visaged, steely-eyed fellow—apparently relatively new to the White House beat—seemed to have taken great offense at our earlier jokes. He said indignantly that we had interfered in the press's interrogation of the president, and even suggested that we had deliberately hindered the public's sacrosanct "right to know." I'd had a bellyful. It was all more than I could take.

"That's a bunch of crap," I hurled at him. That got his attention, so I kept right on going. "What kills me is that you go in there and have your good old fling and that's great. But you know very well that you're not asking him things so you can get answers.

You're asking him things because you know he's off balance and you'd like to stick it in his gazoo."

The reporters scribbled furiously. I probably should have stopped there, but I was on a roll.

"If I were Ronald Reagan I'd just step up at a news conference and say, 'Guys, while you're flunking the old saliva test, I've decided not to take a single question on Iran-contra.' And then I'd talk only about the budget and trade deficits."

Then I really did the unthinkable: I made a magnificently hideous and contorted face and unfurled it for the cameras, my fingers spiraled upward and gnarled like a gnome's.

"Here's the way you look as you go, 'Mr. President! Mr. President!' " I said this in an awful, petulant, whiny voice, the kind you hear from a two-year-old who ain't gettin' his way.

And my, oh my! That little outburst made for compelling television, I must admit. The still photographers also captured my visage in full twist. We politicians know the credo of the truly dedicated news photographer: "Keep taking 'em till you get a bad one!" They sure did. What I did made news everywhere. Too much news. My dear mother and dad saw it and were horrified. Mom called Mary Kay Hill, my press secretary, and sighed, "What did the reporters say or do to Al that he would make such a face?" I had startled my own mother.

Ben Bradlee, then the editor of the *Washington Post,* had a lot of fun with that picture. Ben is one tough cookie with a big heart, strong biases, and a wonderfully ribald and profane sense of humor. He has gigged me several times, but I like him. He sent me the photo with this letter:

The Washington Post

1150 15ᵀᴴ STREET, N.W.
WASHINGTON, D.C. 20071
(202) 334–6000

BENJAMIN C. BRADLEE
EXECUTIVE EDITOR
(202) 334–7510

March 20, 1987

The Honorable
Alan Simpson
U.S. Senate
Washington, D.C. 20510

Dear Alan:

I want you to know that we had a caption writing contest over here about this magnificent portrait. The winner to date:
" . . . and their hearts and minds shall follow".
This comes to you with affection and esteem.
I hate those barking questions.
It reminds me of feeding time at the seal pond in Central Park Zoo. I wish the president wouldn't turn around.

All the best,

Ben

Enc.

The picture wasn't the half of it. The press also seemed to be quite taken with the word "gazoo." A number of reporters indicated in follow-up articles that they had searched for a precise definition of the term. Some insisted that the word I had uttered—or had meant to utter (the media are all too happy to tell you what you meant to say)—was "bazoo," which is defined as "slang for referring to the nose." A *Washington Post* reporter quoted Frederic G. Cassidy, the editor in chief of the *Dictionary of American Regional English*. "Gazoo . . . gazoo," he pondered. "I don't know that one at all. I can't see what it would mean, except the same thing as 'bazoo.' He may just be misspeaking or making a slight variant on it. There isn't any evidence at all for 'gazoo.' "

Mark Russell, friend and comedian extraordinaire, got it exactly right. Like the others, Mark had failed to find a definition for "gazoo" in his dictionary. Still, ever the wry observer, he ventured the comment "I have been to Simpson's home state of Wyoming, and I have figured out that a gazoo is the Wyoming end of a horse facing Idaho!" A toy manufacturer later offered to send me one hundred kazoos, one for each senator. I declined. He misunderstood me. A gazoo is not a musical instrument—or at least is not supposed to be.

Certainly it was great fun to watch people research the meaning of that word. And yet I was trying to make a serious point. I was plumb fed up with the media—not just with their carping about Iran-contra, but also with their general cynicism and hypocrisy. After that day I spent almost another full decade in the Senate, finally announcing my retirement in December 1995. My feelings about the press only ripened during those years. In my view, the media—especially the overheated, Beltway-obsessed Washington media—have largely abandoned all basics of good journalism in favor of slanted, deceptive, and ruthlessly prosecutorial reporting. As a result, the public always gets the story, but seldom gets the truth. Damn seldom.

The media have awesome weapons at their disposal—the First Amendment, the almost limitless resources of the television networks and the huge newspaper companies, and so on. They use these weapons with far too little responsible concern. Many in

America's media elite have become lazy, complacent, sloppy, self-serving, self-aggrandizing, cynical, and arrogant beyond measure. We live in a society in which journalistic ethics—commitment to fairness, respect for privacy, even simple human compassion—all seem to take a seat way in the back of the bus. More and more reporters seem to be asking themselves, "Why just tell the story when I can slant it? Why report fairly on that guy when I can screw him?"

Let me tell you a story—a true one—that will illustrate what the media world has come to. A few years back I was visiting in my Washington office with dear old friends from my hometown of Cody, Wyoming. My friends were accompanied by their daughter, a young lady I had known since her birth. She had recently graduated from Columbia University, one of the top journalism schools in this country. In the course of a pleasant chat, I asked what this bright, intelligent, ambitious fledgling journalist planned to do with her life. She responded with a slow smile and a glint in her eye.

"I'm going to be one of the hunters," she said.

"What are you going to hunt?" I asked.

"People like you!" was her sharp retort.

That bowled me over. Here was this brand-new member of the craft, her degree still practically clutched in her moist, hot hand, and already she was loading and cocking her rifle, as if every person in public life deserved to be shot on sight. Is that the attitude that they teach journalism students at our best universities? Apparently. For a long time, I had been naive and goofy enough to believe that journalism was just as I had been taught it as a kid at Cody High, a sacred public trust that was supposed to give us nothing more and nothing less than the five W's—the who, what, where, when, and why. Little did I know that somebody had painted a target on my dome while I was sleeping and dreaming all that nonsense.

Instead of using the five W's to talk about journalism, maybe we need to use five C's, for the profession today is more interested in conflict, controversy, and cleverness than it is in clarity. During my last years in Congress, we passed bipartisan laws on unfunded mandates, lobbying, gift limits, disabilities, clean air and water, telecommunications, line item veto, immigration, and so on. And yet all we ever heard about in the media was gridlock. No wonder people think nothing gets done in Washington. Conflict, controversy, and cleverness almost always replace clarity in the news reports we watch and read. So what is that fifth C? The fifth C is for coiffure—the television newspeople must always have their hair carefully coiffed. Not that I'm jealous or anything like that!

Today's guardians of the First Amendment would have you believe that they are humble servants of the truth, mere protectors of the public's right to know. Don't believe it. Today's mass media are increasingly dominated by celebrity journalists who are often wealthier and more influential than the people they cover. Most thoughtful, observant, intelligent people know their names—Ted Koppel, Tom Brokaw, Peter Jennings, Dan Rather, David Brinkley, Connie Chung, Bob Woodward, Bob Novak, Sam Donaldson, Diane Sawyer, Lesley Stahl, David Broder, Andrea Mitchell, and on and on. These journalists and their powerful colleagues have lectured us for years about the public's right to know, and they have guarded that right by exposing the intimate private lives and peccadilloes of politicians and public figures far and wide. That is as it should be. And yet the private lives of the "hunters" remain mostly unknown. We may think we know these people; the truth is that we know almost nothing about their possible conflicts of interest and their deeply chambered biases. "But we are not elected officials," they often cry, and that is true. Still, if a high-octane journalist is paid thousands of dollars to speak to an interest group that he or she might later have to cover—and this happens all the time—wouldn't you like to have that information when evaluating that journalist's coverage? I would. But don't hold your breath waiting for the media stars to disclose that sort of thing. Put simply, a lot of people in the media have far lower ethical standards for themselves than they have for others. Some don't have any apparent ethical standards at all.

Nor is there any sure way that you will ever hear about the media's misdeeds. Yes, most newspapers print corrections, and several have reporters whose job is to cover the media. There are also several publications devoted to observing the observers. But unlike doctors, lawyers, accountants, cosmetologists, plumbers, and other professionals and craftsmen, journalists have no governing body that oversees their work and punishes them for their sins and mistakes. Unlike other professions or crafts relying greatly on a high degree of public trust, journalism has no reasonable method of measuring performance. No procedures for truly evaluating credibility and honesty. No testing from time to time, and no periodic certification. I think that is not good.

People in the popular news media will not like to hear me say that. When you complain to journalists about the dirt and sludge they sling at people, they quickly draw a copy of the First Amendment from their jacket pocket or purse and explain that they have a right to broadcast and print whatever they please. Fair enough. Trouble is, today's thin-skinned reporters seem to think the First Amendment applies only to them, not to us. Well, I heartily disagree. Over the years, I have gained a reputation as a fierce—and I hope thoughtful—critic of the nation's media. To put it another way, I have not been afraid to exercise my First Amendment right to criticize the media's abuse of the First Amendment. A lot of journalists see my criticisms as a threat to their profession and to them individually. How come they can criticize what we say but we can't object to what they say? That's sure a double standard, folks—and that is exactly the sort of thing I'm here to talk about.

Now, please, don't accuse me of trying to rewrite the Bill of Rights. Some journalists fear that's what I'm up to. Indeed, in recent years, many have said to me, "I hear you're writing a book about the media, and knowing you, I'm very concerned and disturbed about that."

"Why is that?" I always say.

"Well, I am wondering what you have in mind for us—what you want to do to curb or limit or restrict us."

I render my half-crooked smile and respond, "I haven't the slightest desire to curb, limit, or restrict you in any way—but I do intend to take some of your work and stick it in your ear! Surely that shouldn't bother you if I do it only in order to encourage public dialogue? I mean, you wouldn't want to do anything that would have a chilling effect on me, would you?" That always quiets them down.

Let me say it again: I have never proposed, and never would propose, that we restrict the media in any way. (Indeed, I am writing this book only because someone from the publishing company approached me at a forum for journalists and politicians and asked me to do it.) Rather, the media need to rein themselves in, for the good of their profession and the good of the nation. I think it is not healthy when the American people hold both the media and the Congress in low esteem—and as I write this, they most certainly do. A free society cannot properly function when citizens think the absolute worst about the news makers and the news reporters. Those in Congress will pay the price if they do not straighten up; the voters will oust them. Shouldn't journalists answer to someone? I am not suggesting they be licensed or otherwise regulated by the government. But it might be healthy for the media to balance their immense power by submitting to occasional independent reviews of their work. Journalists, like other professionals, need a standards board and a grievance committee.

And so I have appointed myself the chairman, High Panjandrum, Grand Inquisitor—and sole member—of a grievance committee of my own making. This book is the committee's final report. I feel uniquely qualified to write it. In a lifetime spent in politics, including nearly two decades in Washington, I have learned a bit about how the news media operate. Much of what I know I learned firsthand. I was there in the trenches for the press's Borking of a brilliant and highly qualified Supreme Court nominee, and for its whining, anti-American coverage of the Gulf War. I was a colleague of Gary Hart when some pesky, prowling Florida journalists caught him doing some monkey business, and I have seen many friends—including George Bush—hurt badly by the use of vindictive quotes from anonymous sources. Perhaps most famously (or infamously; you choose), I was among the key players at the Clarence Thomas–Anita Hill hearings, a media spectacle with no parallel this side of the O. J. Simpson trial. Those hearings made my bald head visible across the land and got me into a profane hissing match with one of America's best-known and most biased reporters. I have seen all kinds of media excess.

I have also made some dandy mistakes of my own, the most notable, and most regrettable, taking place during a prolonged dustup with the Cable News Network's Peter Arnett. I will own up to those errors in this book. We will all wait forever for the media to own up to most of theirs.

Having said all that, I should also say that I have had more than my share of satisfying experiences with the press. At various times in my career I have been a true darling of the media, lionized in print and glorified on the tube. Even now, I am always honored to be on *Larry King Live*, do *Nightline*, *The McNeil/Lehrer NewsHour* (now just Jim!), *Face the Nation*, *Meet the Press,* and *This Week with David Brinkley*, and serve as a steady on-the-record source for many ink-stained wretches. I have plenty of friends in the media, and probably will still have some even after this book is published. I would like to believe the media seek me out because of my policy-making wisdom and my ruddy good looks, but probably it is because I sometimes don't know when to stuff a sock in my mouth. This book, I suppose, is the ultimate proof of that. The point is that I have also seen plenty of good in the media, which I believe gives me the perspective I need to point out the bad.

In the front of this book, I reprint "The Famous Creed," by Walter Williams. A copy of this fine document hangs near the elevator at the National Press Club in Washington. Williams refers to journalism as "a public trust," and says that "a journalist should write only what he holds in his heart to be true." I often wonder how many journalists have actually read those words, or the words of the SPJ "Code of Ethics" that are there too. Probably a hell of a lot of them. I wonder how many of them really understood them—probably a similar number. I wonder how many honestly live by them. A hell of a lot fewer than I first thought when I came to this village on the Potomac.

In the course of this book, I'll gingerly suggest a few ways in

which journalists could do better by all of us. But this is not intended merely as an instruction manual. Hey, I want to have a
little fun here, too! Certainly the media like to stick it to us. And
so, when it's appropriate to do so, I'm going to stick it to them—
right in the old gazoo.

CHAPTER TWO

The Wisdom of Miss Gertrude Smith

I learned about good old-fashioned journalism from a good old-fashioned woman. Her name was Miss Gertrude Smith. I wish more of today's fledgling journalists could have a teacher just like her.

Miss Smith was my teacher at Cody High School in Cody, Wyoming, a historic little town founded by the Great Scout himself, William F. "Buffalo Bill" Cody. My hometown is also the proud home of the Buffalo Bill Historical Center, repository for much fascinating Buffalo Bill memorabilia, and of the Whitney Gallery of Western Art, showplace for original works by Frederic Remington, Charlie Russell, Albert Bierstadt, Alfred Jacob Miller, Joseph Sharp, and others. Just fifty-two miles down the road from Cody is the East Gate Entrance to Yellowstone National Park. My father, Milward L. Simpson, a former Wyoming governor and U.S. senator, always described Cody as the Athens of the West. With a 1990 population of 7,987, Cody is far removed from the hustle and bustle, the hype and hoorah, of the nation's great population centers. Life there today really is not too much different from life there in the 1940s, when I was learning about journalism from Gertrude Smith.

Miss Smith (we never dreamed of calling her Gertrude) must have been really over the hill—about sixty years old—when I knew her. She was single and always had been, so far as we in her class knew. Her one true passion, it seemed to us, was teaching. Just teaching. She was a gentle, firm, and thoughtful woman, with gray eyes that widened and sparkled when she felt that one of us duds had finally caught on to something she was trying to teach us. Those eyes were her only youthful characteristic. She was stoop-shouldered and walked with a shuffle. Her crinkly, stringy gray hair was always pulled tautly to the back of her head in a rather stark manner, and she had a wattle of loose skin that hung comically below her chin. Sometimes we would make fun of her appearance, as wiseacre young kids are wont to do. One day she turned her back to write something on the board, and right away we all gleefully started in on her. We belched, farted, laughed, waved our hands, made faces, you name it. While we carried on like the crude knuckleheads we were, this fine, frail person continued to scrawl the day's lesson on the blackboard. Then, suddenly, she stopped, turned, and explained something that put an end to our antics . . . for good.

"I would hope," she said crisply, "that all of you students may come to realize that when a person who wears glasses, as I do, is facing a dark blackboard, that person can see very clearly what is going on behind her!"

No, there is not one of us in the Cody High School Class of 1949 who will ever forget her steadiness of purpose, those radiantly sharp eyes, and that voice, a voice of unusually low key and timbre.

In addition to her regular teaching duties, Miss Smith also advised and counseled the aspiring young journalists—including yours truly—who served with pride on the weekly high school newspaper, the *Bronc Hi-Lights*. It was from Miss Smith that I learned the basic tenets of journalism. She taught us that the practice of the craft rests on this simple foundation: who, what, where, when, and why. We were taught that readers simply wanted us to answer those questions in a clear and straightforward way. Our opinion was not important and did not belong in our stories. We were not to color our stories in any way. Just the facts, please. Opinion was for the opinion pages only. If we wanted to share our own thoughts with our readers, we could write something up, identify it as an opinion piece, and publish it on the editorial pages. Otherwise, we were to keep our opinions to ourselves, and out of our work. There was nothing revolutionary or innovative about what she taught us. She was giving us Journalism 101, the basics, the stuff every cub reporter must know before he or she hits the streets. I don't know if anybody teaches Journalism 101 anymore, but seeing the work product of today's journalists, I damn sure have my doubts.

But what Miss Smith taught us went way beyond the basics. She also taught us the worth of being direct, honest, and forthright in our work, not sneaky or manipulative. She urged us to treat our subjects decently, not to get our kicks by making fun of them or belittling them. (Many journalists I know have completely for-gotten that lesson—else they never learned it.) Miss Smith taught us that journalists wield a powerful and potentially devastating in-strument—a pen or a pencil. These instruments could be used as wands to create wonderment, or as weapons to maim or skewer. And she clearly believed that it was beneath us—beneath any de-cent, conscientious journalist—to wield the scrivener's tools as weapons. To her, journalism was a sacred trust, and journalists an important part of society. It was essential that they know their own strength—that they know the good they could do, and the harm.

When I was eighteen, Miss Smith asked me if I would like to be the sports editor of the *Hi-Lights*. I immediately took refuge in my old "aw, shucks" routine, but the truth is that I was thrilled. Like a lot of boys in Cody, I was crazy about sports. So I took the job. In my senior year I covered the thrilling wins and heartbreak-ing defeats of Cody High's football and basketball teams. The Broncs never read a discouraging word written by this scribe. I was a loyal supporter of the hometown team, the mighty blue and gold.

Of course I was—for I wore the colors, too.

That's right—in addition to covering the teams, I was a member of the football team and was captain of the basketball squad. I played the games and then interviewed myself when they were over. You might well imagine, then, the exciting and vivid press coverage of my athletic skills. Not that I was biased or anything. When I wrote about my own sterling performance on the basketball court—"Lanky, gifted Al Simpson pumped in 18 points for the victorious Broncs"—I was, of course, being completely objective and detached. American newspaper readers had never seen such a paragon of journalistic integrity.

I am joshing, of course. Who in hell can be objective when he has such a tremendous stake in what he is covering? Nobody. Everything I wrote about the Cody Broncs was tainted and tinted by my own passions, beliefs, and prejudices. I'm sure Miss Smith would have preferred to have someone from the outside covering sports—no doubt she understood the potential ethical conflicts inherent in having a basketball player assess his own play in print—but Cody High was a small school and didn't really have any outsiders. That's high school journalism for you. Things are different in the professional journalism ranks. Today's journalists don't cover the U.S. Senate while also trying to serve in it. Indeed, many of them go to great lengths to give the appearance of being objective. Some even register to vote as Independents so they will appear not to be favoring either major party. Some do not register to vote at all, reasoning that merely casting a ballot would compromise their pristine objectivity.

But truly, these people often are not much more objective than I was when I was covering sports for the *Bronc Hi-Lights*. It doesn't take any sensible politician ten minutes in the presence of a modern journalist to know pretty well which side he or she is on. My lack of objectivity as a high school journalist was not a shocker. I was, after all, just a kid writing for an audience of kids. The lack of objectivity of today's professional scribes can have much more serious effects—it can distort reality and warp public policy.

There's a surprise ending to the story of my high school journalism exploits. Quite unbeknownst to me, Miss Smith had entered several of my sports columns in the national Quill and Scroll writing contest. Damned if I didn't win the award for Best Sports

Story in the state of Wyoming. Again I pretended the award was no big deal, but in truth I was really tickled. Still, it was ironic. I had merrily and brazenly violated one of the fundamental principles of journalism—and now had won a nice award for having done so. Had I thought of it, I could have written an article describing my own journalistic greatness, thereby completing the circle of lost objectivity.

I was hardly the first person in my family to form ideas about the media. My grandfather William L. "Billy" Simpson was the first recorded member of the family to declare, "The boobs just don't get it right!" Billy Simpson, a lawyer, was a ruddy, bald-headed human Mount Vesuvius who wore a gold watch chain and double-breasted suits with cigar-ash scars on the vest. He worked hard, played hard, gambled hard, drank hard, and practiced law hard. And when he thought the press was being unfair, he fought back hard. In the late thirties and early forties, Billy—always known as "Popoo" to his grandchildren—watched suspiciously as industrialist John D. Rockefeller moved into Teton County, Wyoming, under the corporate guise of an outfit called the Snake River Land and Cattle Company. Rockefeller was quietly assembling the vast acreage that he would later present to the United States as Grand Teton National Park. That may sound wonderful now, but Popoo saw nothing wonderful then in what those "rich Easterners" were up to. Please understand that public ownership of our wide-open spaces in Wyoming was, and surely still is, anathema to many who enjoy the Western life. Popoo saw what Rockefeller was doing to be a grave threat to the ability of Wyoming residents to control their own land—and their destiny.

Popoo also felt that the local paper was kowtowing to the Rockefeller outfit. He believed that readers should be warned that all the good ranch land was going to be turned over to the detested feds. If this happened, he thought, people would never again be able to pass on their precious land to their kids, or raise hay and cattle, or live the kind of lives they had come to Jackson Hole to enjoy. The local rag refused to tell it that way, so Popoo started his own thoroughly biased rag—the *Grand Teton*. While it had a brief life, the paper masterfully served the purpose of its crusty creator, publisher, and editor, which was solely to tell his side of the story. Now, that's manipulating the media!

My mom and pop were also briefly involved in the press, but in a more serious way. During World War II, when the town was short of men and women to carry on the business of the community, the folks would often contribute pieces to the local paper, the *Cody Enterprise*. Pop was too old to serve in the war, though he desperately wanted to; working for the *Enterprise* was another way to help out. In those different times, publishing a newspaper was not seen as some noble deed performed primarily in service to the First Amendment or to the public's ever-present right to know. Instead, publishing the newspaper was simply a way of providing much-needed information and of unifying the town during a time of war. There was precious little glory to be found in having a byline in the paper. While the *Cody Enterprise* really struggled in those years—more than once, the townspeople had to contribute money just to keep it going—it continued to serve the community well, and today stands tall as Cody's oldest continuing business. Watching my parents work on the *Cody Enterprise,* I gained a lot of respect for the good a newspaper can do—a lesson that was repeated to me with gusto and great gravity by Miss Gertrude Smith.

I graduated in pretty good standing from Cody High in 1949. I very much wanted to go straight to the University of Wyoming, but my parents had other ideas. In those early postwar years, the average age at the university was twenty-two or twenty-three, because so many veterans were enrolling under the GI Bill. Mom and Pop figured—correctly—that all those hard-drinking, fun-loving vets might corrupt me even more than I was already corrupting myself. So instead of sending me to our only state university, Pop shipped me off to Cranbrook School, a prep school near Detroit. Cranbrook is now a coeducational institution (its full name is Kingswood-Cranbrook-Brookside), but in those days it was a boys' school. Pop's old friend Jack Bugas, a vice president of Ford Motor Company, promised to regulate my spirited habits there.

I never worked for the student newspaper at Cranbrook, because I was too busy with other things, by which I mean goofing off royally. And yet I still got my name in the paper. Every now and then, one of the fellows from the newspaper, called the *Crane,* would approach someone on campus and do a brief interview. Once, a friend on the newspaper staff hailed me and asked, "Are you wishing for a white Christmas?" After mumbling for a few minutes and slipping up to my chamber to consult the dictionary, I returned and said, "Ah yes, to once again witness the earth swathed in a hoary blanket of precipitation at yuletide would convoke my loftiest aspirations!" My reporter friend drew his coat and scarf about him and stalked off, muttering that what he really wanted was a simple answer involving how homesick I was. It was then that I began to see how much fun one could have with the press. As much as I sometimes dislike journalists' cynicism and meanness, I have truly come to enjoy my give and take with them—especially when I give more than I have to take.

I have found in my travels that journalists as a group are serious people. Sometimes when I come at them with a good riff of humor they don't know what the hell to do with it. Certainly there are many exceptions. But most of the journalists I meet seem to be engrossed in grave, tortured, serious thought. I often think that they would do a better job, and enjoy themselves more, if they would just lighten up a bit.

After my year at Cranbrook—a damn enjoyable one at a damn fine school during which I ballooned to 245 pounds, thanks mostly to the discovery of Patrick Henry Malt Liquor—I enrolled at last in my beloved University of Wyoming, home of the Cowboys. There I began the studies that would lead me into the law and later into politics. But I also continued to study the media, both as interviewer and as interviewee.

The years at the University of Wyoming in Laramie were growing-up years for me. I spent six memorable years at that fine land-grant institution obtaining a Bachelor of Science in Law (no longer conferred) and a Juris Doctor degree. In addition to wearing the brown and gold for the varsity football and basketball teams, I was president of the "W" Club, a men's athletic honorary, and was also elected a member of the Student Senate to represent the

College of Liberal Arts. Because I was involved in so many things, and because I was, I suppose, considered to be someone with leadership traits, I often had occasion to be mentioned in the press. I was not always happy about it then, either. My clashes with the media did not begin in Washington but in Laramie. Those who have known me for over the full span of my adult political life say I have one very grave, easily definable, testy tendency: I tend to go off like a firecracker when a distortion, inaccuracy, or just plain damned lie is written about me.

I first discovered this trait during the University of Wyoming Student Senate elections of 1954. At the time, the student government had adopted a complicated system for weighing votes and determining senate representation among the different colleges, such as Liberal Arts, Agriculture, Engineering, and Education. I had been appointed to the elections committee of the Student Senate and was therefore one of those charged with monitoring the elections and gleaning the results. Because the system was so complex, it took us quite some time to figure out who had won. After some delay, we released the names of the victors in some of the student election races without also releasing the complete vote totals, which we did not yet have. All candidates were well known personally to the elections committee. Some of our friends won and some of them were hammered.

When we did not immediately release the actual vote totals, the university's student newspaper, the *Branding Iron,* saw something sinister. Surely we were withholding the vote totals for some nefarious reason; we could not have done it simply because they had not been completely tallied. In an editorial plastered on page one, the editors of the *Branding Iron* branded us crooked. According to the editorial, "some students think" that "maybe somebody's best friend got into office without an official ballot count," or "maybe the elections committee thought it was too much trouble to count the numerous votes." And who were these "some students" who thought such terrible things? The editorial didn't say. Yes, these budding journalists were going to do well in the shadowy world of the press.

The author of the piece was the student editor, Paul Holtz.

Years later, Paul served splendidly as executive secretary to Wyoming's well-loved and respected governor Cliff Hansen. And when Cliff became a Wyoming U.S. senator, Paul went along as his administrative assistant. After that, Paul served me loyally and most ably as my legislative director, and as the top transition member of my staff during my early months in the United States Senate. Small world, eh? Obviously our relationship took a cheerful turn for the better after our college days. But back in 1954, I was just plain po'd at him.

After reading the *Branding Iron* editorial, I sought out the chairman of the elections committee and told him how I felt about the piece. He felt the same. Then the chairman and I and a third member of our committee sat down and banged out a response. Our letter dinged the *Branding Iron* pretty hard: I hand-delivered the stink bomb to Paul. At first, Paul wasn't willing to publish our screed on page one, where he'd had his and we wanted ours. But he finally relented, and I experienced for the first time the rare thrill of sticking it to the press in just the same way—and same place—as it likes to stick it to us. Forty years later, I still feel a rush whenever I sit down to fire off a volley at some reporter or editor who has gone too far.

A lot of people—friends and critics alike—have told me over the years that my insistence on lobbing 'em back when I am fired upon is evidence that I have thin skin. True enough. I am thin-skinned. So are a lot of the journalists I have met, beginning with the student editors of the *Branding Iron* whom we chided back in '54. I have also been advised many times to keep my mouth shut on the theory that one should never pick a fight with somebody who buys ink by the barrel. If you criticize the media, they'll often come at you even harder. I have learned that lesson well—the hard way! If writing a letter to the editor makes me a masochist, writing this book must make me the Job of our times.

Many years later I participated in a spirited public discussion presented by the Joan Shorenstein Barone Center on Press, Politics, and Public Policy. I am proud to serve as a member of the senior advisory board of that fine organization, which is affiliated with Harvard University's John F. Kennedy School of Government. I guess you could call me its resident goad. In that forum I related something I had learned in my college days—that an attack unanswered is an attack believed. At that point, the ever-alert Bob Squires spoke up. Bob—adviser and consultant to Democrats far and wide and especially left—said, "Simpson, I'll go you one better. An attack unanswered is an attack agreed to." At that moment, I found myself in the unlikely and surprising position of agreeing completely with Bob Squires. That was a first, and probably a last.

I finished college in 1954 and immediately married my dear Ann, a native of the little town of Greybull, Wyoming. The first time I ever saw her, she was waving the blue-and-gold pom-poms of the Greybull Buffalos at a high school basketball tournament. She is just as beautiful today as she was then. She is so many wonderful things. Wise. Trusting. Gracious. Intelligent. Stunning. Exciting. Sexual. Smart. Witty. Sensible. Kind. Direct. Nurturing. Loving. I'm an awfully lucky guy, and I know it. Knew it then, too.

That was a big year for me and my family. Also in 1954, my father, Milward L. Simpson, was elected governor of Wyoming. Pop, as I always called him, was born in the primitive grandeur of Jackson Hole, Wyoming, on November 12, 1897. As a kid he lived with his parents, William L. "Popoo" and Margaret L. "Nanny" Simpson, in the small frontier towns of Jackson, Lander, Meeteetse, and Cody. He went to high school in Cody, college at the University of Wyoming, and law school at Harvard. He briefly practiced law with his dad in Thermopolis—irritating the old man by hanging a shingle painted "Simpson and Father." In 1929 he married my beautiful mother, Lorna—the daughter of a Dutch coal mine owner who founded the now–ghost town of Kooi, Wyoming. They headed back to Cody. My dear and loving only brother, Peter, was born to them in 1930, I in 1931. He opened a law practice that would eventually include this son and two of his grandsons, William and Colin. My father spent his whole life in and around politics. And now, in 1954, he was making the transition from country lawyer to frontier-state governor. His experiences in that office would shape many of my views of public service—and of the press.

A few days after Pop's election in 1954, I reported for military duty at Fort Benning, Georgia. Soon I was shipped off to Germany for a tour of eighteen months. In 1956, Ann and I returned to Laramie, where I attended law school. I passed the bar in 1958. I was preparing to move east to enroll in the New York University tax school when events unfolded that would immediately and drastically change my plans.

I could see by early September of that year that dear Pop was in a difficult—if not doomed—race for reelection as governor. His opponent, a fine lawyer named Joe Hickey from Rawlins and Cheyenne, had kept nailing Pop with straight jabs, flurries, and left hooks. I said to Ann, "I have a bad hunch that Pop is going to get beat, and I'm not sure if I want to do this postgraduate work in tax law, since I don't know tax law from a left-handed hook shot"—a basketball shot I never mastered. "But I sure know Pop is in for a real tough one, and I feel I ought to stay here in Wyoming and help him out."

Ann responded with her typical class, style, wisdom, and common sense. "The decision is yours. But you don't want to be studying in New York and see your dad beaten and know you could have contributed something that might have turned it around." So I stayed in Wyoming.

I learned a good bit about politics and the press that year. Indeed, I learned more than I ever wanted to know about the ability of the media to distort and manipulate the facts—and at the same time warp the public's perception of certain people. That same fall, Frank Barrett, Wyoming's steady, constituent-centered, conservative Republican senator, was up for reelection. Somewhere along the line, Barrett had made the enemies list of the syndicated columnist Drew Pearson, whose name still makes some old-timers shudder. A few days before the '58 election, Pearson wrote in his national column that Barrett was guilty of criminal and unethical wrongdoing in a tax situation. The charge was heatedly denied, but of course it received great attention in Wyoming. Indeed, it came to dominate the campaign at a critical moment. Barrett lost the election by a whisker—1,913 votes—to my former American History professor at the University of Wyoming, Dr. Gale W.

McGee, who served Wyoming honorably, capably, and with distinction for eighteen years thereafter.

Pearson's story was not true. He admitted that himself. After
the election, the intrepid, ignoble, and arrogant Pearson curtly
apologized to Barrett for getting his facts wrong. But the apology
did not undo the results of the election. Indeed, I'm sure Pearson
was pleased with himself. Without even troubling to publish a true
story, he had ensured the defeat of his old enemy. That was a hell
of a disservice to his readers, and to the Wyoming body politic.

At the same time, Ann and I were witnessing the collapse of
Pop's reelection campaign. Joe Hickey kept attacking, but Pop
never fought back—a real mistake. Pop had a wonderfully loyal
executive secretary named Bob McManis, an earthy, savvy, salt-
of-the-earth guy with finely honed political instincts. The two of
us tried to prod Pop to strike back, but he refused. I never forgot
that lesson.

Pop was also getting hammered in the press—but not unfairly.
He was richly criticized for what I considered his strong and prin-
cipled stand against capital punishment. I disagreed with him, but
respected his point of view. As governor, he had commuted several
death sentences—not the best way to endear yourself to voters in
the old vigilante country of Wyoming! He was also damned in
print for the choice of location of a federal interstate highway (a
choice he didn't make), for the closing down of gambling houses
in Jackson Hole, and for his fresh, strong, direct, and stubborn
personality. I witnessed that last one up close. During the closing
days of the campaign, a reporter asked him, "Governor Simpson,
do you think you have been treated fairly by the press?" Pop said
unhesitatingly, "I sure have. I just wish you hadn't said what I'd
said!" I loved my father's candidness, along with just about everything else about him.

Pop went down the tubes with Senator Barrett in '58, losing
by 2,582 votes. After that, he returned home to Cody, where he
and I went into the practice of law together. I really didn't know
whether Pop would ever run for anything again. He was stung
hard by that defeat. Still, he eventually put a cheerful spin on what
had happened. "I would rather be a lamppost right here in Cody,

Wyoming, than have all of the honors this state could ever confer at home or away," he would say. Little did he know what turns his life would take.

There were now some pretty damn popular people holding public office in Wyoming—U.S. Senator Gale McGee, U.S. Senator Joseph C. O'Mahoney, Governor Joe Hickey, Secretary of State Jack Gage. They were strong and well regarded. The trouble was, they all belonged to the wrong party!

The single bright shining Republican light was our fine congressman, a beloved and spirited young man named Keith Thomson. In 1960, Keith ran for the U.S. Senate and was elected big. But almost immediately after his election, tragedy struck—Keith died in the office of his old friend Kenny Bailey, an accountant who worked just down the hall from Pop and me. What a blow that was. This rugged symbol of energy, independence, and vitality was gone—long before we were ready to let him go.

You could hear the political wheels start cranking immediately. In politics, death never gets in the way. Pop's former opponent, Joe Hickey, governor for two years now, suddenly had the responsibility of filling, by appointment till the next general election, a vacant seat in the U.S. Senate. Hickey wanted the job for himself. He could hardly appoint himself to the job, though, so he resigned the governorship, automatically making Secretary of State Jack Gage the new governor. One of Jack's first official acts was—you got it—to appoint his friend Joe Hickey to the Senate. That kind of caper really never has worked out well in politics. It didn't work in Wyoming either.

Soon after Joe appointed himself, I saw Pop standing with hands in pockets, looking out the window of our law office at one of those incredible Western sunsets. He had that look in his eyes, and I knew what he was thinking.

"Pop," I said, "if you're going to get into politics again, at least let me be your campaign manager."

He said, "Let's go get 'em, boy!"

And we really did. In 1962, we put together a damn good strong campaign with some awfully good people who worked like dogs for Pop. Among them was a young man fresh out of the

University of Wyoming law school who went on to serve his country loyally, energetically, and controversially as secretary of interior—James G. Watt.

Pop was duly elected to the United States Senate in 1962, and so he and Mom headed off to Washington. Although immediate family members were still allowed to serve as paid administrative assistants or staffers in those days, Pop and I agreed that I should not accompany him to Washington. Instead, Ann and I stayed there in our beloved Cody, where I continued to pour my energy into the practice of law. We also continued to raise a dear family: Bill had been born to us in Laramie on February 24, 1957; Colin entered the world early on March 5, 1959; and Susie came just seven weeks after the election, on December 27, 1962.

It was in Wyoming that I had my first significant experience with what has become a fine friend and occasionally a bitter enemy—television. One day in July 1964, I received a call from my old college friend Jack Rosenthal, a bright and articulate man who then owned Wyoming's first and only statewide television station, KTWO. (He has since sold the TV station but now owns a 50,000-watt clear-channel radio station with the same call letters.) Jack told me, "We're going to provide some great statewide primary-election-night coverage on KTWO. Our signal reaches almost all of Wyoming now, and I want you to be there as an analyst throughout the night." I tried not to sound too excited when I said yes, but I couldn't really contain my enthusiasm. I was greatly looking forward to sharing my ideas and views on that still-young (in Wyoming, anyway) communications medium whose true power was still not fully known.

And yet I had a pretty fair idea about its power even then. As I drove from Cody to Casper for the broadcast, I began to think about how much was at stake. A good showing on statewide television could only help me later in any run for elected office, should I decide to tread my father's career path and go into state or national politics. And a bad night could hurt any public perception and sour chances of ever going into public service. This was not an off-the-cuff speech at a rubber-chicken dinner. This was an entire evening spent talking to the whole state. Anything could happen. About twenty miles outside of Casper, I stopped at a remote phone booth and called Jack to tell him I would be there soon; I'd had a late start. Apparently Jack had been reading my mind. He said, "Hurry on, Al, we're going to have a hell of a lot of fun—and we're going to get your name and face aired around this state too. Never know when it will come in handy!"

We went on the air on KWTO in the early evening of August 18, 1964, and stayed on for several hours. All through the night, folks from Wyoming's twenty-three counties called in election returns, and we quickly began to analyze them for our viewers. We tried hard to talk like the pundits who appeared on the national political shows even then—the savvy, wizened "insiders" who analyzed the news for the poor, dull, addled masses. Yes, we were all doing our best imitations of those guys, and enjoying ourselves to boot. We used charts and diagrams. We told jokes and made predictions. Maybe most of all we talked about some of the political figures who had represented the Cowboy State. We spoke of U.S. Senator Francis E. Warren, whose daughter married General John C. "Black Jack" Pershing, and of U.S. Senator Joseph C. O'Mahoney, the great liberal statesman and trust-buster who served in the time of Franklin Roosevelt. We even told some good stories about my dear pop, who was U.S. senator then. Jack Rosenthal had christened him "the GAT"—Great American Tourist—because he was always traveling somewhere. I felt so exhilarated that I hardly noticed the camera. Indeed, I was surprised at how easy being on TV was for me. And I couldn't help thinking that my appearance that night helped the people of Wyoming get to know me, and maybe even like me. Here I was appearing in people's living rooms after the dinner hour, and I was really pumped up! I had done it.

Things have changed. Gone are the times when all a politician had to do was be seen on TV in order to have some degree of credibility in the public mind. The American public watches television now with an increasingly discerning and critical eye. The medium still has the power to glorify politicians, but more and more it seems to diminish them. We all saw what happened to the usually solid Gerald Ford when he "misspoke" his answer to a question about Eastern Europe, Poland, and Communism. We all tensed up as Michael Dukakis was asked what he would do if his wife, Kitty, was raped and murdered. When he answered that bizarre question in his cool, almost detached way, people saw him in a new way, and not a flattering one either.

But back in 1964, long before those events, I was only too happy to chatter away on the tube. I liked doing it and felt I had something important to say. I also saw television as a powerful way to share my ideas, beliefs, and dreams with larger numbers of people—people I was beginning to think I would like to serve.

CHAPTER THREE

Persistence

I began my own political career a couple of years after Mom and Pop moved to Washington. In 1964, when I was thirty-three, I was elected to the Wyoming house of representatives. It was a terrific place to learn about lawmaking—and about dealing with the Fourth Estate.

The Wyoming legislature was, and is, a remarkable place—a blend of Democrats and Republicans, conservatives and liberals, ranchers, radio announcers, businessmen and businesswomen, teachers, retired teachers, teachers-to-be, accountants, professors, and lawyers. Wyoming is probably one of the few states that can still honestly say it has a citizen legislature. This is—by God—government by the people and for the people, and the people did not let us forget it. Years ago, Wyoming voters decided to exercise control over their lawmakers by setting a forty-day limit to the length of a legislative session. All the business of that vast and diverse state had to be done in less than six weeks. For us as legislators, that sometimes meant working round the clock. We used to joke that the session lasted forty days—and eighty nights. Those were extremely intense and concentrated legislative sessions. Nothing I have experienced in Washington—not even the two-hundred-plus-day marathons we routinely run—has ever left me as pooped out as those sessions in Cheyenne. On a couple of occasions, we all realized that the last hour of the last day was going to drain away without our having finished our work. So we did what we had to do: One of us stood on a chair and jammed a broom handle into the face of the clock above the speaker's chair. Years later, the Wyoming Supreme Court ruled sagely that the broomstick trick was against the law. But it was a caper that came in mighty handy during my tour of duty.

And the time limit was just one of the restrictions placed on us. Wyoming's constitution even requires the legislators always to balance the budget—something we sure as hell didn't ever accomplish in Washington as long as I was there. What's more, the governor has the line-item veto. Often we would painstakingly arrive at a compromise, only to have the governor turn the bill into Swiss cheese. Probably it's heresy even to discuss such ideas as these inside the Washington Beltway—but these things really do work out there in the real world. Both measures have served Wyoming well.

When I arrived in Cheyenne for my first session, the Democrats were in the majority in the house of representatives for the first time in twenty-five years. The speaker was Walter Phelan, a gregarious, steady, cerebral, big-hearted, expansive man. If death had not taken him at a young age, he might someday have become governor. Phelan was fair and firm and marvelous to work with. He told me, "I'll treat you right. Just get in there and get down to work. Pull your share. We need all the good heads in both parties so we can come together and try to get this old state running right." That sounded good to me. Before long, I became involved in some spirited political scraps, but like Walter Phelan, I tried always to fight fair and to carry no grudges.

It wasn't possible to carry grudges anyway. We lived and worked in such close quarters in Cheyenne that you simply had to put aside your differences to get the job done. During the session, many lawmakers stayed at the Hitching Post Inn, a wonderful lodging owned and operated by Harry and Mildred Smith and their son Paul. Each night after work—if we weren't working into the night—members of both political parties and quite a few thirsty Wyoming citizens would check their partisan handguns, dirks, knucks, and daggers at the door and throw back a few drinks at the "Hitch" bar. I might even have been there once or twice myself. Still, my consumption level had dwindled considerably in the ten years since college. At the University of Wyoming, I weighed 260, had hair, and thought beer was food. By the time I was elected to the legislature, I had dropped much of the weight and most of the hair. I had also figured out that Bud was not dinner.

I did not stay at the Hitching Post Inn. Instead, I rented an apartment downtown, near the capitol. I found I had to be by myself in order to research an issue, form my opinions, and craft my own legislation. I also wrote my own bills, something I have never done as a United States senator. I pasted, cut, and cobbled them together—and saw them made into law. Writing those things was a lot of work, considering that I was also attending hearings, participating in floor debates, and trying desperately to keep up with my correspondence. Still, I felt damn good about being so productive.

And yet all was not well. The letters from my constituents told me so. Again and again, the people who had elected me would write me letters saying, "Al, why are you doing this?" or "How in the world could you ever have passed this one?" These people were really upset. The trouble was that they did not really understand the issues they were writing about. That was not their fault. My constituents were reading about my legislative activities in the *Casper Star-Tribune,* the state's largest daily, the *Wyoming Tribune-Eagle* in Cheyenne, or the *Billings Gazette,* a Montana paper that had a heap of readers in the northern part of Wyoming. From my little apartment in Cheyenne, it was easy to see what was happening. The news coverage did not accurately reflect the real work of the legislature. And as I looked into what was happening, I could see that some organizations in the Wyoming media had their least experienced people covering some of the toughest issues. Some of the reporters simply did not know what they were doing. There we would be, going at full tilt on some piece of legislation, eyes blazing with enthusiasm, and up to us would come some pool-table-green reporter who had been on the job for maybe six months. "Can I ask you a few questions, Representative Simpson?" Sure, I always said. What could go wrong?

I soon found out. When good reporters ask you good questions, you realize how much they know. And that's impressive. When bad reporters ask you bad questions, you know right away that they don't know a damn thing. I had the latter experience a bit too often in Cheyenne. I would make the mistake of thinking that the reporters who approached me were just as interested as I was in the work we lawmakers had been doing that day. It never took long to see that I was wrong. Instead of asking questions about the day's legislation—stuff readers should care about, stuff that touched their lives—the reporters would generally ask about some minor but obvious disagreement between a couple of legislators, or about some "sexy" but insignificant bill that was either sure to pass or sure not to. When offered a plate of T-bone, these reporters always seemed to eat the parsley.

Let me give you an example. During my early days in the legislature, we worked hard on some strong and sensible mined-land-reclamation laws. The work was as complicated as its name would suggest. The bills were all about mining practices and types of reclamation, the moving of soil, the placing of the removed soil in piles, contouring, seeding and revegetation, fertilizing, and so forth. I had trouble understanding some of the technical stuff in the bills myself. Many of my colleagues did, too. And so did the media folks—though unlike many of the rest of us, they were loath to admit it. Reporters would sometimes pretend they understood. They would ask a couple of simple questions, the kinds of questions you could come up with just by reading the first page of the legislation, then turn quickly to a sexier and much more controversial subject. "So, Representative Simpson, what's going to happen to the abortion bill?" Always it was the abortion bill. I would say patiently that the abortion bill was stuck in committee and probably was going to stay stuck because the chairman felt it was too hot to handle. The reporter would then thank me and ask, "Well then, what about Casper College becoming a four-year institution?" That was always a hot one too. Most citizens knew that neither the abortion bill nor the Casper College bill would ever get to the floor. But because those issues had been bandied about for years, they were clearly easier to cover than mined-land-reclamation bills. The hotter, sexier, less important story was the one that always got into the paper, often on the front page. And what kind of play did the media give to the technical parts of minded-land-reclamation bills? You guessed it—those stories, when they were written at all, usually ended up embedded in the bowels of the paper, back there with the weather report, the funnies, and Jack Anderson's column.

Every once in a while, on a slow day, a reporter would track me down and ask me to explain some of those complicated bills. I soon found that I was spending an awful lot of time educating these good people. In short, I was doing what they were supposed to be doing—providing the who, what, when, where, and why. As I did this, I would often mumble to myself, "But why the hell don't they learn more about the issues?" I thought they were the ones who were supposed to do the dry research, and then come at us with the tough questions. Why was it that they asked me the easy—or just nutty—questions, and expected me to do their research for them? I still mull that one over.

Giving those lessons was frustrating. Still, I learned more by doing it. When I learned how little some reporters really knew, I quickly learned to stop commenting on issues in an arcane, whimsical, esoteric way. Irony is always lost on a person who doesn't know what you're talking about. I also realized that the reporters were doing me a favor with their questions. They were forcing me to articulate my own views, clearly helping me to communicate my ideas better to them and to others. So I owed the reporters some gratitude.

In Wyoming, I learned that some in the news media are lazy, biased, inept, cynical, and even indifferent. I had many print and TV reporters ask me at the beginning of an interview, "Now what is it you want me to ask you today?" I would always think testily: Enough of that. You do your job and I'll do mine.

It would be unfair—and untrue—to say that every reporter I encountered in Cheyenne was lazy or inept. One of the finest journalists I met there was Pete Williams, the NBC correspondent who served as Pentagon spokesman during the Gulf War. In those days, Pete was covering politics for what is still Wyoming's only statewide television station, KTWO in Casper. Pete was a real professional, even at the tender age of twenty-two in 1974. He made the state proud then, just as he did during his stint working for the Department of Defense. Lee Camlet worked alongside Pete at KTWO. His probative and earnest style has since made him one of ABC's top news producers. He has always had a quiet but intense interest in the news—the real news, not the gossip, tripe, trash, and crap.

Dave Espo, now a well-respected national correspondent for the Associated Press, was peerless when it came to extracting all the vital information from a dull, dry, leaden state budget. He was also great fun to be around. Some of today's journalists would feel insulted if I said that about them, as if being human and being a reporter did not go together. Some of these people are so afraid to be seen as decent that they stop being decent just to be safe.

There were other real pros. One was Bob Leeright, who later went on to become head of the Associated Press in Idaho. He loved reporting on the legislative wars, but you couldn't always keep wonderful people like that in Wyoming. There was Jim Flinchum, the editor of the *Wyoming State Tribune*. His columns were pungent, partisan, and, I must admit, well researched.

I know I have been critical of the way some reporters worked, but the truth is that I had a healthy and pleasant relationship with the media while in Cheyenne. Indeed, they named me the Most Effective Orator in 1971. I was always accessible and still am, even when I think the media are out to get me. Indeed, I wasn't in the Wyoming legislature very long before I adopted my pop's philosophy of dealing with the press: "When they're after your ass, answer the phone!"

Still, that is easy to say and often tough to do. Any longtime Washingtonian can describe how it feels to know that the hounds of the media are coming after you. There you are, standing in front of the television cameras, trying to look cheery and unconcerned, when in fact you have a lump in your throat the size of a hockey puck and a wad of cotton in your mouth. At such times I feel vulnerable, or even picked on. Sometimes I withdraw from action for a while, just to collect myself. But eventually I always get to a phone and return my calls, even though I know the questions won't be pleasant. When the ordeal is over, sometimes you don't even know what hit you, or where the blows came from. I am reminded of some of that wonderful, whimsical—yet painful— line from Larry King's *The Best Little Whorehouse in Texas*: "I didn't even know it was hungry—until it et me!"

The media tried to devour me during one of my sessions in Cheyenne. Why? Because I introduced some legislation they didn't like—at all.

I was inspired to sponsor the legislation by a lingering and painful sense of loss. When my friends and I were at the University of Wyoming, we all thought we had every God-given right to suck down a few beers, then hop in our cars and cruise merrily down the highway, the wind in our hair (I still had mine) and a cold can of suds wedged between our legs. But as I got older, I realized that we were dead wrong—and some were just dead. Over the years, I had lost, or nearly lost, several good friends who had made the grave mistake of driving drunk, or of riding with someone who was soused. I can still picture one wonderful young friend, Joe Temple, a gifted athlete with an open, freckled face, who was killed in a hideous drunk-driving wreck. Another intimate pal, Bill "Chink" Chambers, the handsomest guy I've ever come across before or since, died of internal injuries from a car wreck while on the way to see me while Ann and I were living in GI housing in Laramie. And a friend named Lloyd A. "Buck" Buchanan— then my best friend, next to my wonderful brother, Pete—was killed when he was thrown from the bed of an old pickup that was being driven by a mere boy.

When you're eighteen, nineteen, or twenty, you don't dwell

long on that sad waste of life. At that age, you think you're bigger than life, omnipotent and immortal. But when you are thirty-five or thirty-six and you think back on the friends you've lost, you start to see things differently. And now that I was in the Wyoming legislature, I could do more than just lament those tragic accidents. I could do something to ensure that fewer such accidents would happen. And so I did. I sponsored Wyoming's first implied-consent law, which required all drivers to consent to sobriety testing when stopped by a police officer. Anyone who refused to take the tests would automatically forfeit his or her license. If you were going to have the privilege of driving, you were going to have to submit to testing when stopped by a police officer.

The media harangued me pretty well over that legislation. Apparently some of the state's less enlightened editors saw things the way my college buddies did. To them, any effort by the government to make the streets safer in this fashion smacked of intrusion and invasion of privacy. I was lambasted in several editorials, but I kept pushing my bill, because I thought I was right. The final legislative result was a dramatically watered-down version of what I had really wanted. Still, I was happy to get as far as I got. Today, Wyoming has one of the toughest implied-consent laws on the books of any state. And I'd bet a wad that the state's newspaper editors would squeal like hell if anybody tried to repeal it.

Probably my greatest struggle with the press came later, when I decided to take on one of Wyoming's most sacred cows—the Union Pacific Railroad. It would not be an exaggeration to say that the UP once was Wyoming; the territory had grown up around the railroad tracks laid down by the company. Even in the 1960s, this gigantic railroad company seemed to hold fast to the belief that it owned Wyoming, as it once nearly had. In the 1860s, the federal government had enticed the UP into expanding the West by giving it vast segments of land in the areas where it laid its tracks—plus twenty miles on either side of the line. And Uncle Sam threw in the mineral rights to boot! The Union Pacific quickly became so powerful, and so adept at exploiting the laws of eminent domain, that it could practically put a railroad depot in your living room. The UP also made sure always to have a legislator serving in the state house or senate. This person was either a manager, worker, company lawyer, or former lobbyist. Now that's what I call really laying the track!

But to truly understand the UP's power, one need only look at the layout of our beautiful capital city of Cheyenne, where the lovely, gold-domed capitol building faces a similarly majestic building due south: the Union Pacific Depot. These were the most potent symbols of power, influence, and strength in Wyoming.

This, then, was the powerhouse I and a few other legislators decided to take on. The issue at hand was the underground mining of soda ash, or trona—a product used in the making of all glass products. There are vast deposits of it in southwestern Wyoming, where, you'll remember, the UP owned most of the earth's surface and also whatever was underneath it. In order to get to the trona buried deep in the earth, miners had to ask the UP for an underground easement, even when the miners owned the land. The UP was always happy to grant one—at a cost of about 40 percent or more of the action. In one case, the UP demanded a positively outrageous 51 percent cut.

Some of the more experienced members in the legislature couldn't believe our Wyoming statutes would ever allow that kind of extortion. But the railroad had made sure it was legal during an earlier session by quietly passing a change in one of the transportation laws. This "modest change" was sold to the legislature merely as a "clarification," nothing more. The whole thing had a rank and fishy smell. What the UP had done was wrong, so a bunch of us set out to make it right.

I had some mighty worthy and wonderful allies in the fray. One was Ed Herschler, a Democratic legislator who later became governor. This was a man with a marvelously rich vein of common sense and a magnificent sense of humor. Another ally was Harold Hellbaum, a wise, businesslike, and witty wheat farmer from Chugwater. The three of us were joined in the common effort by one Michael J. Sullivan, a lobbyist and lawyer who represented the Allied Chemical Company. He was a pleasant young man, steady, articulate, and thoughtful. A Democrat, he too would eventually serve as governor of our state.

Ed Herschler, Harold Hellbaum, and I split up the tough task of educating our colleagues and seeking their support. For the final house floor debate, we divided our presentation into three parts. I described the sneaky and dishonest way in which the law had been changed; Ed spoke of the history of the Union Pacific and its dramatic effect on Wyoming; Harold talked about the need for the new legislation. It was during this gripping debate on House Bill 208 that I discovered the best way to destroy somebody else's emotional, hysterical, or phony argument: to bury 'em with facts. We all did our homework—and did it damn well. I can tell you we really worked our asses off.

If only the media had worked as hard. Instead, the newspapers and TV stations too often got caught up in the emotion of the thing. Remember, this was a state that owed its very existence to the railroads. Some people felt strongly that what the UP wanted, the UP should get. Some in the media felt that way too, and too often it showed in their coverage. It was during this time that I added another arrow of a saying to my quiver: "Emotion will always triumph over reason, but reason will always persist."

I persisted. As a politician, you learn the hard way you must always keep telling your story. You must repeat it and repeat it and repeat it, else it will never be heard. I had a truly great saying hanging on the wall of my office, which was located on the first floor of the southwest corner of the Dirksen Building. The words are imprinted on leather, and rightly so, because they are tough and strong, yet soft and supple.

Nothing in the world can take the place of persistence.
    Talent will not;
Nothing is more common than unsuccessful men with
        talent.
    Genius will not;
Unrewarded genius is almost a proverb.
    Education will not;
The world is full of educated derelicts.
    Persistence and determination alone are omnipotent.

Our persistence paid off well in the case of that UP Railroad legislation. We went up against the most powerful political force in Wyoming—possibly in the West—and beat it. I think the state was better for it. And the UP is a damn fine corporate citizen now.

I served in the Wyoming house from 1965 to 1977 and enjoyed every minute of it. And yet, as the years went by I began to feel an urge to raise the stakes a bit, to take on a greater challenge. Don't ever believe politicians who say they were drafted or persuaded to run for office. When politicians say that hundreds of their friends and supporters urged them to run, the truth generally is that a few close relatives or friends really did the urging. Some politicians can walk into an aerobics class and be convinced they're getting a standing ovation. No, most politicians take the plunge with the help of their spouses, a couple of drinking buddies, and their own grand ambitions.

So it was for me. In 1977, Ann's twin sister, Nan, went through a painful divorce. When it was over, she went to Paris and rented a $500-a-month apartment, where she and her youngest daughter fully intended to work through a blue period. Is there a sensitive person alive who, if given the chance, would not want to live through a blue period in Paris? I would hunch not. The City of Lights certainly worked its magic on Nan; after eleven months there she called Ann and said, "I'm now healing and ready to come home. You can have the place for the final month." Soon Ann, our daughter Sue, then fifteen, and I were on a plane to Paris. I wasn't going to batch for thirty days.

What a delicious month the three of us had. One beautiful June evening we were sitting at the kitchen table with a jug of wine, a loaf of bread, and thou . . . when the landlady knocked. We opened the door and she handed over a telegram posted from my folks' address in Cody. At first we feared something was wrong; Dad was nearly eighty then, Mom about seventy-seven. With some trepidation we tore open the envelope. The news was not bad. The message said, "Senator Cliff Hansen announced today at the Wyoming Stock Growers convention he will retire from the United States Senate. Wanted you to know. Your mom and I hope you are having a great time. Love, Pop."

Ann and I read and reread that yellow slip of paper. Then I placed it down on the table. A breeze rustled through the open windows as Ann and I sat there, just looking at each other, both thinking the same thing. All at once we started talking excitedly, our words coming out in staccato bursts. Should I run? Over the years, a run for higher office had always been something we had discussed and then put aside for another day. Once, the Republican Party asked me to consider a run for Congress, but the kids were small and I was deeply involved in my law practice, so I declined. Later, I became interested in following my father's footsteps with a run for the Senate, but Cliff Hansen seemed sure to occupy the seat for a long time. The door seemed to be closed for good. Well, now the door was open again. We both strongly felt that it was time to do more in politics.

But what were the risks? We poured out two glasses of a nice chilled white wine, sliced up some rich goat cheese, broke off a good chunk of fresh bread, and started talking the pros and cons. We recalled what Pop always said about politics: "Hell, the worst thing that can happen to you is you could lose." But was that really the worst thing? What would a Senate race do to our family? To our three maturing and wonderful children? To our lives? To our marriage? We were coming up on our twenty-third wedding anniversary, and we didn't want to do anything that would prevent us from having a good number more. What would I do with myself if we lost? I could make a living, I knew, but how would I feel?

I did not know, but I was willing to find out. Right there and then, on a cool evening in Paris, we decided to take the chance of a lifetime and run. Here was my chance to serve the people of my beautiful state, and our wonderful country, in a lasting and meaningful way. I couldn't pass it up. And so we excitedly kissed Paris goodbye and hurried home to Wyoming, elated and excited about working toward the goal ahead.

Politics in the 1990s now seems to require candidates for public office to burnish their media images carefully even before beginning the race. I had no intention of doing that in 1977. I have never been one to enroll in charm school, or hire a consultant to teach me to smile, or get somebody to plaster pancake makeup on my bald head so it won't shine under the lights. Still, I knew it was critical that I go out and meet the press if I wanted to get elected. After further discussions with Ann, I decided to go around Wyoming's 98,000 square miles and introduce myself to all of the big- and small-town newspaper editors and reporters and the electronic media people. I wanted to let them meet me, let them see what made me tick.

And so in late 1977 I started up the old panel station wagon and headed out. Before I arrived in each town, I would call ahead to the local media people and make an appointment to see them. When I found the address, I would push open the door, doff my hat, and say, "Hi, I'm Al Simpson. I'm going to run for the United States Senate. I was raised here. I've been in the state legislature for thirteen years and I have a good reputation for doing my homework. I'll try to always listen to what you are saying to me and I will make you only two promises: I'll try to make you very proud and I'll work my butt off." I would then answer any questions they might have, introduce myself to all of their employees, and be on my way. I visited with editors, reporters, camera people, clerks, secretaries, you name it. I spoke with a great many of the journalists who worked in that big expanse of Wyoming. And I enjoyed myself immensely while doing it.

While I had no plans to change my public image, I understood that I had to be careful about how I got my message across to the people. In planning my campaign, I looked to the success of my old friend Malcolm Wallop, who had run a first-class U.S. Senate campaign in 1976. Malcolm had engaged the services of a media consultant, Bob Goodman, who developed a campaign that people still talk about today. Wyoming people are highly resentful of any intrusion into their lives by federal officials, whom they call "the feds." Goodman's campaign strategy played on that sentiment by producing an ad critical of all the fussy regulations imposed by the Occupational Safety and Health Administration (OSHA). In one ad, a cowboy heading into the backcountry was shown strapping a portable toilet onto the back of his horse. Brilliant. Another ad was about an errant letter that always seemed to need more stamps but never got to the addressee. Malcolm's Democrat op-

ponent, Senator Gale McGee, was on the Senate Postal Committee. Those ads hurt him, and he lost the election. I saw Malcolm's
success and did what came naturally: I, too, hired Bob Goodman
to do my media work. As we used to say at the pool hall in Cody,
I was going to go to school on Malcolm's shot.

By the fall of 1977 I had not officially announced my candidacy
for the soon-to-be-vacant U.S. Senate seat, but the word was out
that I would make a run for it. My anticipated presence in the race
apparently didn't scare off people, because other Republican chal-
lengers quickly began lining up their support. Four of us would
face off in the primary—Gordon Barrows, James G. Maxey, Sr.,
Hugh "Bigfoot" Binford (he chose the nickname himself, believe
it or not), and me. Bigfoot was the one who concerned me most.
He was cocky and ornery, and besides he had big bucks. I didn't
take him lightly in any way.

Again and again during the campaign of 1978, I reaped the
dividends of the many media visits I had made in my old station
wagon. Throughout that primary race, Bigfoot Binford tried to tar
me with all kinds of outrageous accusations. For example, he said
I was for gun control. What a statement to make in Wyoming! In
the Cowboy State, gun control simply means how steady you hold
your rifle. I was in no way aligned with the antigun fringe, and I
said so. Bigfoot then said I was a "100 percent environmentalist,"
as if I were one of those barefoot, rheumy-eyed bark eaters who
go around hugging trees. I answered that one by saying we could
make good use of our resources while also protecting our precious
environment and preserving our unique way of life. Bigfoot's accusations never got much play, because the state's journalists already knew me and knew where I stood on those and other issues.
I had met virtually all of them in person. So whenever Bigfoot
tried to hang a label on me, they would think, "But I talked to Al
Simpson, and he said just the opposite."

I might even go a bit further and say that the Wyoming media
may have liked me because I had taken the time to meet with
them. Their coverage of my campaign would suggest that they
did. The newspeople treated me well, and the editorial writers
touted me, sometimes letting me get away with more than they

should have. I had set off on that long station-wagon tour of Wyoming with a simple wish—to let people come to know me. But I'll also admit that I hoped the media would like and respect me, and sure enough, I think, they did. I liked them, too. I later decided that my car tour was much more effective than any full-bore professional media campaign could ever have been.

That campaign also gave me a chance to meet many, many just plain folks, something I truly enjoy doing. I carried with me a little black book full of the names of people I had met over the years, going way back to when I worked on Pop's governor's campaigns in 1954 and 1958 and on his Senate campaign in 1962. I saw many of those people in my travels. What a fine and fascinating citizenry my state has. Only four states have a higher percentage of people who have completed a twelfth-grade education. As I say often, the people of my state are thoughtful, articulate, well read, and highly opinionated. And they damn sure expect their candidates to get out there and get to know them. You have to go door to door, making time for each of them, because there are not many of them. We really are the state of high altitude and low multitude. And you must treat Wyoming people fairly, kindly, and with respect. That's all they ask.

And then, of course, they also want you to leave them alone. I'm reminded of the story of the fine-looking young cowboy who was out fixing his fence one day when a tourist lady pulled up. "Young man," she said, "I understand you have more cows than you do people out here. Why is that?" He looked at her with a steady gaze, cocked his head, hooked his thumb in his belt, and replied, "We prefer 'em." So we do.

Though the media and I seemed then to belong to a mutual admiration society, I got my share of tough questions on the campaign trail. There were always two ways to answer those questions. I could give the political answer, meaning the one that sounded good but probably didn't mean anything, or the nonpolitical answer—the sharp, pithy, clever, honest one that people would remember right up to the minute they pulled the lever and voted for somebody else. Oh, how my campaign staff feared the second kind of answer! And how my loved ones still do!

Sure, it is always easier to give the political answer, because that's the one that people most often want to hear. The political answer is like a lullaby; it soothes people and puts them to sleep. Many politicians have mastered the art of the political answer. They'll toss off some line of babble such as "I am doing this unselfish deed for our deserving downtrodden of America," or "I take this compassionate action on behalf of the oldest and most fragile of our citizens," or "We must always think first of the dear children," or "We must never forget the sacrifices made by [fill in the blank]." When hit with a guided missile of a question, the best of them will always find a way to present their side—even if it pertains to another issue entirely.

But I never felt comfortable with the political answer. Nearly makes one gag. While Pop was in the governor's office and in the Senate, I would always roll my eyes heavenward when I heard his fellow politicians give the political answer. A powerful voice inside me always wanted to shout, "Why the hell don't you answer the damn question?" Instead, these people were most likely to deliver only a great gooey wad of God, Flag, Country, and Apple Pie. None of that crap for me, I thought. I decided early on in my days in Cheyenne that I would always at least try to give the nonpolitical answer, even if it meant taking some pretty good lumps afterward.

There I was, trying to be virtuous and forthright with the media, when suddenly I found myself about to hire a masterful media manipulator. One day, my fiercely loyal campaign manager, Joe Ratliff, told me, "We have an appointment for you with Roger Ailes, the media consultant, in New York City when we're back there next month raising funds." Roger Ailes! This was a guy with a reputation for crafting and shaping people into salable political commodities, a man who packaged and peddled politicians. I knew he had done very good and effective work for a lot of people, but I just didn't want anything to do with it. I was highly offended at the idea that some slick media consultant was somehow going to change me, dammit! I didn't care to have someone teach me how to speak without a nasal twang, show me how to look into the camera with syrupy sincerity, or recommend that I get rid of the goofy half glasses. I said, "Hell, Joe, I'll go to New York to raise the money, but I don't want to see Ailes." But when Joe, Ann, and others working on the campaign insisted that I pay the man a visit, I grudgingly agreed.

Early in our meeting, I told Ailes exactly how I felt about becoming one of his products. This earthy, gentle, energetic, and sometimes gruff man just listened. And then he flipped on his video camera and just talked to me. For three hours we spoke. When we were finished, Ailes said, "I gather you are a rather strong-willed, independent, and half-ornery guy. I haven't the slightest desire to change you. I wouldn't even try. But I do have a couple of suggestions—recommendations, if you will. Want to hear them?" Since I was paying cash money for his ideas, I said yes.

Ailes began by summing up my performance on camera. "You really don't hold your head up. You don't look at the camera correctly. You have a real nasal twang. Those half glasses look goofy on you, and you also have a strange half-smile playing about your chops. Yet, all of that is you," he said. Somehow, I wasn't too flattered.

Then Ailes gave me the two suggestions that turned out to be among the most useful and valuable bits of advice I have ever received in public life. "Just remember two things, Al. First, there is no such thing in politics as repetition. By that I mean you can talk about the same issue or the same thing day after day, and week after week, and people might not hear it or pick it up until the eighth, ninth, or tenth go-round." Truer words were never spoken. The people whom you are trying to reach in a campaign are not hanging on your every word; they're simply going about their lives. They're doing their jobs, raising their kids, coaching Little League, whatever. And so they don't absorb your message in any way until they have heard it a few times. During that 1978 campaign, Ann would sometimes go almost numb from hearing me deliver the same stuff in the same way over and over again. She would say, "Don't you think you really ought to change the message a bit or tell them something new?" And, repeating Ailes's words, I would stubbornly say, "Nope, Annie—there is no such thing as repetition."

Roger Ailes's other invaluable tip to me—one I didn't fully comprehend at the time—was "Let the microphones come to you." He said this with his eyes afire, stiff beard bristling, and jowls jutting. Then he switched on the video player. "Now watch this— watch what happens to you in this video clip. Here you and I are, visiting in a conversational tone. I suddenly say to you, 'All right, Al, imagine you've just stepped out of an important meeting with some constituents and the media are standing close by. Suddenly they shove a battery of mikes and booms, recorders and notebooks, into your face. What do you say to them?' Watch and listen to yourself. See how your voice goes up a full range or two until you hit first tenor? See what I mean?" I could only smile in agreement as the tape rolled; he was right. I could see and hear the excitement creeping into my voice as I spoke. The mere idea of encountering the big press pack had me singing the high note.

Ailes told me to settle down. There was nothing to be anxious about, he said, for I'd be talking often to the cameras in the life I'd chosen. He told me to speak to the media as if I were sitting right there in front of a fireplace, visiting with a friend. Then he added, "When the TV producers tell you 'Give me a voice level,' never alter your conversational tone or timbre of your voice. Tell them, 'It's all right here, just like this.' They will pick it all up. They have all the sensitive and fancy equipment to do that. Then the microphones will come to you. You don't have to change your delivery or raise your pitch to get the cameras' attention. You just stay comfortable and at ease. By doing this, you're not straining and you are not suddenly pressing forward in voice, body, and presence." Damn good advice it was—and is. It works well for me.

That is not to say I became an Ailes creation. I was not, and will never be, a dazzling performer on the tube. I still unconsciously use my hands too much. I still make faces when I talk. My spoken sentences will always be disjointed—unpunctuated and overlong. But if not for that session with Roger Ailes, I might never have reached my present level of comfort and confidence in front of the pack. I'm most grateful to him. There is an old axiom in politics: "A candidate's press will never be any better than the candidate." Maybe that should be changed. Maybe it should be "A candidate's press will never be any better than the candidate's ability to cope with the press."

I must have coped pretty well, because almost everything in that first Senate campaign went my way. When election day finally came in November 1978, Ann and I found that we had won handily; our efforts with the media, and with the Wyoming people, had paid off. Soon, Ann and I and our only daughter and youngest child, Sue, were headed off to Washington, D.C., to begin adding pages to this new chapter in our lives. I was humbled and quite moved by it all. I had watched my pop closely during my youth and had seen that political success did not change him in any way. Nor did it change dear Mom. They remained perpetually the same inspirational, faithful, caring, and loving persons they always had been, and they retained their passion, zeal, drive, and energy about what was right. Ann and I only hoped we might bring that same degree and sense of commitment and conviction to our own tour of duty in the nation's capital.

CHAPTER FOUR

Western Breeze
Through Stuffy Senate

M y rapier wit, dapper haberdashery, and dashing good looks were not alone going to be enough to get me ahead in the United States Senate! I knew from my father's experience in Washington that only one thing truly assured legislative success: seniority. Nothing more, nothing less. Others knew it, too. In calling some of my fellow soon-to-be freshman senators, I became well aware that many of them were urging their predecessors to resign early so they could gain a little extra seniority on the rest of us. After a while, I began to wonder if I should call my old friend Cliff Hansen, Wyoming's retiring senior senator, and ask him to do the same. Indeed, I wondered that so many times in Ann's presence that she finally said, "You seem to keep talking about it a lot, so why don't you do something?"

So I did. I called Cliff and asked him, as tactfully as I could, if he would step aside early. He was tentative at first. He said, "Let me think about it, Al. I'll call you back in a day or so." I could tell he didn't want to give up the seat any earlier than he might have to, and I didn't blame him. The next day, Cliff called me back. He said, "Fine with me. I'd be glad to help."

That left only one small final detail to be taken care of. With the seat open, I would have to be officially appointed to the Senate. And that could only be done by our governor, Ed Herschler—a Democrat. Fortunately, Ed and I had been very close friends in my Wyoming lawmaking days, even if he was from the wrong party. We knew each other well. We respected each other. When he died, I gave the sole eulogy at his funeral. When I called Ed, he said, "Sure. Great, Al. I'll do it. It's my chance to finally appoint a Democratic senator." I chuckled and told him that wasn't exactly what I had in mind. Then Ed leveled. "It really is a hell of a nice and generous thing for Cliff to do for you, resigning early. If he's willing, I'd be honored to appoint you, old friend." I was touched, and very pleased.

Those two acts of kindness by Cliff Hansen and Ed Herschler helped me to make an early mark in the United States Senate. Instead of being one hundredth on the seniority list, I leapfrogged to eighty-eighth. That put me ahead of most of my nineteen freshman colleagues. I was designated the ranking member of the Senate Subcommittee on Nuclear Regulation, part of the full Committee on Environment and Public Works. On a subcommittee or full committee, a ranking member is the senior member of the minority party. I thought this assignment would be a rather obscure one. And I assumed that I would have plenty of time to learn about commercial nuclear power and its regulation by the Nuclear Regulatory Commission.

Wrong. On March 28, 1979, bulletins flashed across the world that a reactor at the Metropolitan Edison electrical plant at Three Mile Island, Pennsylvania, was leaking radiation and would be shut down as an emergency measure. It was the most serious "transient"—that's the Nuclear Regulatory Commission euphemism for "accident"—involving the nuclear industry in the country to date. Minutes after the accident was discovered, I received a call from the subcommittee chairman, Colorado Democrat Gary Hart. He told me that our subcommittee would conduct a complete investigation of the accident. He said we would also eventually propose legislation to address the plant's operation and assess the government's full regulatory process. Gary concluded, "They have a chopper waiting for us at Andrews Air Base, and we'll head for Pennsylvania to take a look at it all. See you in a few minutes."

Before I left, several of my Republican Senate colleagues took me aside. One said, "Now, watch out for Hart on this one. He's obviously going to run for president at some point. Don't get sucked in here." My colleagues were afraid that Hart would use this dramatic moment to advance his own political career, possibly at my expense. You see, Hart was no avid supporter of nuclear power. Some of my Republican friends feared he would tell the press, "Senator Simpson and I have agreed that this accident heralds the end of the use of commercial power nukes in America," or some other wild statement I wouldn't be ready for. Well, I wasn't ready for much. This was happening in March, and I had just been sworn in in January. I was brand-new, really a green pea.

I was thinking about my colleagues' advice—and about a hundred other things, not the least of which was the safety of people near the plant—as I headed to Andrews to board a rickety, beat-up old military helicopter for the short flight to Pennsylvania. As we ducked into the chopper, I remembered what one of my Army instructors had told me at Fort Benning: "Relax, Simpson, nobody has ever been injured by one of those rotors. They've all been killed."

As that old crate whop-whopped toward Pennsylvania and the Susquehanna River, I turned to Gary Hart and asked him point-blank, "Are you going to do this thing responsibly, Gary? Or are you going to try to turn this thing into some big media circus?"

He looked at me with hard, piercing eyes and asked sharply, "Who the hell put you up to that? Who said I would do it that way?"

"Some in my party in the Senate," I said.

"They're dead wrong," he said. "Watch me. See what I do. I intend to do this one very well and very fairly."

Seeing would be believing. I would watch him like a hawk—all the way.

Forty-five minutes later, we were hovering over Harrisburg.

Gary told the chopper pilot to circle the reactor before landing. That was the first time I ever saw the place that was even then becoming a household name. We circled the plant for several minutes, learning only later that radioactive gases were at that moment issuing from the imposing hulk of the reactor. Gary would later say that it was while we were hovering there that I lost what was then left of my hair.

Gary then directed the pilot to put down near the reactor at the headquarters of Metropolitan Edison. We landed swiftly and clambered out of the helicopter. We were immediately ushered into a building, where we received an extensive briefing from officials at the plant and from Nuclear Regulatory Commission personnel. Gary asked a good many questions. I asked damn few; I was just trying to learn as much as I could as fast as I could.

Then we stepped out of the briefing building into a crush of reporters the likes of which I had never seen. This was my first— but by no means last—look at a real media feeding frenzy. I saw television camera people muscling each other out of the way and radio guys shoving each other around. I saw folks jerking cables and wires out from under each other, and others in the throng pulling, yelping, shoving, cursing, and shouting questions. Why was everyone so excited? Partly it was because they saw the very real potential danger of an accident at Three Mile Island. But partly it was because they all considered themselves experts based on something they had recently seen at the movies. That was the year of *The China Syndrome,* a film about hazards of a core meltdown, starring Jane Fonda and Jack Lemmon. The movie had nothing to do with what was happening in Pennsylvania, but the media nonetheless believed it might be a similar disaster.

A few of the reporters we met outside the building asked thoughtful questions. But most asked hysterical, silly questions, usually delivering them in the most dramatic and solemn tones. One reporter said, "We understand a plume of radiation is now headed directly for our nation's Capitol in Washington, D.C. What will be done?" Even at that early stage we knew there was no plume of radiation. The experts had told us so. Yes, there was plenty of dangerous radiation trapped in the containment vessel, but what had escaped through an open valve was later found to be the equivalent of a sparrow fart. And yet the media persisted in reporting what could have happened instead of simply what actually had happened. And by doing this, they created a greater crisis than the one that actually existed. The media types were all trying to look very wise and profound, and of course were demanding answers from the nation's leaders. At the same time, they were bombarding the populace with terrifying tales of howling destruction that would soon rain down upon the land. When the story first broke, *Newsweek* magazine's cover featured the steaming cooling towers in ominous, shadowy outline for emphasis. Stories on radiation, fallout, and exposure levels dominated the newspaper and the tube. And of course you couldn't cross the street without hearing the word "meltdown"—a word that did not, in any way, describe what had happened at Three Mile Island.

Gary Hart handled the whole situation most responsibly. Throughout that first stressful day and the following days, he was accessible, knowledgeable, level-headed, and even-handed in the face of rampant conjecture and speculation. That weekend on one of the Sunday talk shows, he proved that he had put aside any of his antinuclear feelings and was dealing honestly with the facts of exactly what had happened—and had not happened. I was impressed.

Like Gary, I was right smack in the middle of a huge international story, but unlike him I did not feel at ease in any sense. I was not yet knowledgeable about the complexities of the operation of a commercial nuclear power plant. I did not yet fully understand the mission of the subcommittee, nor did I know how much power it had to investigate such an accident. I was not even sure what was required of a ranking member of a subcommittee. Remember, I had been in the U.S. Senate only a couple of months. I knew where my office was, knew how to find the cloakroom and the john, knew the names of my staff, and that was about it.

When it came to nuclear power—the raw, hot fissionable force that had caused all the commotion—I didn't know zirconium cladding from a Zippo lighter, but I sure as hell knew I had to learn pretty fast. Because of the media's overheated coverage of the accident, the good citizens of this country promptly became completely and utterly terrified.

One able guy finally settled the country down. His name was Harold Denton, and he was director of nuclear reactor regulation for the Nuclear Regulatory Commission. He was sincere, direct, steady, thoughtful, and articulate, and a man of great good humor. In many, many televised interviews, he dispensed with the arcane and technical language of nuclear science and put things into words a layman could understand. He spoke realistically about the dangers of operating a power plant, not hysterically as the media were doing. Every few hours, Gary and I would communicate with him on secured phone lines, and he would patiently explain all of the immediate problems at the site. Soon we knew what had gone wrong and had a pretty good sense of how it could be fixed.

I had another fine teacher at the time, an exceptionally able subcommittee staffer named Jim Asselstine who would later serve with distinction as a member of the Nuclear Regulatory Commission. Jim and I had known each other for only a few weeks, but we worked together well from the start. He gave me a crash course in commercial nuclear power. With his help, I learned about pressurized water reactors, criticality, turbine operations, cooling legs and water flow, the role of control rods in the fission process, shutdowns, and so on. At times I didn't think I could ingest another one of Jim's comprehensive memoranda, but what choice did I have? I had a serious responsibility to know the issue before I could sensibly comment on it in the media, much less suggest new regulatory law.

With hearings on the accident set to begin in our subcommittee, I found I was getting just as tired of the "Hell no, we won't glow!" crowd as I was of the "Nobody's ever been killed!" contingent. I was then—and still am—a supporter of commercial nuclear power. But I was, and am, cautious in my support. The accident at Three Mile Island raised extremely serious questions about the way such plants are operated. Plant licensing procedures needed to be reviewed again, as did construction and operating permits. The training of various technicians needed a thorough overhaul. A few executives from the power company needed to go into some other line of work. We subcommittee members were also startled to learn how poorly some of the power plant employees were compensated. Shift supervisors in a multibillion-dollar facility were being paid $30,000 a year. That did not seem to us to be fair pay for someone charged with such an awesome responsibility. Running the control board at a power plant is not like flipping burgers at Freddy's Fast Food.

With the help of our staff and some fine outside experts, our subcommittee was able to publish a thorough and readable final report. We tried to keep the report as free as possible of drama and hyperbole, and I think we did that pretty well. I felt that I helped Gary Hart as best I could, and hunch that he would agree. Hundreds of thousands of words were written about the Three Mile Island incident, countless pictures taken and distributed. And though many media people and commission members carefully studied what happened, I still honestly believe that the members of our subcommittee compiled the fairest and most complete account. Not that I'm biased or anything.

I am about to make a statement that will shock some journalists: Each and every fact in our report was attributed to some clearly identified person or written source. We substantiated every single jot and tittle. I think our footnotes may have comprised more words than the rest of the report! The document might have made for pretty dull breakfast reading—the *New York Post* it wasn't— but it was meticulously and fully researched. And to me, doing good research is one of the fundamentals of good legislating, not to mention good news reporting. When I read, I want attribution. Don't tell me that an "unnamed source" said this or that. I know plenty of journalists who understand the raw persuasive power of an attributed fact—and plenty others who apparently don't.

My work on the Three Mile Island accident taught me how a reactor works—and showed me a hell of a lot more about how reporters work. I saw how some in the media arrived at the scene of a fire and quickly started pouring on gasoline and fanning the flames—how they abandoned any attempt at fostering understanding and instead fostered only fear and doubt. It was during the

Three Mile Island mess that I first noticed what I consider to be a sad and all too common trait among reporters—the almost palpable sense of excitement they feel when something goes wrong. I know, I know—when things are working right, reporters don't have anything to report. Five schoolchildren crossing the street safely is not news. But I couldn't understand how anyone could arrive at a scene like Three Mile Island really harboring the hope that this was going to be a huge story. And yet some reporters did. Many in the media seem to thrive on chaos instead of charity or clarity. Rather than report, they distort. In those first days of the crisis, Gary Hart and I worked hard to educate ourselves, and then to pass on what we learned or knew to an anxious American public. If only we had not needed the news media to help share our knowledge.

Though I had learned a thing or two about nuclear power, I knew I could not be a single-issue legislator. No member of the United States Senate has that luxury. Three Mile Island dominated my thoughts during those first months in the Senate, but I knew I also had to be concerned with other issues of concern to me and to my constituents in Wyoming. Every lawmaker seeks committee assignments that will make his or her work and life relevant and important. I made it one of my priorities to seek membership on the Senate Judiciary Committee. I had chaired such a committee in the Wyoming house of representatives and had enjoyed the work. Here is where you deal with all the "stuff" that other committees don't handle, or don't want to. It was from my seat on the Judiciary Committee that I would later come face to face with Robert Bork—and with Clarence Thomas and Anita Hill, that tragic pair of the 1990s.

Malcolm Wallop, our senior senator from Wyoming and my longtime friend, had resigned his seats on the Senate Judiciary Committee and on the Environment and Public Works Committee in favor of other assignments, leaving both committees open to me. I also filled the ranking-member vacancy on the full Veterans' Affairs Committee, which was then chaired by a man I came to know very well, Senator Al Cranston, the Democrat from California.

It was in the Environment and Public Works Committee that I first tried to make a name for myself in the Senate. At first, things didn't work out too well. I stuck my neck out—and almost got my head lopped off.

At the time, the committee was reviewing the budget of the Army Corps of Engineers. Now, that struck me as an interesting subject. The absurdly large size of the government and its appalling unresponsiveness have always been of keen concern to those of us who live in the West. And to my way of thinking, no agency symbolized the excesses of the federal government better than the Corps of Engineers. I was, and am, a fiscal conservative, and I believed strongly that the Corps had spiraled out of control during previous administrations—it even had its own air force. Indeed, my interest in the Corps had peaked immediately after my election when three different regional offices invited me to come and see their vast facilities. No need to book a commercial flight, they said. They would send a Corps aircraft to Cody International to pick me up.

I thought, What the hell kind of an outfit is this? In my brief study of the agency, I discovered that it was full of people who didn't have enough work to do, and who were therefore looking for ways to make work. For most, that meant building something, whether the thing was needed or not. The agency's most bizarre and stunningly wasteful project of the eighties was the Tennessee Tombigbee Waterway, which ran from Demopolis in Alabama to somewhere in Mississippi. The final cost of this unnecessary project: billions. It was called a cloning of the Mississippi River. The people at the Corps had gone way, way too far.

Right off, I went after them. In that early Environment and Public Works Committee budget hearing, I offered an amendment to reduce the Corps of Engineers' budget by 10 percent across the board. That would show 'em. That's the way I was thinking, anyhow. I was just new enough, naive enough, and goofy enough to think the amendment made sense. And so, hour after hour, I kept pushing. I wasn't going to let go of the idea.

The amendment made much less sense to the committee chairman, the redoubtable, sometimes irascible Ed Muskie, Democrat of Maine. He knew such a deep cut would never get through the committee, much less become law, and he didn't appreciate having his time wasted on that kind of foolishness. He was plenty po'd. And yet I hung in there. We worked right through the lunch hour, and I couldn't have cared less. When Ed and some other members of the committee got hungry, they started to bully me, but I insisted that my views counted, and so did those of my constituents, by God. I asked why the Senate was afraid to cut the budget of that bloated bureaucracy. Why, I asked, was everybody so paralyzed?

Muskie assuredly was not paralyzed, because when I said that he came right out of his chair. Speaking without notes, he poured out a long, rich, colorful, and spirited dissertation on his philosophy of budgeting, which, he pointed out, he had developed and honed after many years in the Senate. In other words, he was no greenhorn, wild-eyed rookie, like some people. Ed, his voice rising, said he would never subscribe to what he called "the meat ax" approach to budgeting.

By the time he finished, my face was flushed and my ears were ringing. But I still stubbornly insisted that the committee vote on my amendment. I wasn't going to back down from a fight if I believed strongly in the cause, even if I was just a freshman senator from the wilds of Wyoming. Still, I got creamed. The vote was 10–2, which should tell you exactly what my more experienced colleagues thought of my great big idea.

I was still pretty steamed and, yes, embarrassed when I left the committee room on the way back to my office. I was boarding one of the Dirksen Building's old, slow elevators when Muskie and some of his staff crammed into the car along with me. I found myself facing Ed as he stood near the back of the elevator. In that dignified and measured Maine way of his, with that tremendously deep and rich voice, and with his face crinkling with good humor, he told me, "You hung in there, young man," even though I wasn't that young. "I do admire that. In order to succeed around this place, Simpson, you have to be about half a son of a bitch—and I see you are!" Then he clapped his hand on my shoulder and told me about his first big scrape; it was with Wayne Morse of Oregon. I felt better. Damn right I loved Ed Muskie.

Only later did I learn that a reporter had witnessed my brow-beating in the committee room. In the audience that day was one of Wyoming's most beloved and respected newspaper publishers, Bruce Kennedy. Bruce, who died in an accident in 1993, owned a chain of weekly community newspapers, the kind that serve as town crier, town watchdog, and chronicler of all events great and small. He quoted Ed Muskie as saying that freshmen senators should wait a little before speaking out, and that only the most experienced senators knew how to do things. Bruce wrote, "Simpson got a lesson from old veteran Sen. Ed Muskie that when you rock the boat you're gonna get a little wet." I sure did. I got soaked—but ended up a bit drier behind the ears.

In the early spring of 1980, just as I was finishing my first year in the Senate, I had my first opportunity to work on legislation that would really affect the way the media did business. The legislation was drafted in response to a 1978 U.S. Supreme Court decision involving the Stanford University student newspaper, the *Stanford Daily*.

These were the facts. In early 1971, student demonstrators at Stanford occupied the Stanford University Hospital. At first, the university tried to persuade the students to leave peacefully so the hospital could go about its business. The students would have none of it. Finally, local law enforcement officers were called in to remove the demonstrators. When the police entered the building, some of the demonstrators came at them with sticks and clubs. A few cops were seriously hurt, but no officer was able to identify the attackers.

Then the *Stanford Daily* published its stories on the incident. The paper also published numerous photographs. After seeing them, the Santa Clara County district attorney's office applied for—and obtained—a warrant to search the newspaper's offices for all pictures taken during the incident. No one on the newspaper staff was a suspect in the attack; the district attorney simply wanted evidence that would show what had happened. The search was conducted according to the terms of the warrant. A month later, the *Stanford Daily* filed a lawsuit asserting that the search had violated its First and Fourth Amendment protections.

The case crawled through the courts. The federal trial court found for the plaintiffs, as did the Ninth Circuit Court of Appeals. That court held that the Bill of Rights also prohibited searching the premises of any third parties who were not suspected in the commission of a crime. The Ninth Circuit held that such searches are even less appropriate and permissible when their object is a newspaper.

The U.S. Supreme Court disagreed. Writing for the majority, Justice Byron White—"Whizzer" to those of us who knew of his football heroics at Colorado University—said it was generally true that search warrants cannot be obtained to conduct third-party searches—that is, searches of people not suspected of a crime. And yet he said there was nothing in the Fourth Amendment nor in the First Amendment that prohibited law enforcement officers from issuing a subpoena for information—and following it up with a search warrant if the information was not produced.

The Fourth Estate went nuts, immediately decrying the Supreme Court's ruling as an assault on the press. Editorialists complained that it would have a chilling effect—always it's a chilling effect—on the gathering of news. Columnists said the ruling impinged on the public's vaunted and oft-cited right to know. It seemed to me that journalists were reading a hell of a lot into a very precise, very understandable, and extremely well-crafted opinion. Never mind that Justice White had been quite specific about what the law would be. Journalists nonetheless insisted that all sacred newsrooms somehow would now be fit subjects for police searches at any hour of the day or night.

Two years after that ruling, the Senate Judiciary Committee began considering a piece of legislation that would require prosecutors to issue a subpoena for certain documents held by journalists. Such a new law would thus partially conform the federal statutes to Justice White's opinion. The difference between a search warrant and a subpoena is this: The search warrant is a judicial order authorizing the law enforcement officer to search someone's personal home, boat, car, you name it, either in or out of that person's presence; the subpoena is the legal order requiring someone to appear in court to give testimony and provide evidence, and a subpoena duces tecum orders a person to come to court bringing along certain documents.

After reading the draft legislation, entitled "The Privacy Protection Act," I generally supported what it tried to do. I felt that it recognized the unique tools that journalists need and the protected role the press must have in our society. As a conservative, I am inclined to believe that less government is better than more government, and thus I agreed that the government should employ the least intrusive possible means to gather information for a criminal trial. In that sense, issuing a subpoena seemed okay. And yet the new law did not go far enough for me. The requirement that prosecutors must always serve media outlets with a subpoena before seeking a search warrant struck me as overly burdensome, especially in light of the facts in the *Stanford Daily* case. Remember now, this campus newspaper had a clear policy of destroying any photographs that might aid in the prosecution of students who had attacked and injured the nine policemen. The attorney for the newspaper stood before the justices of the Supreme Court and freely acknowledged that fact.

I therefore tried to amend the proposed legislation so it would be more to my liking. I felt that journalists—yes, Lord sakes, even journalists—have certain obligations and responsibilities when it comes to the prosecution of a criminal case. With that in mind, I proposed that "police officers be given the right to enter a newsroom unannounced [with a search warrant] and search through files for evidence, *if* they think use of a subpoena would result in destruction of documents sought." Basically, I was trying to outmaneuver the *Stanford Daily*. In my book, as a lawyer, the destruction of any evidence makes it impossible for a person to get a fair trial, and therefore must never be permitted. The national press corps paid little attention to me at the time, but I remember several Wyoming journalists thumping me hard for proposing that amendment.

The final bill became law without my amendment. Still, I felt

I was right. It still troubles me that journalists seem to actually think there should be a completely different set of laws governing them as citizens. The journalism profession flourishes without any form of formal regulation, and that is as it should be. But is it necessary for us to bestow such sweeping and awesome powers to the media? In the final committee report on that bill, I said, "The lack of a destruction of evidence exception for work product is particularly regrettable in that it can only serve to benefit the few highly ir-responsible members of the journalism profession who seek to withhold evidence from the criminal justice system. The over-whelming preponderance of press in this country are not likely to destroy evidence or refuse to cooperate with law enforcement of-ficials. Documentary materials in their possession would normally be available through subpoenas. These journalists have no need to be afforded any enhanced protections since there would be no reason to believe that they would destroy, alter or conceal docu-ments. It is only the irresponsible press which will have the op-portunity to seize upon the absolutist protections in [the bill]."

Again, the lightweights and reactionaries of the profession were given all the same protections as the true professionals. Sadly, there may be far more in the former group than in the latter. And yet even the good journalists stood up for the bad ones. The ancient, arrogant creed of the profession—"We stand by our story"—should be edited to say "We stand by anybody who ever wrote a story." I am reminded of a quotation attributed to Zachariah Cha-fee, Jr., the grandfather of my great friend and Senate colleague John Chafee, a rock-solid product of Rhode Island. Zachariah got things just right in 1948 when he said, "The press is sort of a wild animal in our midst—restless, gigantic, always seeking new ways to use its strength. The sovereign press for the most part acknowl-edges accountability to no one except its owners and publishers."

I didn't like a lot of the things the media did, but the fact is that I was in those salad days enjoying a very cordial relationship with most of the Washington press corps, and with some reporters in particular. I suppose they considered me something of a novelty. My distinctly Western style—alarming nasal twang, odd vocal and facial expressions, earthy or even ribald sense of humor—apparently endeared me to a press corps that was accustomed to a much more buttoned-down crowd. And let me be the first to say that I also enjoyed the reporters and—yes, sure—the attention they paid to me.

An example of my early favorable press attention was a story by Ward Sinclair in the January 11, 1980, edition of the *Washington Post*. The piece was headlined "Freshman Simpson: Western Breeze Through Stuffy Senate." That headline came as a relief when I picked up the paper that morning: You never know which way a story is going to go. Here's how the story began:

A senator who finds renewal in Thurber and Mencken, keeps Western originals by Russell and Remington on his walls and sees the Senate as something of a funny farm deserves a closer look.

Actually, the word about Alan K. Simpson, a Republican from Wyoming, got around rather quickly after he showed up in the Senate last year.

The guy is different, they were saying. He talked back to senior senators, always with courtly deference, but he talked back. Don't tell me how to vote, he cautioned committee staffers accustomed to telling senators how to vote.

Simpson, 48, came here last year labeled as one of those new hard-core conservatives hell-bent on standing big government on its head.

The game of politics, alas, is played with labels and codes and Simpson is stuck with his label. What a yuk.

He is conservative and big government doesn't enamor him, but his link with the label pretty much ends there. He idolizes some of the liberals he's supposed to abhor, cosponsors their bills and trades ribald stories with them.

Simpson turns out to be one of the most refreshing breezes that occasionally gentles their way through Congressional pomp and fustian to remind that all is not lost; it hasn't even been found.

Sinclair also reported, accurately, that my "profanity can reach lyrical levels," that I rarely issued a press release or sent a newsletter to constituents, and that I sometimes answer my own phone. He told the story of the day somebody called and said, "Where is that skinny bastard?"

"Speaking," I said.

Sinclair's story was a delight. I loved it. And why not? His premise—that I was an exciting new player in a stuffy old game—was completely benign. He apparently could not find even one person to say anything negative about me, though God knows more than one must have been out there. When people asked me how I liked the piece, I would say, "I enjoy sniffing it but I try not to inhale." (I don't use that response anymore, and anybody who followed the 1992 presidential campaign knows why.) I think Sinclair was—I mean this exactly—more than fair. He was also a lot of fun to know. He had a wickedly delightful sense of humor you could spot in a moment. He went on to cover agriculture for the *Post* and eventually ended up running a farm of his own—and loving it! Which makes me wonder: How come a lot of the people who should be reporters are farmers? And how come a lot of the people who should be farmers are reporters shoveling the stuff farmers shovel? Ward is gone from us now. We miss him.

I forged many friendships with Washington journalists during those early years in the Senate. Do not be misled by some of my harsher criticisms—there are some damn fine people in Washington who practice the craft. Meg Greenfield, editorial page editor at the *Post,* was one I met early on. She is just about my vintage—high school class of '49. We would talk animatedly about our high school and college days; she has a wit and energy and irreverence that I find quite pleasing. Al Hunt, of the *Wall Street Journal,* was another friend. Sometimes Al gets very intense, but you can see that he is only probing, seeking, questioning. The syndicated columnist Mark Shields is a delight. He is a ribald, earthy, robust guy with a piercing sense of humor. Al, Mark Shields, and I would have lunch together. I have always richly respected the work of *Post* columnist David Broder, and David himself. If there is a more thoughtful, pungent, prescient, and instructive journalist in the business, I do not know that person. The leaders of our nation would do well to pay closer attention to Broder's thoughtful and well-grounded columns. Helen Dewar, the finest of print journalists covering the Senate. Kay Graham, a strong and trusted friend. I also came to know the irrepressible Sam Donaldson, who is just as tough on the Democrats as on the Republicans. Behind that impish and sinister gleam is a solid, delightful, sincere fellow. Jim Lehrer is extraordinarily bright, patient, and kind. Columnist Rollie Evans always delighted me with his marvelous wry smile and his incredulous looks. And Bob Novak always managed to smile thinly while saying, "You can't possibly and really honestly be telling us this. Can you?" A good egg. Among other journalist friends were TV's Ann Compton, a genial and gracious woman; "Budge" Sperling, an "oh shucks" down-to-earth chap who can get a lot out of you at breakfast; and pungent columnist Carl Rowan, who greatly honored me by selecting me to give the Republican response at the Gridiron Dinner. I also enjoy Ted Koppel, William Raspberry, Charlie McDowell, Gloria Borger, Karen Tumulty, Ben Wattenberg, Elaine Povich, Miles Benson, and many more. Each of these relationships was important to me—not because they were with journalists, but because they were with people I consider special.

Early in my tenure, I became involved in an issue that would eventually put me at odds with some of those fine journalists, and with many others too. The issue that caused the rift was immigration—legal and illegal. Faced with public concern and even fear over the number of refugees and illegal immigrants arriving in the United States, President Jimmy Carter had, near the end of his term, appointed the Select Commission on Immigration and Refugee Policy. Among the appointees were academics, business leaders, government types—and, to my great surprise and dismay, me. But why? I had no interest in the subject whatsoever. I went to Howard Baker, my party's superb and steady leader in the Senate, and asked him if he knew why I had been appointed. Yes, he did. The president was required to have a bipartisan commission, he said. And since I was a junior member of the Judiciary Committee, Baker had decided to dump—I mean, confer—the appointment upon me! Lord! I tried to get out of the job, but I was stuck. Little did I know then that the issue would eventually consume a large portion of my Senate career.

At the same time, great change was taking place in the nation. On election night in November 1980, Ann and I watched the returns at a joyful Washington gathering of Senate colleagues and other loyal Republicans. Ronald Reagan was winning big, but that was only part of the story. On that dramatic night, the entire base of political power in the nation would shift. As the networks sped through the state-by-state results, it became clear that a lot of once-powerful Democrats were going to lose. Down went John Culver; down went Herman Talmadge; down went Birch Bayh; down went Gaylord Nelson. These venerable senior Democrats would soon be joined in defeat by Warren Magnuson, Frank Church, George McGovern, John Durkin, and Robert Morgan. These icons of liberal democratic politics were being unceremoniously toppled by energetic Republicans. The Reagan Revolution had begun; now there would be a Republican majority in the Senate. Suddenly the Grand Old Party had power.

One exhilarated chap grabbed a microphone that night and shouted to the faithful, "Do you honestly realize what all of this means—the real significance of all this?" Oh yes, sir! We realized. Howard Baker would be the new majority leader of the United States Senate. Strom Thurmond—that courteous, disciplined, rock-solid conservative Southerner—would be the chairman of the Judiciary Committee. Affable Bob Stafford of Vermont would head up the Environment and Public Works Committee. Bob Dole, the most powerful, practical practicing politician of our time, would now chair the Finance Committee. Bob Packwood, a re-markable fact-gatherer and debater who encouraged me in that first run for the Senate, would lead the Commerce Committee. Dogged, determined Pete Domenici would lead us as chairman of the Budget Committee. Change upon change. As for me, I would, in my third year in the Senate, become the new chairman of the Senate Committee on Veterans' Affairs, replacing my old mentor and friend Al Cranston, the liberal, anti-nukes Democrat of California. As chairman of a full standing committee, I would now be part of the Republican Party's executive committee, and therefore would be among those who set the Senate's agenda. No more would we be just a ragged band of ranking members. Now we would all be committee chairmen, and as such would have political power and influence unseen in our party for years and years. What a giddy evening!

The first call I received the next day was from Al Cranston. "Congratulations, Mr. Chairman," he said. Later that day, Strom Thurmond bounded up to me, grasped my hand, and said, "Alan"—pronounced "Ell-en"—"I've been in the Senate twenty-six years and never been a chairman. You've been here two years and here you are! Your daddy would be proud. I'm very proud of you." I appreciated that so much, especially coming from the likes of Strom. Becoming chairman was pretty heady stuff. I was off and running!

My whole life changed. No longer was I minor player on my committees. As chairman of the Veterans' Affairs Committee, I would constantly be trying to answer the nagging question of whether we had really done enough for our Vietnam veterans. I would take on such emotional issues as Agent Orange, prisoners of war, outreach centers, and so on. With the change in leadership, I also became chairman of the Nuclear Regulation Subcommittee, replacing Gary Hart. The committee still had much work to do if we were going to restore public confidence in the regulation of commercial nuclear power after Three Mile Island. My responsibilities on the Environment and Public Works Committee also increased exponentially. I was cosponsor of the Superfund legislation. I worked long, hard hours on such issues as clean air, clean water, acid rain, the protection of truly endangered species, and so on. And I was most assuredly not politically correct on some of those issues.

But without question the most difficult and nagging issue I dealt with was immigration. On President Jimmy Carter's Select Commission on Immigration and Refugee Policy, I had served with some of the finest people in this country—Democrat and Republican, liberal and conservative, labor and business. The Rev. Theodore Hesburgh, then president of Notre Dame University, chaired the panel. What a true leader he is. With Father Ted's guidance, our commission presented a thorough, accurate, and well-researched report to the nation. Now it was time to take the commission's recommendations and try to legislate them into law. The Senate Judiciary Committee would be the venue for doing that. With the change in power in the Senate, Ted Kennedy was replaced as Judiciary Committee chairman by Strom Thurmond. Ted—who had worked with me on Carter's select commission—felt that it would be sensible and timely to establish a separate immigration subcommittee, and I agreed. So did Strom Thurmond. Thus, three members of the select commission—Kennedy, Senator Dennis DeConcini, and I—became charter members of the Subcommittee on Immigration and Refugee Policy of the U.S. Senate Judiciary Committee. I was chairman. Soon we were ready to address some highly controversial legislation on a highly emotional and critical issue.

Democratic and Republican senators and congressmen had for years been trying to address the problem of uncontrolled illegal immigration into the United States. These same legislators—understanding that some unscrupulous employers loved to hire illegal immigrants and pay them slave wages—tried to pass laws that would penalize such businesspeople. But a farcical part of the law known aptly as "the Texas proviso" always stood in the way of sensible reform. The Texas proviso made a mockery of immigration law by making it legal to hire an illegal, but illegal for the illegal to work. That's right—you could hire all the undocumented immigrants you wanted, and if you got caught, they paid the price. Clearly this was a pressing national issue that needed some kind of honest, understandable, sensible resolution. I intended to give it my very best shot.

I sought help from one of the finest persons I know. Dick Day is an old lawyer pal of mine from Cody, Wyoming. A former college professor, Dick is a solid, intelligent, and marvelously nonpolitical man with a strong sense of fairness and a whimsical and elegant sense of humor. In January 1981, he and his wonderful wife, Judy, were my guests at Ronald Reagan's inauguration. During his visit, I gave him a tour of my modest office digs on the sixth floor of the Dirksen Building, showing as much enthusiasm as I could possibly muster about the new challenges I faced. And then I asked him to come to Washington and work with me on immigration.

"Think hard before you say no," I told him. "Be my chief counsel and staff director on the immigration subcommittee. You may know nothing of the issue now, but you will learn quickly enough. Study the issue just as would the steady former college professor you were, and the fine lawyer you are." Dick said nothing. I went on, "Dick, I'm heading into an issue that will be fraught with bigotry, racism, and xenophobia. I'll be hit with full bucketloads of bullshit. People will try to use emotion, fear, and guilt to hurt me. I need somebody who knows me and loves me and will help me cut through the crap. I need you."

Dick Day still said little. But when he finally smiled that wry smile of his, I knew that he had sniffed the bait and it would be only a matter of time before I would set the hook and reel in my prize Wyoming catch. Sure enough, Dick called a few days later and accepted my offer.

By then, the House was also taking up the immigration issue. Normally, the House and the Senate would draft bills, hold separate hearings, conduct votes, and then try to reconcile the bills into one functional law. That approach did not make sense to Dick Day and me, not this time. We both saw immigration reform as an issue that transcended partisan politics. And we saw no sense in holding a hearing in the Senate one week and then watching as the same hearing, with many of the same witnesses, was conducted in the House the next week. So we decided to see if there was some way to work jointly with the House of Representatives.

That wasn't going to be easy. For one thing, the two houses of Congress typically work separately, as I've said. For another, the legislator who was overseeing the issue in the house was—egad!—a Democrat, Romano "Ron" Mazzoli of Kentucky. Ron, a Notre Dame graduate, had served on Father Ted's select commission with me. I already knew him to be a prince of a guy and a hardworking and truly industrious and committed legislator. At first, both parties resisted the idea of a partnership—neither party wanted to be seen as giving aid and comfort to the enemy—but partisan politics were soon pushed aside and Ron and I began our work.

Our aim was to craft a law that would undo the Texas proviso—a law that would hold all employers accountable for hiring undocumented immigrants. Ron and I held five joint hearings, and I conducted nine additional hearings in the Senate. We heard hundreds of hours of testimony from more than a hundred witnesses. We had clear heads and brass butts. Those hearings weren't just the standard nine-to-noon jobs. Hell no! They ran from breakfast until lunch, and after that until the dinner hour or beyond. One of us was present at all times. So was Dick Day, who was mastering the subject as swiftly as we were.

I also busted my fanny to make certain that people with views different from ours would get the chance to testify. Sometimes I would ask Dick, "Who is the orneriest rascal in this country on the other side of this particular aspect of the issue?" He would name a person or two—he always knew exactly who the extreme ones were—and we would then invite them to testify. These people would say their piece, and often they would take a few shots at us. We would then fire a few shots in return. And I think both sides enjoyed themselves.

I remember only one occasion when things got out of hand. The witness was the Reverend Monsignor Salvador Alvarez, a Roman Catholic deacon who worked with an organization that represented the interests of Mexican-Americans in the church and in the United States. Part of our legislation would have created a group of temporary farm workers who could enter the country and work here legally for a fixed period of time. The idea always was to try to reduce the number who crossed the border illegally in search of work. Alvarez didn't care for our plan. He felt that these workers would be made to work like "slaves"—he used that word—only to be unceremoniously sent home when they were no longer needed. He also believed that the temporary workers would take away work from people already in the country, legally or otherwise. Alvarez said, "Your bill is directed to provide a deathblow to the United Farm Workers of America."

I had a question for the deacon. "You testified that here is a blatant attempt to destroy the United Farm Workers of America. If you can, sir, answer me this, because I do not understand it. I really do not. Today we have a situation where hundreds of thousands of illegal, undocumented farm workers enter the United States every year. Hundreds of thousands. How can we provide protection for either the U.S. farm worker or the undocumented farm worker with the situation that exists today?" To my way of thinking, the undocumented workers were being exploited and were filling jobs that could have been done by legal immigrants. How would the status quo possibly help anyone he was speaking for?

Alvarez did not have a very good answer. But he sure had plenty of inflammatory accusations. He said, "What you are proposing in your legislation is racist. . . . Racism has extended itself into immigration policy in this country." He insisted that the United States allow greatly increased immigration from Latin America "the way it was done for other groups."

Finally, I got fed up. "Let's you and I visit. How would you like to do that, chum, instead of babbling into the airwaves at each other. Why do not you and I have a little appointment and talk about things? Because if you want to just come in and be incendiary, you do it. That is not the way I do my business, so I will visit with you, and you and I will have a chat and talk about things that are of importance to you and to me, instead of just playing Ping-Pong. Eighty-five percent of the legal immigrants in this country last year were non-Europeans, so do not come in here and truck that load of stuff around in this chamber."

Alvarez snapped, "That is good campaign rhetoric, Senator."

I drew a breath. "You know, I try to use facts. When everything else fails, it is usually a hell of a good thing to do. I am not trying to be rude or a dink with you, but if you want to come in here and just shoot it around the room, why, you have got the wrong chairman." With that, I pushed away my microphone and turned over the witness to Senator Paul Simon of Illinois.

Paul looked wide-eyed at me and said ruefully, "I thank you. I am glad I got on this noncontroversial subcommittee here, Mr. Chairman."

Senator Ted Kennedy, the ranking member of the Judiciary Committee, sat through many of the long hearings and always provided helpful ideas. Kennedy knows most of the procedures better than almost anybody in the Senate. He guided me around some pretty gargantuan boulders strewn along the path. No one knew the agendas of the various advocacy groups better than he. When someone was out to get me, he warned me. He also got Ron and me to make some suitable compromises that we might not otherwise have made. Ted voted against the bill in the end, as I expected he would. And yet he almost cast a yes vote in one of our last committee hearings. At least, I think he did. When the clerk called his name, he just kind of grunted. When his name was called again, he mumbled. The clerk took that as a no. I asked him later, "What the hell did you say when you voted?" I think he wanted to say yes, but his mouth could not form the word. His tough ethnic and activist constituencies in Massachusetts would simply not allow that. Let the record show that I enjoy Ted Kennedy very much. Forget his past. Forget partisanship. Forget judging others. A good and true friend he is.

The news media were also present for our hearings, day after day, hour after exhausting hour. I was impressed with the work they did. They covered this complex matter in a straightforward and truthful way, whether they were writing about those I agreed with or those with whom I strongly disagreed. My staff worked hard to help them, and to strengthen relationships with them. My knowledgeable, likable, and efficient press secretary, Mary Kay Hill, was available whenever a reporter needed her, and so was Dick Day. I also tried very hard to meet with all journalists. They needed my assistance, and I knew I couldn't get support for immigration reform without constantly stressing my side.

Getting balanced news coverage was one thing; getting the support of media opinion-makers was quite another. To really sell the reform package to the American people, I had to win over columnists and editorial writers at all of the major media outlets. So again, I went out on the road to meet the press. My first stop was New York. At the *New York Times,* I met with Jack Rosenthal (not the one who was my college friend—this is another Jack Rosenthal). He knew more about immigration than perhaps anyone else in the media. He also knew lawmaking: Jack had been a congressional staffer. He knew the Hill, knew the players, and knew their games. Jack asked, "How goes the battle? What are your views of it now? Did the last amendments tear it up badly? Where are you headed at this very moment?" Then we would have a good visit—not as reporter and politician, but as friends. He was always supportive.

From Jack's office I hied myself off to the *Wall Street Journal,* where I met with members of the editorial board for about forty-five minutes. That was the real low point of all my national trips. I began by making my case for illegal immigration reform and answering a few questions. Then I became aware of a certain still-ness in the room, a certain glaze in the eyes of my silent audience. I had a sinking feeling. One of the senior editors stirred from his near-slumber and said, "Senator, I live in Teaneck, New Jersey. I drive into the city every morning and I've never seen an illegal alien. I think your solution may be unnecessary and uncalled-for." Well, well. He had never seen an illegal alien on his drive in from Teaneck, so unchecked immigration was not a problem. Wow! That myopic and ill-informed statement basically sums up the *Journal*'s editorial treatment of the issue over the past decade. When that fellow made his statement, I figured the smartest thing for me to do was to grab my hat and coat, get the hell out of there, and suck up some fresh air. And so I did.

I started up a running gun battle with the *Journal* on that day, and it's been going on ever since. Things later got so bad that they would just regularly love to whack away at me and seldom give me the fair opportunity to respond in their biased pages. Nothing has changed. What a bunch.

Other prominent editorial writers got out of their cars or limos long enough to see the need for reform. Among them was Pat Shakow of the *Washington Post* editorial board. Pat had once been a Senate staffer, serving with the brilliant and inspirational Jack Javits of New York. She wrote much thoughtful commentary, adeptly and seriously analyzing the issue. Tony Day, the earnest and yet laid-back editorial page editor of the *Los Angeles Times,* understood what we were trying to do, and why. His work often shed light where it was needed. I can't say the same for *Los Angeles Times* cartoonist Robert Conrad, whose dark, foreboding, macabre drawings played to people's most irrational fears. In one drawing,

Conrad rendered the American flag as a prison door, with the white stripes as bars and the red stripes as dripping blood. Poor defenseless immigrants were shown standing behind the bars. That cartoon was a cheap shot at Mazzoli and me, and he damn well knew it. Conrad never understood immigration, refugee, or asylum issues at all. Still doesn't.

Jonathan Friedman of the Copley papers in San Diego poured enormous time, effort, and energy into understanding the issue and explaining it to his readers. He won a Pulitzer Prize for his efforts. Friedman was superb, an extraordinary ally in a part of the country where we surely needed all the thoughtful support we could muster. And speaking of Pulitzer, it might be timely to relate what he said in 1907: "A cynical, mercenary, demagogic press will produce, in time, a people as base as the world itself." Words to live by.

Ron and I introduced our bill on March 17, 1982—St. Patrick's Day. This was in the heady early months of Ronald Reagan's presidency. Senators O'Simpson and O'Mazzoli were going to try to win one for the Gipper. That was a memorable day for me. Up to that point I had participated in various press conferences but had never called one myself. Now it was time. We were proposing important, sweeping legislation and would need the whole nation's support to pass it. Ron Mazzoli and I met the press in the historic caucus room of the Russell Senate Office Building. Many of the reporters present had plumbed the issue in extraordinary depth. They all asked good, tough questions.

The *New York Times*'s lead editorial was headlined "Not Nativist, Not Racist, Not Mean." It said, "A Republican Senator and a Democratic Congressman joined yesterday to introduce a rare piece of legislation: a responsible immigration bill. . . . As a general proposition the Simpson-Mazzoli bill is at once tough, fair and humane." We considered that to be a pretty damn good review.

We got generally favorable reviews from most of the major media outlets. The papers were full of positive editorials and op-ed pieces. Still, I would hunch that most of the nation's editorial writers would be most uncomfortable with any idea that they served as cheerleaders or even supporters. Those words make journalists blanch, and rightly so. And yet journalists need not be so uneasy about supporting good ideas. There seems to be a feeling in the media—among editorial writers and news reporters alike—that supporting what is best for the country or the community compromises one's journalistic integrity. I disagree. Most major media companies definitely supported the Simpson-Mazzoli legislation, even though they might not always have been comfortable admitting it.

Most, but not all. There was always the *Wall Street Journal* to contend with. The *Journal* regularly used—and still uses—its editorial pages to trash any kind of workable immigration reform. The paper offered no solutions, mind you, just biting and haughty criticism. One must always remember that media outlets are first and foremost profit-making businesses, not the benevolent, community-minded institutions they often posture to be. The *Wall Street Journal* is not just a repository for journalism, but a salable product tailored carefully to those in the business world. And make no mistake: The people in charge of the *Journal* decided that their readers did not want illegal immigration reform. They apparently also decided they had no obligation to print my thoughts. My many attempts at presenting my side in an op-ed article or even a letter to the editor went for naught. I finally sought the advice of my old friend Al Hunt, the Washington bureau chief of the *Journal*. His urging seemed to help. The paper's editorial page continues to display absolute and wholesale ignorance of immigration, refugee, and asylum problems, but every now and again the *Journal* condescends to print one of my letters to the editor. Seeing one there is like finding a ruby in the dung.

I recall one that appeared in 1990. The *Journal* had even tried to link me to racist David Duke—the Louisiana guy with a white supremacist platform—by saying I was against all immigration, period. A xenophobe *cum laude*. This after I had proposed a 35 percent increase in legal immigration. My October 18, 1990, letter said, "You imply that I am a racist. Not only is that crude and unprofessional, but it masks the real truth. Your editorial board really longs for the good old plantation days, when workers were subservient, worked their butts to the bone, and were fearful of the sting of the lash. You apparently would want to return to those days through open-border immigration. However, that is assuredly not my vision of America's future."

I went on: "I believe we must close the back door to illegal immigration. If we do that realistically and compassionately we can then open the front door wider to legal immigration. Very few Americans would agree with you that both doors should be thrown wide open—or blasted right off their hinges."

I often wonder how the *Journal* feels now that we have seen some of the consequences of too-liberal immigration—shootings at the CIA in 1993, the bombing of the World Trade Center, and the passage of the hard-edged Proposition 187 in California in 1994. I don't suppose those things bother people at the *Journal* much. No doubt the *Journal* would still like to see a national immigration policy that allows fat-cat businesspeople—that is, many *Wall Street Journal* readers—to import, exploit, and then casually discard wasted illegal aliens.

We worked on illegal immigration reform for five long years. And during that time, we never once changed our behavior or our attitude in an effort to curry favor with the media. We never tried to produce a seven-camera hearing by calling some irrelevant but well-known person as a witness. Remember when the actress Jessica Lange testified in Congress about the terrible shortcomings of the nation's farm program? At that moment, Congress was spending something like $26 billion a year on farm programs, but never mind. The point is, Jessica Lange was not an expert in agriculture. She was testifying simply because she had starred in *Country,* a poignant movie about tending of the soil. The use of such star witnesses lends a phony feeling to a serious subject. We could not afford to do that with immigration reform. We were not about to call Meryl Streep as a witness just because she had played people from various countries whence immigrants had flowed. We felt we had to deal openly and honestly with the true issues of illegal immigration, and just hope that people would hear the message. They did, thanks to some hardworking newspeople.

Time to name names. We had a stellar crowd covering illegal immigration reform—Ben Shore from the Copley newspapers, Karen Tumulty of the *Los Angeles Times,* Robert Pear of the *New*

York Times, Nadine Cohadis reporting for *Congressional Quarterly,* Karen McPherson of Scripps Howard, Bill Choyke representing the *Dallas Morning News,* Kathy Kiley of the *Houston Post,* Judy Weissler from the *Houston Chronicle,* Sue Schaeffer and Larry Margasak of the Associated Press, Jessica Lee from Gannett, Beth Fehrking of the *Denver Post,* and Mary Thornton from the *Washington Post.*

Many years have passed since Ron Mazzoli and I began our efforts, and yet I still remember each of them well. They were diligent, committed, and always professional. And they asked some damn good questions. Were we afraid that employers would avoid hiring people of, say, Hispanic descent if we passed employer sanctions? Didn't the Statue of Liberty urge us to accept all the poor, huddled masses yearning to breathe free? How would amnesty for some illegal immigrants be perceived by Americans who might be out of work themselves? What are the honest concerns over a national ID card? What effect would our legislation have on people who simply "look foreign"? By asking these questions, the reporters pressed us ever harder to do our work well.

The Simpson-Mazzoli immigration bill passed the Senate on August 17, 1982, by a strong vote of 80 to 19. Then it went to the House. It lay dormant there for many days until my old friend Thomas "Tip" O'Neill, then the speaker of the House, made a solemn promise to me to bring it to the floor very late in the legislative year. He did so, and took a hell of a lot of criticism for it. A wonderful man he was. Still, the bill came up too late to be fully and fairly debated in the House, and so it died there in December 1982.

We introduced the bill again during the next Congress. This time, it passed the Senate by another good vote of 76 to 18. It bounced around the House for a while before Tip O'Neill again brought it to the floor. This time—by now it was the fall of 1984— the House fully debated our immigration reform measure, and passed it. But we still had much work to do. Because there were serious differences between the House and Senate versions, the bill was sent to a conference committee at which members of both chambers would try to work out a compromise. I served on the committee. For ten often contentious days we slogged away. We resolved a number of controversial issues, but then we came to one we couldn't resolve. The conferees could not agree on how much money to appropriate to help settle and assimilate the previously illegal immigrants. We could offer no more than $4 billion because the Reagan administration said it would veto the bill if we went a penny higher. The House conferees said unanimously that $4 billion was not enough. They told me, "Oh, come on, you're a friend of the president. Go back and tell him we need more." I was firm. "I know the president. It won't work," I said. I wasn't even going to suggest such a thing again to the president. I had tried before.

After many months of delays, deep disappointments, and soaring successes, we were stuck. There was nothing I could do. I just swallowed hard, took a deep breath, and said, "I guess that's it. We don't have a bill." And then New Jersey Democrat Peter Rodino, the old pro of the Watergate hearings and a fine gentleman, hammered down the gavel for the last time on that conference. I shall never forget the stunned look on the faces of those in the hearing room—the faces of people who had worked so hard, and so long, for nothing. People from all sides of the issue, pro and con, gathered around Ron and me as the media began asking questions. "Couldn't you have sold the Administration on a higher price tag?" "Why would you take it this far and let it die here?" I don't know that I really answered the questions—I was too hurt and stunned to think clearly. And yet I knew that we had perhaps only one more chance to get the legislation passed before Ronald Reagan left office. He was always tremendously supportive of my efforts, and of the cause. Others in his administration, most of them Californians, were not so enthusiastic.

The anguish of our failure passed, and soon we cranked up for another try in the session that began in January 1985. When I introduced the Senate bill that year, I told reporters, "I am not a three-time loser. I intend to get 'er done this trip!" The Senate passed the bill by 69 to 30 that time; we could not help but notice that we were getting fewer votes each time out. In the House, the bill passed by a solid vote of 230 to 166. Again the bill was sent into the jaws of a conference committee. But this time, I would be serving as chairman, and Peter Rodino, who had chaired the previous conference, would be vice chairman. The Senate Judiciary Committee chairman, my sturdy friend Strom Thurmond, gave me free rein to deal and loaded my pockets with proxies. I was going to need them.

The conference committee lurched along, but made good progress. But then we got hung up again. It seemed our final conference gathering was going to fail too. Then Peter Rodino called me aside for a word. He said, "Meet me in my office. Let's see if you and I alone can't hammer something out. If so, we'll take the rest of them along with us. We know the issues. I've been working on them for over fifteen years, since 1970, and you've been at it for six years. If you and I don't know what we have to do, who the hell does?" That reasoning sounded pretty damn solid to me.

So on a bright, sunny morning before the next (and possibly last) conference meeting, the two of us sat down. Peter said, "Where are you on legalization?"—meaning amnesty.

I drew my line in the sand. I said, "Where are you on funding for the states and counties after legalization?"

He stated his position.

We asked each other, "How do we lessen the fear of illegal immigrants who might want to seek temporary resident status—but will have to present themselves to the Immigration and Naturalization Service in order to do so?"

There were many other questions to answer. "What about discrimination?" "What about additional agricultural workers?" We gave and we took. We thrusted and we parried. We shoved and jousted. We pushed and we pulled. When we were done and the deal was closed, we shook hands, smiled, and headed back to the conference.

Looking down the long table at Peter, I gaveled the conferees to order. Peter laid out the terms of our agreement, and we made good progress. We all knew the alternative—failure. But then we came upon two tough sticking points. One was a House provision that called on the Justice Department to investigate possible discrimination against legally documented workers. I didn't like that idea. Leave that to the Equal Employment Opportunity Commission, I argued. The other involved agricultural workers. Growers across the country were rearing back and snorting fire over the possible loss of cheap and available labor to harvest America's crops. Some of the House members agreed with the growers. We were snookered again. This was all happening near the end of the 1986 session. Members of Congress were eager to recess for the election. Once again, we were running out of time.

About that time, Peter said, "Mr. Chairman, may I be recognized?"

I recognized him.

"Mr. Chairman," he said, "I have an idea worth considering. Let's go back into the large room just outside of this hearing room. Just us members. No staff. If we can do that, I think we can come to closure on this conference."

The whole thing was a planned performance. Peter and I had agreed that, if necessary, we would do exactly what he was proposing. Following our script, I said, "I respect the suggestion of my vice chairman from the House. We will conclude the public portion of this meeting and members will meet immediately at the appointed place."

And so we did. Peter stepped into the middle of that room with a steely, determined look on his face. My expression matched his. We were determined. Vital. Powerful. Persuasive. Tired of the crap. Right away, we started crushing knuckles. We issued threats, veiled and unveiled. The Senate conferees responded appropriately—they graciously followed the official line. Most of the House people did too. When you are flashing proxies all day long—especially ones given to you by Howard Metzenbaum and sometimes Ted Kennedy—the House knows you're there to do business. But I will never forget one House member—a liberal Democrat—who tried to slip out of the room. He told Peter Rodino, "I simply have to visit with a member of my staff before I can agree to that proposal."

Peter said, "You are not going anywhere. Remember the conditions: no staff. No lobbyists. Nobody else here. Just make your decision. And make it right here and right now, one way or the other. I will tell you, though, that I think you want to be voting right. And in this situation, voting right means being with your chairman."

I will never forget the look on that chap's face. He knew who had won that round.

Three hours later, we all walked out of that room—with a bill! I laid the final product on the table and announced, "The conferees have agreed. The staff will prepare the final report. I deeply thank my good friend Peter Rodino and each and every one of you. This conference is adjourned." Hearty congratulations went out all around. We were all pleased and proud.

Before the agreement could be put to a final vote in both halls of Congress, I had a promise to keep. I had promised my colleagues that I would get the president's support for the bill. That wasn't going to be easy. That year, 1986, was an election year, and some Democrats in the House thought President Reagan might veto the bill just to hurt them in the coming elections. And they had ample reason to think so: Attorney General Edwin Meese and many others were advising the president to veto the bill. I could not let that happen. Ronald Reagan and George Bush had always supported the immigration reform effort, so I went directly to the president. I told him I thought we had the best deal we could ever get that would still accomplish meaningful reform. Before long, he gave me his word that he would sign the bill. What a day!

After the House and Senate approved the final version, the president kept the promise. The date was November 6, 1986. I was right there, and I was proud as hell. I had crisscrossed this great country making the case for immigration reform for six years. During that time, I had worked my ass off. Some had painted me as a bigot, a devil, pure evil. And yet I had gotten the thing done. Rarely have I been so satisfied, so deeply pleased, so moved.

Several weeks later, many of us involved in immigration reform—legislators, staff, supporters and detractors, reporters—got together to celebrate the end of our work. The party was held in the D.C. apartment of one of the reporters who had covered the issue through the years. The invitation described the event as a "survivor's party." The place was festooned with banners, signs, sketches, slogans, and graffiti, all of them commenting on our long journey together. That night, we shared the knowledge that we had all done our jobs as well as we could, whether that meant trying to pass the bill, kill the bill, or just explain the bill to the world. The system had worked, and it felt damn good to know that.

My experience with immigration reform also underscored an irrefutable fact of life in Congress: Any major legislation dealing with any complex, tough, and emotional issue will take six, eight, or even ten years to pass through the legislative Cuisinart. That is as it should be. But that fact of legislative life can be hard to accept when you are the impatient principal sponsor.

During the time I worked on the immigration issue I was also doing what every other member in the United States Senate was doing—sitting on too damn many "A" committees, such as Appropriations, Foreign Relations, Commerce, Armed Services, Finance, Judiciary; sitting on too many "B" committees, such as Budget, Rules and Administration, Small Business, Veterans Affairs, Aging, Intelligence; sitting on too many "select committees" such as Taxation, Ethics, Indian Affairs; and too many subcommittees. I was up to my gazoo in committee and subcommittees. I was also eternally trying to find time to visit with constituent groups from Wyoming who had traveled 1,740 miles to Washington and damn well expected to see me when they arrived. And certainly they had a right, because they were the ones who sent me to Washington in the first place. My constituents always got in to see me ahead of lobbyists, interest groups, staff, media, and all the rest.

In late December of 1982, I had heard from my constituents in one big way. At that time, the Senate was involved in a hellacious wrangle over a nickel-a-gallon tax on gasoline that was proposed as part of the transportation funding bill. Some members saw the tax as a reasonable revenue enhancement—that's our euphemism for a tax—while others saw it as a harsh and overly burdensome hit on any number of individuals and enterprises. The Wyoming trucking business—one of the state's most important industries—

felt such a tax would be harmful to its statewide operations. As a result, I got the word from my constituents that supporting the gas tax would not be rollicking good for my legislative future. Hearing that message, and agreeing with them anyway, I vowed to oppose the new tax "with vigah," as John F. Kennedy used to say. Even so, it looked as though the tax would sail on through because we were about to recess for the Christmas holidays.

Or maybe it wouldn't. A number of vehemently opposed members decided to stage a filibuster—unrestrained debate resulting in unending delay. The filibuster was led by the determined, dedicated, wily, sometimes stubborn Senator Jesse Helms, Republican of North Carolina. With Jesse standing there at the bridge of the Senate ship, there was no way that bill was going anywhere.

The hours and days rolled by, with Christmas drawing ever nearer. President Reagan visited with Jesse and personally urged him to allow the bill to go forward. With the antitax Reagan supporting the bill, I began to change my mind about it. The Christmas break was beckoning to me, too. Travel plans for members, families, and staff had already been changed, and changed again and again. By December 22, tempers were flaring, and frustration and irritation were elbowing aside our well-practiced senatorial civility. I was as frustrated and irritated as anybody—and that's what got me in real trouble.

My wonderful pal Bill Cohen of Maine, who came to the Senate when I did and who shared my Senate life fully, heard me bitching and whining about the filibuster in the Senate Dining Room. Finally he said, "Well, what are you going to do about it?"

I said, "Here's what." I took out some notes I had scribbled earlier and said, "That's what I'm going to say in a few minutes."

He read them and said, "Well, good luck!" But he did not leave it at that. Cohen—a wonderful prose stylist and poet, but mostly a pure friend—read the notes again and suggested a few ways in which I might soften my message.

But I wasn't having any of it. I knew—by God—exactly what I was going to do.

Late in the evening, on the Senate floor, I rose to seek recognition. I said, "Seldom have I seen in my legislative experience of seventeen years or more a more obdurate and obnoxious performance. I guess it is called hardball. In my neck of the woods we call it stickball. Children play it. It seems the whole issue of the senator's tenure, as I have observed it in my short term, is, 'How is it playing in North Carolina as to peanuts, tobacco, and family hog farms?' Let them know in North Carolina that the next time those issues come before this body, and are presented to us, there will likely be a veritable phalanx of opposition which will likely be most demeaning and disturbing to the senator's constituency."

When I sat down, I was trembling. I wondered if the words had really come from my mouth. There was absolute silence in the Senate. Jesse was slumped in his seat just a few feet in front of me. He was terribly hurt and stunned. The hurt was in his eyes. I fully knew I had overstepped all bounds of Senate propriety. Perhaps the chair would admonish me. I did not know or care. I had said what I felt I had to say. I became aware of a great deal of milling around after my remarks. I heard hushed comments, saw smiles and frowns. People avoided eye contact with me. I wondered what would happen next. Before the tense evening ended, Jesse and I spoke briefly, then shook hands. Within hours of my unfortunate outburst, an agreement was reached that was satisfactory to Jesse, the president, the committee chairmen and ranking members, and a majority of Democrats and Republicans alike.

The media distorted the whole episode wondrously. It was reported that Jesse and I both stalked from the Senate chamber without speaking after my tirade. Not so. As I said, he and I exchanged a few muttered words and a handshake. And you should have seen the enthusiastic, almost gleeful, coverage given to my comments. I had taken on a fellow whom the press loved to hate, a man they considered an ogre. I was hailed by many media outlets everywhere in America, except perhaps in North Carolina. Reporters said to me, "Senator, many Americans were very pleased with your remarks last night. Do you have anything more to say?" "Has Jesse finally gone too far?" "Will Jesse ever get anything passed again?" Several TV producers asked me to "expand" on my Senate "speech." What speech? I had merely been ranting! I declined all interview requests. I did not want to give the media an opportunity to compound my mistake—an opportunity they were so desperate for.

The day after my outburst, I saw Jesse Helms sitting dejectedly in the cloakroom. I said, "Jesse, you must surely wonder why I did that."

"I certainly do," he said sadly. "I was so stunned and hurt by that. I am very disappointed in you."

"I can understand," I said. "I did it out of a terrible frustration. I just got fed up with the tactics of it all. And because you have such a total mastery of the system and its parliamentary procedures, many of us feel wholly inadequate to the task of ever taking you on. We all have families, and we've had a rugged and tough session. I wanted to get the hell out of here and I was damn determined to do it. But I do want you to know something else—I have not responded to the requested interviews with any of the television or print media, and believe me, they would dearly love to prevail on me to continue whacking on you. I don't intend to do any of that. But I meant what I said, and I said what I meant—and I'll leave it right at that!"

He was now sitting deep in the leather chair in that cloakroom. He stared up at me in his owlish way, then snuffed out a cigarette, stood up very straight, and looked me square in the eye.

"Alan, that is good enough. At least I understand a little better why you did it. You are new here. Someday you will need to use these tactics. One day you will see the true worth of the protection you have under the Senate rules. But for now, I must say that I am still very hurt."

I mumbled that I hoped someday to learn those parliamentary skills and procedures as well as he had. We parted civilly, and I headed for Wyoming. Snowstorms had closed the airport in Denver, my usual point of entry to the West. I spent the night of December 23 hunkered down in a little motel room in Billings, Montana, waiting out one hell of a winter storm. The next day— Christmas Eve—I finally made it home. I was still plenty flustered and embarrassed—yet somehow elated too. I was sorry about what had happened, but yet not sorry. Anyway, I was home.

Jesse and I long ago made our peace over what happened that late December night. But sometimes when I am with Jesse, especially in North Carolina—where I have actively and eagerly campaigned for him in all his reelection efforts since then—the media still ask me about that incident. And Jesse and I both know they'll never quit.

Though I was disturbed with the way the media covered that incident, the fact is that I was still getting along well with them most of the time. As I have said, my early days in the Senate were brightened by many user-friendly profiles and flattering mentions. I figured things would always be jake and just that way. Not everyone thought so. One evening near the back of the Senate chamber, Bill Cohen said, "How you doing, Al?"

"Well, I'm loving it," I said, and then, puffing myself a bit, I mentioned some of the nice things that media people were saying about me.

"They love you," he said. "But simply because of that, watch out. Be very careful. I've been through a similar experience. When I served on the House Judiciary Committee and voted to impeach Richard Nixon, I became the darling of many of those same folks. Then later as they reflected on it, they realized they had abandoned their objectivity when praising me to the skies. Then it didn't take long for them to come down hard, thinking, 'Hey, time to drill this guy's teeth.' In your case, Al, they're going to say, 'He's been getting away with murder and now we're gonna cut him down to size.' They will. Believe me. Count on it."

That was hard to believe at the time. In the early to mid eighties I was often invited to speak at or participate in many media social events in Washington—the annual cartoonists' dinner sponsored by the *Washington Post*, the summer and winter dinners of the Gridiron Club, the Washington Press Club dinner for congresspeople, gatherings at the National Press Club, breakfasts with Budge Sperling and the leading reporters of the day, and many more. At these events I would often tell some of my corniest and most colorful stories. I would say, "Now let me tell you a quick

Wyoming story. This couple hits the sack. At three in the morning the phone rings and the guy answers and says, 'How the hell do I know . . . that's two thousand miles from here!' Then he hangs up, and his wife says, 'Who was it?' 'I dunno, some nut called and asked if the coast was clear.' " And if I didn't tell that one, I'd tell the one about the two guys serving time in another state. One turns to the other and says, "The food was better here when you were governor!" Oh my, how the press folk would smile and laugh. Then they would clap me on the back and chuck me under the chin with their praise. Those were delightful times.

But Bill Cohen was so right. In later years, those sweet times began to wither like squash vines in the wintertime. As time passed, I became more and more familiar with the Washington media— with their intrusiveness, arrogance, cynicism, sarcasm, righteous- ness, and especially their clear and contemptuous and contemptible bias. I became appalled at their lack of accountability, with their abject failure to take any responsibility for the needless hurt, injury, and anguish they caused others. The more clearly I understood their shortcomings, the more inclined I became to point them out as clearly. I did this in a jocular and humorous tone at first, and then with increasing stridency. Our country was facing awesome problems—budget deficits, rising Medicare and Medicaid costs, the impending demise of Social Security, rising national debt, buildup of nuclear waste, the instability of the Soviet Union, un- controlled population growth, immigration problems, dirty air, acid rain, and so much more. Were the media earnestly, thought- fully, and honestly helping to educate the American public on these grave issues? They were not. Mostly they were just trying to dish the dirt. And I said just that, loudly and often. That did not go over well. Yes, the media just loved it when I took on Jesse Helms. But when I turned my heavy guns on Peter Arnett, Nina Totenberg, Anita Hill, and the "borkers" of Robert Bork, well, the press didn't like me quite so much anymore, didn't consider me a great jokester, or a genial wit, or, as the *Washington Post* had said, a "Western Breeze Through Stuffy Senate."

Things got tighter and tenser. You didn't have to be a West- erner to sense that pretty soon there was going to be a shootout.

CHAPTER FIVE

The Secret Code...
of Ethics

igma Delta Chi/The Society of Professional Journalists (SDX/
SPJ) is, as the name suggests, a national organization for journalists. My first experience with this organization was in 1982,
when I took part in a panel discussion at its national convention,
held that year in Washington. The forum was a session called
"Meet the Op-pressed!" In it, politicians turned the tables by asking questions of the media. I was one of the politicians, and firing
questions at the likes of CBS's Phil Jones, ABC's Carol Simpson,
and National Public Radio's Cokie Roberts was a lot of fun. We
all enjoyed ourselves. I admire that journalism society's work.

SDX/SPJ first adopted a code of ethics many years ago (see
page ix). Over the years the group has revised it several times. The
code is the only document I know of that actually attempts to
define honorable and ethical journalism practices. Its preamble ad-
dresses "the public's right to know the truth." When today's journalists use that phrase, they tend to leave off the last two words.
They often speak of the public's right to know, but show no concern about the public's right to know *the truth*. Those two simple

words are absolutely critical to the ethical practice of journalism. It's my strong belief that the public does not have a right—or even a desire—to know only gossip, rumor, innuendo, lies, damned lies, and fables. It has a right to know the truth. Many in journalism seem to have lost sight of that. But if you are goofy or bold enough to say so, the media will treat you like a stupid, lunkish, unreconstructed, boneheaded, evil-eyed, punkin-eatin' poophead. Merely suggest that the media go too far in fulfilling the public's supposedly sacred right to know, and you will be met with muffled gasps, chokes, dirty looks, or plain garden-variety derision. "Oh, my God," they'll say, "you really don't understand, do you?"

At times in my Senate career, I used the SDX/SPJ code of ethics during public speeches to evaluate the work I saw journalists doing. Was the work fair? Had the reporter behaved ethically and responsibly? If you went by the code, you often had to conclude that the answer was no. And no wonder! Most of the journalists I met didn't even know they had a code. How could they adhere to a code of ethics if they didn't even know it existed?

By October of 1991 I had made reference to the code of ethics many, many times. My harping on the subject finally caught the attention of writer Joel Achenbach of the *Washington Post*. My speeches must have really stung poor old Joel! He wrote a cynical and drippingly sarcastic piece in the Style section of the *Post*. In it, he thoroughly ridiculed the idea of journalists having such a code, and berated me for my ugly, incredibly stupid and numskulled habit of referring to it. This guy really jammed a pencil in my ear—or someplace.

He began by saying, "No wonder American journalism has become a gutter profession—we forgot we have a code!"

He went on, "The 'Code of Ethics' is an industry secret. Which is to say, hardly anyone in the industry knows it exists. All across America, reporters are shouting questions at public figures and rifling through government documents and taking two-hour expense-account lunches totally unaware that these actions are governed by a code, a code that is three pages long and has a section on Fair Play and a section on Accuracy and Objectivity and concludes with a Pledge.

"A copy was obtained by the *Washington Post* (after efforts to find one inside the building failed) from the office of Sen. Alan Simpson (R-Wyo.), who carries the code with him to any event where a journalist might be lurking. 'He's had this for years,' spokesman Stan Cannon reports. 'He keeps a copy right in the drawer of his desk.' "

Achenbach ridiculed me for thinking journalists should have standards. Then he seemed to ridicule journalists: "What happens when an entire profession ignores its own code? That should be obvious: anarchy. Horrible explosions of . . . unstandardized journalism.

"Imagine, for example, what would happen if reporters routinely ignored Rule 5 of the Accuracy and Objectivity section, which states: 'Sound practice makes clear distinction between news reports and expressions of opinion. News reports should be free of opinion or bias and represent all sides of an issue.'

"Sounds reasonable, right?

"I don't think so.

"Sorry. The writer has to stick his own stupid opinions in here!"

Finally, he gets to his ridiculous point: "The truth is, this Code of Ethics is a load of malarkey. Whatever malarkey is. No self-respecting journalist would be caught near this thing. Sure, most of it's fine—let's hear it for someone pointing out that reporters shouldn't take free plane tickets from the people they cover. But it never gets specific enough—it ought to say things like 'Journalists should never use the scientific name for snot when they can just say snot.' "

How's that for searing analysis?

As Major Amos B. Hoople used to say in that delightful old comic strip, "Egad!" Nobody that I know of has any problem whatsoever with the written expression of opinion by journalists. But most reasonable people agree that their opinions belong on the opinion pages, not in the news columns. I know this is an annoying and numbing and silly idea to Achenbach, and to many others in the Fourth Estate, but I'd bet that most common folks would side with the code on that one. For any journalist to smirk at the code of ethics is elitism at best, and unprincipled, unethical, and unprofessional conduct at worst. Achenbach's piece might even lead some to believe that he doesn't much care about the facts. His closing idea—that no self-respecting reporter would adhere to the code—says it all about the arrogance of today's journalists. Surely Joel is not alone in his vacuous views; they are shared by many of his colleagues.

Hubris is plenty dangerous no matter what profession you're in, be it law, medicine, education, business, or politics. I know from painful experience the damage that prideful arrogance can do to someone, and I'll be talking about that in coming pages. But I can't honestly think of a profession more infected by hubris than journalism. What I find vexatious and tiresome—and I think many Americans would agree with me—is the absolute unapologetic nature of so many in that profession. I have often seen someone ding—or hammer!—a journalist in a letter to the editor, but I have damn seldom seen a reporter answer the letter with an apology, or even an acknowledgment that he or she might have been wrong. Instead, most journalists offer an indignant and haughty self-defense, usually backed with the puerile pronouncement "I stand by my story." Sometimes it seems the point of American journalism is merely to stand by a story, not to get the story right in the first place. Lord, spare us! Again, the truth is the only thing that the public has a right to know. Nothing more.

In my Senate years, I gained much personal experience with reportorial hubris and indignation. Again and again, I discovered that Washington journalists were almost universally unwilling to admit when they had screwed up. It did not matter if the error made was large or small. They all suffered from what I call the I-Never-Make-a-Mistake Syndrome, a terrible malady that diminishes them and compromises their credibility. I had an experience with one *Washington Post* reporter that illustrates this problem fairly well. His name was Charles Babcock.

The brush with Babcock came in 1981, when I was at work on the complicated and highly emotional issue of immigration reform. At the time, the Reagan administration was preparing its own package of reforms, not all of which jibed with mine. Babcock called me on the phone to discuss the administration's reaction to my proposals. He and I had a fairly cordial and informative conversation lasting perhaps ten to fifteen minutes. When it was over, I went back to work and thought nothing more of it—until the next morning.

When I opened a copy of the *Post* the next day, I felt as if I had been kicked hard in the tailbone. According to the article, Babcock had asked me what I expected workers to do in order to verify that they were indeed in the country legally. Babcock quoted me as saying, "I want to hear alternatives. We'll consider everything but tattoos." There was just one problem—I hadn't said anything about tattoos. In fact, I had scrupulously avoided saying any such thing, for I knew well the impact that a word like "tattoos" could have. If I had ever used such a word, my critics in that debate would have compared me to the Nazis, who branded some people in order to identify them. The immigration debate was hot and emotional enough without the introduction of such raw, inflammatory ideas. The last thing I needed was any perception that I could have been that flip about such an important issue, for the legislation was hanging by a thin, very frayed thread. I felt terribly abused and deceived.

Most of the time, the victim of a misquote has only his or her word against that of the intrepid reporter. You can imagine who wins that war. This time I had more. By that time, my press secretary had done a range of interviews on immigration reform, and in the process had gained a strong sense of which reporters could be expected to get things right and which couldn't or wouldn't. When Babcock called asking to talk, this press secretary got a bad feeling. He suggested that I place a small recorder on my desk during the telephone interview, and I agreed. I myself had no previous reason to be suspicious of Charles Babcock, but my aide did, and that was good enough for me. So there the tape recorder sat, whirring away as I talked. I hasten to add that in no way did I record or try to record Babcock's voice. Doing so without his knowledge would have been illegal. Only my end of the conversation was recorded. And guess what—the tape of my words proved beyond a doubt that I had never uttered the words he attributed to me in quotation marks.

I called Babcock immediately and told him he'd misquoted me. He denied it. I told him that I had taped my end of the conversation and therefore could prove that I was right. Even so, he vigorously denied any possibility that he was wrong. As I recall our conversation he also seemed to be highly irritated that I would record my part of the conversation. How dare I not trust him? No, he would not back down. He even used that tired old phrase "I stick by my story." We argued for a while, and then he asked if he could hear the tape. Absolutely, I said.

Babcock came to the office, which I appreciated. We showed him a typed transcript of the tape, and then let him listen. The offending word, "tattoos," was just not on there. But even having heard that for himself, he would not admit his mistake. He said only that he had the words right there in his notes, and so there would be no correction. Sorry, Al.

I couldn't believe it. Here was a level of arrogance that I had not often encountered during my time in public life. I was plenty pissed. At that early stage in my Washington life, I was not yet ready to get into a big cat fight with the town's largest and most powerful newspaper. But I sure as hell intended to correct the record and cut off any future dealings with that reporter.

I knew only one person at the *Post* who might help me try to set the record straight—Meg Greenfield, the op-ed page editor. I called Meg and told her the whole story, including the part about the tape. She said, "Send me the tape and the transcript. We want to try to be fair here."

I sat down and wrote a letter to accompany the tape and the transcript. I stated that the word *tattoo* "generates inflammatory and barbaric overtones that could only hinder our ability to deal with this most sensitive issue in an atmosphere of calm and reason. The *Post*'s past editorial and reportorial coverage of this issue has been of superb quality. But in an issue as sensitive as this one, one misfire or inaccurate attribution can be most damaging." I told her that I wanted nothing more than to tell my side of what happened.

And I added that I would never again grant an interview to Charles Babcock.

Meg wrote back on July 30, 1981: "I gather that you and the *Post* reporter involved have discussed the matter; that you and he still differ, but that you see no need to challenge each other's veracity in public. Thank you for expressing your concern for the record. Yours, Meg." I appreciated Meg's letter, but I felt—and still feel—that a simple correction of the error would surely have been in order. The rabid, almost pathological unwillingness of some reporters to correct their mistakes continues to astound me.

One would think by now that the media—especially the *Washington Post*—would have learned the dangers of manufacturing quotes. The sad story of Janet Cooke should have taught them that lesson, but good. Surely you remember Cooke—she was the *Post* reporter who won a Pulitzer Prize with her account of the life of Jimmy, an eight-year-old heroin addict. Her two-thousand-word story, which appeared on September 28, 1980, began this way:

> Jimmy is eight years old and a third-generation heroin addict, a precocious little boy with sandy hair, velvety brown eyes and needle marks freckling the baby-smooth skin of his thin brown arms.
>
> He nestles in a large, beige reclining chair in the living room of his comfortably furnished home in Southeast Washington. There is an almost cherubic expression on his small, round face as he talks about life—clothes, money, the Baltimore Orioles and heroin. He has been an addict since the age of five.
>
> His hands are clasped behind his head, fancy running shoes adorn his feet, and a striped Izod T-shirt hangs over his thin frame. "Bad, ain't it," he boasts to a reporter visiting recently. "I got me six of them."
>
> Jimmy's is a world of hard drugs, fast money and the good life he believes both can bring. Every day, junkies casually buy heroin from Ron, his mother's live-in lover, in the dining room of Jimmy's home. They "cook" it in

the kitchen and "fire up" in the bedrooms. And every day, Ron or someone else fires up Jimmy, plunging a needle into his bony arm, sending the fourth grader into a hypnotic nod.

Gripping stuff. A few months later, in April 1981, Cooke was awarded the Pulitzer Prize in feature writing, the most coveted award in journalism. With it, she received a $1,000 prize. The Pulitzer board said the story was "met by a wave of shock and disbelief." In its article announcing the prize, the *Post* noted that Cooke's story "led to a fruitless search for the boy by District of Columbia officials, who once threatened to subpoena Cooke for his identity."

That wouldn't have done 'em any good. Cooke was getting Jimmy's quotations from the same place Charles Babcock got mine—thin air. Indeed, that is where Cooke got Jimmy. She made him up. Jimmy did not exist. The whole story began to unravel a couple of days after the Pulitzer was awarded. In her biography submitted to the Pulitzer board, Cooke had claimed to have a couple of degrees she didn't really have. Parts of her résumé got into the newspaper when she won the prize. People from the colleges called reporters, and the reporters called the *Post* asking for comment. First, Cooke stood by her résumé. Then she admitted it was falsified. Still, she stood by her story. Not strange— they all do. Finally, after much interrogation, she acknowledged that the story, too, was malarkey. (Perhaps this will help my old pal Joel Achenbach: Malarkey, Joel, is the stuff that the *Washington Post* makes up.)

The *Post* stood by Cooke's story, too, until it was no longer feasible to do so. Oh, in the days after the publication of the story, the *Post*'s editors insisted that the whole thing was true. District of Columbia police officers were out there searching the neighborhoods for Jimmy in the belief that an institution like the *Post* couldn't possibly have made up such a story. Even after the Pulitzer Prize was announced and people began asking the hard questions, the *Post* stood its ground. It took a couple of days before the newspaper publicly admitted its grave mistake. "The credibility of a newspaper is its most precious asset, and it depends almost entirely on the integrity of its reporters. When that integrity is questioned and found wanting, the wounds are grievous, and there is nothing to do but come clean with our readers, apologize to the Advisory Board of the Pulitzer Prizes, and begin immediately on the uphill task of regaining our credibility. This we are doing."

Uphill is right.

The story of Janet Cooke brings us to another Janet—Janet Malcolm, who wrote an extraordinary article for *The New Yorker* about a psychiatrist of some renown. In presenting the story of this fellow—who may or may not have had some serious character flaws—Malcolm placed quotation marks around some words, sentences, and comments that were never uttered by her subject. Nice, eh? Such a shoddy, crude, contemptuous practice is a true assault on the credibility of journalism. Naturally, the subject of the story sued. And what did the great institutional powers of the profession do then? Well, they rallied in deep-throated defense of Janet Malcolm, the "aggrieved" journalist. The real shocker was still to come: It came out in the trial that there are plenty of journalists who genuinely believe that a reporter is entitled to generalize here and compress quotes there. Come on! What bullshit! That's not the way it's supposed to work in this fine country. Reporters should have great latitude to select their story, choose their sources, and figure out their angle. I don't have any problems there. But they sure as hell do not have any right ever to manufacture quotes. There is no honest way to try to explain that one away. Forget it. It's lying. Why not just say and report what is said? Seems pretty easy to do, doesn't it? Pretty elementary? Pretty fair? I think so.

I was reelected to a second term in the Senate in November 1984. The next year would be a time of significant change for the Republican Senate leadership. Senator Howard Baker, Republican of Tennessee, a loyal and consistent friend who had steered the Republican minority and majority through thick and thin, was retiring. With Republicans in control of the U.S. Senate, the new Republican leader would become the majority leader of the U.S. Senate. A host of highly talented members announced their intention to run for the top job. Senator Ted Stevens, a bright and tough scrapper from Alaska and our party's assistant leader for nearly eight years, declared he was ready to move up. His candidacy left open the job of assistant majority leader. After consulting with friends, colleagues, family (heh, heh!), and my own expanding ego, I decided to run for the leadership role. Though still a relative newcomer—I was just beginning my second term in the U.S. Senate—I believed I could do a good job. The election took place in the historic old Senate chambers in the Capitol Building. Senator Bob Dole, the Kansas Republican, was elected as our leader. He is the essence of that. And sure enough, I was elected his assistant. A truly great thrill it was for me—a most memorable day.

Life would never be the same. Just as the 1980 general elections had vaulted Republicans to majority status in the United States Senate, the leadership election of 1984 hurtled me into a more intense setting. My schedule became more hectic; I began to assume all the obligations—and enjoy the privileges—of working in a closer way with Dole, President Reagan, and my fellow senators.

As I became more aware of the inner workings of government, I also became more conscious of the press's shortcomings in reporting them. More than ever, I noticed the media's biases and inaccuracies. This was an odd feeling, because the media were generally being quite kind to me. "Leadership from the responsible center" was the headline of a David Broder column in December 1984. Broder wrote: "Along with Sen. Alan Simpson of Wyoming, the newly elected Whip, the Republicans now have a leadership team as wise and witty, as humane and as humorous, as the Senate has ever seen. It is a team that will be at least a match for the Democratic duo of Minority Leader Robert C. Byrd of West Virginia and Minority Whip Alan Cranston of California on legislative tactics. . . . " He went on, "Their election is evidence of the dominance in the incoming Senate of what might be called 'the responsible center' of the political spectrum and the subordination—for now, at least—of both right wing and left wing ideologues."

And there was more.

In an editorial, the *Washington Post* said, "Sens. Dole and Simpson are tough, realistic men." That piece went on: "Sen. Simpson made a sustained and heroic effort in the last Congress to get much needed immigration reform enacted and, against great odds, almost succeeded. He has also built a solid reputation—in both houses of Congress—as a person who can work out sensible compromises on other red-hot issues, such as nuclear waste disposal, Agent Orange compensation and Superfund."

And from way out West, the *Denver Post* editorialized: "Simpson, something of a Senate phenomenon, is a conservative still in his first term, and is arguably one of the best-liked and most highly respected members of the upper chamber. His natural gift for humor and good grace is rivaled by his abilities as a legislative technician and architect of compromise—a combination most legislators seek, but rarely achieve."

Pretty heady stuff! But my election as assistant majority leader would lead me into more conflict with the media. As a leader, I would have a clearer observation platform from which to see how key legislative efforts could collapse, sometimes because of the media's inability or unwillingness to tell the story without their usual guff. Besides, now that I was in the leadership, I was a convenient target for the media—and, at six feet seven inches, a pretty hard one to miss.

After some very productive years came the fall of 1991. I'm not just talking about the autumnal equinox; I'm also referring to my own personal fall. That was when the nation witnessed the drama of the Clarence Thomas Supreme Court nomination hearings; the failings of journalists in that story will take a later chapter to describe. To lay the groundwork, let me describe a much less noted exchange I had that fall with a reporter from the *Billings Gazette*. See if you don't think there is something terribly wrong with journalism as I relate this short tale.

As a U.S. senator from Wyoming, I have always considered it a significant part of my job to follow closely the management of public lands. Among the most important of these lands are Yellowstone and Grand Teton National Parks. For decades, controversy has raged regarding the parks. Certain overly enthusiastic environmentalists work diligently to limit public access to these great parks, in hopes of actually turning them back into wilderness.

They have never succeeded. The Organic Act that established Yellowstone National Park was unambiguous: It created the park as "a pleasuring ground for the enjoyment of the American people." For which I think most Americans were grateful.

Lorraine Mintzmyer, an able and articulate woman, was a highly respected and highly professional employee of the Park Service in those days. As it happened, she shared some of the goals and frustrations of the activist environmentalists. She often heard from environmentalists who wanted people to have less use of the parks. Just as often, she heard from the other side—people who thought the parks were all for them. As a dedicated professional, Mintzmyer participated in the preparation of a "Vision Document" that sketched out the future use of the parks and their environs. The original draft was—perhaps not surprisingly—quite acceptable to the environmentalists. That alarmed some of what I'll call the "user groups," who asked to meet with the Wyoming congressional delegation to discuss the troubling document. We agreed to meet. After the meeting, we suggested certain changes in the Vision plan—changes that would make the park and contiguous areas user-friendly for years and years to come. Mintzmyer reacted. She felt her professionalism had been questioned. She soon announced her resignation because of "pressure."

Later, she was called to testify before a highly partisan House committee whose chairman wanted to lay a little load on President Bush, Chief of Staff John Sununu, and others. Mintzmyer testified that she felt she would have liked to participate in the constituent meeting that was held in my office but was "not invited." Some reporters came and told me what she had said.

"Not invited by whom?" I said.

The press's response was "We don't know. Was it you?"

Well, she had not been "not invited" by me, but if I had known she was anywhere in or near my office she could have come by that meeting—without any question.

Mintzmyer's supposed exclusion from that meeting was not the only dramatic part of her testimony. She also fingered Sununu as the one who had exerted the political pressure to alter the document. But apparently that message didn't enter the foggy consciousness of the *Billings Gazette* reporter, one Elizabeth Lesly, who obviously was eager to tack a bit of my hide on the wall. The banner headline on the *Billings Gazette* on September 25, 1991, read, "Simpson draws fire in hearing." That was followed by the subheadline "Park Service Official accuses him of unjust political pressure in 'Vision' draft." After several paragraphs of background at the top of the story, Lesly got to the dark heart of the matter:

"Mintzmyer, who was subpoenaed and testified under oath, said that political pressure regarding the Vision document from Republican Sen. Alan Simpson of Wyoming and White House Chief of Staff John Sununu resulted in the document being gutted."

One tiny problem here. Mintzmyer never accused me of exerting pressure on her or anyone else. The headlines and the story were untrue. Plain damn false. Period. The only time Lorraine mentioned me in her entire testimony was when she referred to the meeting in my office. And the truth about that one was that her superiors had told her she could not attend. I certainly never disinvited her. The hearing transcript fully bears me out on these points.

Armed with the facts, I sallied forth to the *Billings Gazette* to demand a correction. When I asked for one, the *Gazette* editorial staff suggested that I simply issue a statement on the matter—as if correcting the newspaper's mistake was my responsibility. I said I preferred to have an open, clear, and honest admission of the error by the reporter and the paper. The editors refused. Pure arrogance? You damn betcha! Seeing no alternative, I did as they suggested and put together a statement. The first copy went to the *Billings Gazette*.

"Certainly I had real problems with the draft Vision Statement for Yellowstone," my statement said in part. "I felt it was very narrow in scope and that it lacked any thoughtful economic consideration of the life of the surrounding communities. I also felt that it had been written in a vacuum without any public participation—something which undermines the democratic process. But while I did disagree strongly with the direction of the document, I never did, and never would have, suggested that Lorraine Mintzmyer be removed from her position."

I went on, "I challenge the *Billings Gazette* to find one single mention in Lorraine Mintzmyer's testimony where she says that Al Simpson was responsible for the 'political pressure' regarding the Vision document. The *Gazette* story is plain damn wrong. Their biased reporter drew conclusions which are simply not supported by the testimony. No wonder people get a bellyful of the media. I ask only honesty and fairness and for the *Billings Gazette* to recognize and admit their mistake, not just shove it under the rug, as can be the tendency."

I then suggested that the *Gazette* publish Lorraine's testimony so readers could see the truth for themselves. "I hope they do it," I concluded, "but don't hold your breath."

Instead of doing as I suggested, the *Gazette* did something truly incredible—it assigned the same reporter who had made the mistake, Elizabeth Lesly, to interview me about what had happened. This little antic was supposed to clear up the error. The editor who called me said the only subject of the interview would be the paper's mistake. What a chuckle! To my surprise, disappointment, and pure disgust, the eager and terminally biased reporter arrived at my office and immediately began seeking comments about another aspect of the story. When she wrote her piece, she used this new information in the lead paragraph—and artfully buried a very small correction deep in the story.

By now I was completely flummoxed. I whomped up a letter to the editor and—give the editors credit—they published the whole thing. The letter said, "The citizens of my State of Wyoming and of the nation have it within their right to hold me accountable for all of my actions. So why is it that when the *Billings Gazette* should stumble and make a mistake, it can't simply own up to it and honestly set the record straight? All I asked for was truth and fairness. That's the vital stuff good newspapers are supposed to be made of." Yes, yes, a bit of bad grammar with that.

I went on, "And the truth is this: No matter how many readers will see my words buried here on the letters page, not everyone who saw that headline will read this correction. The truth is that some readers will never know the difference—or care. But I do. That's my good name that is so loosely and falsely being used."

While the manufacture of quotes or the clever twisting of someone's words remains a persistent evil in journalism, another distasteful practice is growing perhaps more common—plagiarism. The SDX/SPJ code of ethics states that "plagiarism is dishonest and unacceptable." Sounds good. Pretty clear, too. But as I've said, many journalists don't know the code.

Here's an example from July 1991. A very conservative dean of the Boston University Communications College gave a speech in which he used words written by another person. No proper credit was given to the author. The media covered this case of academic plagiarism closely, and with intense interest. The *New York Times* reporter on the story was Fox Butterfield, the paper's man in Boston. But wait—Butterfield's own journalistic effort apparently relied partly on a story that a *Boston Globe* reporter had published only the day before. Now, if ever there is a time when a reporter should not plagiarize, it is when he is writing an article about plagiarism. When the *New York Times* got wind of the similarities between Butterfield's story and the *Globe*'s, it published an editor's note. "The *Times* article included a passage of five paragraphs that closely resembled five paragraphs in the *Globe* article," it said, adding that Butterfield's story was "improperly dependent on the *Globe* account." The article was played on page three. This is known as burying your dead swiftly. All the news that's fit to print? No. All the news that's fit to hide.

But the story had not reached its climax. Persistent and hawk-eyed *Washington Post* media reporter Howard Kurtz—who regularly skewers the media, God bless him—picked up on the story, providing more information than the skimpy *Times* clarification had given us. "Asked if any action will be taken against Butterfield, [*Times* spokeswoman Nancy] Nielsen says that is 'under consideration,' " Kurtz wrote. "Butterfield could not be reached yesterday." Kurtz's piece carried the catchy headline "What's Black, White and Red All Over?" And I'll bet he wrote the whole story all by himself.

I wish I could say the same for one of his colleagues. A couple of days after reporting on the *New York Times* fiasco, Kurtz wrote another story on plagiarism for his paper. This time the story was about—oops!—one of the *Washington Post*'s own minions. So much for the *Post*'s apparent glee in reporting on the *New York Times*'s travails. Still, I have to hand it to Kurtz, and to the *Post*— they told the story pretty fully even though the *Post* was embarrassed by it. Here's how Kurtz's second story began:

"The *Washington Post* apologized to the *Miami Herald* yesterday for publishing a story on mosquito infestation in Florida that lifted substantial information from three *Herald* stories, including several quotations, without giving credit."

One of the most disturbing elements of the story was a quote from John Pancake, the *Miami Herald*'s state editor: "I wish I could tell you this never happened at the *Miami Herald,* but I suspect it has. I think stuff close to this goes on a lot in journalism." Maybe so, but the readers of the *Miami Herald* never heard that opinion. The *Herald* picked up the *Washington Post* story on the incident— but deleted Pancake's comment. What a bunch.

Kurtz also reported, "Managing Editor Leonard Downie Jr. said that the reporter who wrote the story, Miami bureau chief Laura Parker, had left the paper. He would not say whether Parker had resigned or had been fired, calling that an internal personnel matter." Downie was then quoted as saying, "She's left our employment. That is all I can say."

Really? Why? If the reporters accused of such shoddy journalism that week had been public officials or politicians, the media would have probed every single remote corner of their personal and professional lives. We would have been treated to story after story, each one more searing and lurid than the one before. But these media plagiarists were allowed to slink away to lick their wounds, far from the cruel and prying eyes of the reading public. Wonder why people get fed up with the press? This is the kind of crap that can give you a pretty good inkling. I can already hear the banshee shriek of the media folk—"But Simpson, we are not public figures!" Fair enough; nobody elects newspeople. But they are as much a part of the democratic process as any of us in Congress.

They have the awesome power to shape or alter public opinion, and yet they are not accountable to anyone except their editors. If you don't think reporters haughtily hold themselves to a different standard from the one they apply to politicians, well, you must be a reporter.

Let me give an example of this double standard. In 1988, Senator Joe Biden, my solid and special friend from Delaware, was a candidate for president of the United States. He delivered a speech or two which were strikingly similar to some given at previous times by British Labour Party leader Neil Kinnock. When the media were informed of this, they had themselves a high old time of it. Every paper in America opened up Joe Biden as if he were a can of tuna. They were savage. They were lusty. They were cruel. Some in the Fourth Estate even seemed to be having fun covering what was, for Joe, a tragic mistake. And please understand that I know he made a serious mistake. I can respect and appreciate the public's interest in knowing that each presidential candidate is an honest person and an original thinker. But the media did not keep things in perspective. Was Joe Biden otherwise a good man, a fine legislator, and a strong presidential candidate? He was. But you wouldn't have known it from the beating he took—a beating that eventually forced him from the presidential race.

By way of contrast, let's discuss the case of Texas newspaper columnist Molly Ivins. Not so long ago, she used a few jokes that bore a strong similarity to those published by another writer. Did you know that? Probably not. If you did hear of it, you sure as hell didn't hear as much of it as you heard of Joe Biden's story. Again, yes, yes, I know that Joe was running for president. But Molly Ivins is not exactly an anonymous soul. She's a best-selling author, popular speaker, and famous newspaper columnist. The near noncoverage of her adventures is, I think, a powerful example of the media double standard.

Indeed, the media don't pay much attention to media plagiarism in general. The Laura Parker incident might have provided a good opportunity for print journalists to assess the extent of the plagiarism problem. After all, here a *Miami Herald* editor had gone on the record in Howard Kurtz's story as saying that plagiarism "goes on a lot in journalism." But did the papers investigate themselves, or even each other? They did not. What they did was report energetically—and absurdly—on President George Bush's brash declaration that he did not care for broccoli. Seriously, that is what happened. We learned who grows it, who eats it, who likes it, who hates it, you name it. The broccoli story sprouted for three weeks, but the plagiarism story—well, that limp cucumber died on the vine.

The mainstream media are forever trying to distance themselves from the tabloids—the *Star,* the *National Enquirer,* the *Weekly World News,* and so on. But how great is the distance, really? Not as great as it should be. The lines between responsible and irresponsible publications have been grotesquely and hideously blurred. Here's an example. In the late spring of 1992, many mainstream media outlets reported solemnly and with a straight face the story of the Filipino man who was endowed with both male and female sexual organs. What was even more remarkable was that this fellow—this woman—this whatever—was pregnant. Could it be true? Had to be! All the vast media outlets carried the story—even the half-vast! Well, don't believe everything you read in the papers. The terribly confused lad (he was a he) in the story had made the whole thing up in an effort to snare back his boyfriend. When the mainstream media realized they had been duped, some of them admitted that they were embarrassed. But most didn't. As for us in the reading public, we just laughed—not with the media, but at them.

That was an extreme case. Yet stuff that is almost that shocking gets published quite often, and with much more serious consequences. During the 1988 and 1992 presidential campaigns, George Bush was widely considered the "family values" candidate, the person whose life best exemplified the strength of the American family. Yet both campaigns were sullied by a persistent rumor alleging some extramarital affair years before. The first media story on the subject appeared in the *Village Voice* in the fall of 1988. The woman who was supposedly involved was at first not named. Later she was. Many other reporters later published stories, cleansing themselves at the confessional by emphasizing that the tale was only a rumor. Now, I hate to have even mentioned again this stupid, dead rumor about my old friend. But I think it stands as a strong example of the kind of crap that the media sometimes serve up. If something is a rumor, they should leave the junk alone. Instead, one paper publishes a story, and the rest bellow that the rumor is now in the public domain, and therefore must be reported. The story goes nowhere; the reader gets nothing; but the subject of the story is needlessly embarrassed and made miserable. What's fair about any of that?

Please, do not babble to me about the public's right to know. If the media know the story, let them tell it honestly, with attribution for every fact. If they can do that, we'll all be able to make a clear distinction between the tabloids and the responsible press. If they can't do it, we're all headed for a heap of trouble.

How did the media become so arrogant, so sure that the public has the right to know everything, truthful or not? My thought: It was the U.S. Supreme Court case of *New York Times* v. *Sullivan* that seduced them. This landmark ruling granted extraordinary First Amendment protections to the news media—and breathed icy air down the bare necks of every public official in America. Journalists say the ruling gave teeth to the First Amendment. I say it gave it fangs.

A little background. This 1964 case involved an Alabama state law which allowed a public official in that state to file—and later win—a libel suit against the *New York Times,* which had published something untrue about him. The Supreme Court found the Alabama law unconstitutional and threw out the judgment. In doing so, the Court declared that public figures could not successfully sue for libel just because a story was wrong and the reporter knew in advance that it was wrong. No, the only way a journalist could shed his blanket First Amendment protections would be to publish such a story with "actual malice." No joke! According to the Supreme Court, there is nothing wrong with being wrong, even knowingly wrong, as long as you're not malicious too. With this ruling, the Court basically painted a bright red target on the foreheads of public figures everywhere.

The ruling made it virtually impossible for public officials to seek redress for libelous conduct in reporting. The Court did not merely address whether the *Times*'s right to free speech had been violated by the lawsuit. In deciding *Sullivan,* the Court seemed to be trying to prevent any situation in which free speech might be restrained. The message this ruling seemed to send to the media was "Don't worry. Hammer the bastards. They are a lousy lot in society and they deserve everything they get. Just print it. Roll 'em!"

Here's part of the ruling: "A rule compelling the critic of official conduct to guarantee the truth of all his factual assertions—and to do so on pain of libel judgments virtually unlimited in amount—leads to a comparable 'self-censorship.' Under such a rule, would-be critics of official conduct may be deterred from voicing their criticism, even though it is believed to be true and even though it is in fact true, because of doubt whether it can be proved in court or fear of the expense of having to do so. They [would] tend to make only statements which 'steer far wider of the unlawful zone.' "

Justice Arthur Goldberg cautiously added: "In any event, despite the possibility that some excesses and abuses may go unremedied, we must recognize that the people of this nation have ordained in the light of history, that, in spite of the probability of excesses and abuses, certain liberties are, in the long view, essential to enlightened opinion and right conduct on the part of the citizens of a democracy."

In its zeal to protect the First Amendment, the Court obviously was willing to overlook the possibility that the media would libel some public officials, sometimes with stories that concerned these officials' private, not public, conduct. Still, given a choice between absolute truth and the unchecked freedom of the press, the Court chose the latter. In the Court's view, it was all right for the media to get something wrong; the important thing was that they be able to get it.

Here comes a portion of this book which will be savaged by many in the Fourth Estate—and probably others, too. *Sullivan* turned public officials into raw meat. That is true whether you are a member of the Park County Weed and Pest control District or the president of the United States. In the years after *Sullivan*, the judicial system confirmed its basic holdings in the cases of *Sharon* v. *Time Magazine, Westmoreland* v. *CBS,* and others. The powerful effect of the decision pretty much comes down to this: As long as a story is referring to a public figure (a definition that is often disputed mightily in the courts), a reporter can lie, and a reporter can defame. And unless one of us public figures can prove actual malice, we have no standing to seek damages for injury to our reputations.

There are grave consequences. One is that a hell of a lot of good, thoughtful, honest, and decent men and women stay out of politics because they know what the media can do to them. These people tell their spouses, family, friends, and potential supporters, "Boy, I don't have to take that crap." Some people have the tenacity to go into public life anyway. When they do, they subject their families and friends to the same intrusive probing and prodding that they must endure. Want examples? How about the things that were written about Dick Nixon's wife, Pat, and his daughters, and his brother, Don? Ask Geraldine Ferraro about the reporting that was done on her son and husband. Ask Jimmy Carter about the hits on his brother, Billy, or sister, Jean, or his mother. No, it is not only the public figure who is held up to scrutiny, oh no, no, no. It is also the errant daughter with the drug problem, the wastrel brother who is an alcoholic, the aunt who cut corners in her business dealings, the "funny" uncle, or the cousin who was involved in certain questionable financial activities. And so a lot of people stay away from politics, away from public service. Who needs the hassle? This sad phenomenon will not change until a law is passed—or another case tried—undoing the damage of *New York Times* v. *Sullivan.*

Here's a personal story on this subject. When I was a damn foolish kid of seventeen, a bunch of my pals and I went out and started shooting up mailboxes just for kicks. We really ventilated a bunch of them. What we didn't know was that a guy could get six months in jail and a $100 fine for each hole! If we had been given the maximum, I would probably still be in jail. Lucky for me, all I got was two years' federal probation and a regular meeting with a parole officer. That's right—I was a federal outlaw. And when I was at the University of Wyoming, I got myself into a brawl or two, including one that won me a free night in the Laramie lockup. Now, I told the voters about all that stuff when I first ran for the Wyoming legislature. The things I did were stupid; I didn't kill anybody (though I did seriously wound a few of those mailboxes). Still, I don't know if a person with that kind of record would want to venture into public service today. Would it really be worth the exposé that well might result if such a person was not entirely upfront about past mistakes? I think not.

The true result of the *Sullivan* decision, in my view, is that we wind up with some extraordinarily vacant, inept, and lackluster candidates for public office. Too often, the only people willing to subject themselves to relentless media scrutiny are those who will eventually be found wanting. Now, what kind of system is that? Of the ones who aren't simply damaged goods, too many get into politics just to boost their own egos—to see how much ink or tube time they can capture. These sedulous, spunkless non-risk-takers may well pass muster with the media, but they bring little to public service. These are people who will attempt to avoid controversy at all times, and at all costs. And so they never take on the tough issues, never stand up to the strong constituent groups or the powerful special interest groups. Often, today's politicians talk a pretty good game—they know just what to say on TV—but they vote with temerity and trepidation.

We often hear about freedom of the press as guaranteed by the First Amendment. Now, think about who is most protected by that part of our Constitution. Freedom of the press is the only fundamental freedom in the Bill of Rights which cannot—especially in these media-dominated 1990s—be effectively exercised by an individual. In my reading of America's tumultuous history, the First Amendment became the law in order to protect the rights of some spirited, alarmed, and zealous citizens who were cranking out seditious literature in their Philadelphia basements. CNN didn't exist in those days. Today, freedom of the press protects and emboldens an entire industry—a very large, profit-making, growth-oriented industry, too. Today, media companies are listed on the New York Stock Exchange; taken together, they rack up billions of dollars in profits.

I'm sure the framers of the Constitution would be appalled to see the way we interpret the First Amendment today. They didn't put it on the books to protect a child pornographer, or to ensure that a person could spend his personal fortune in order to buy himself a governorship or even the presidency. In its original noble simplicity, the First Amendment was meant to give voice to everyone in the new land—poops, pricks, princesses, panderers, promoters, politicians, pressmen, potentates, and panjandrums. All were supposed to be heard; let the educated citizens figure out whom to believe and whom to ignore. Today, we have a small number of gigantic media companies exercising enormous power over what people see, hear, read, and yes, think. Sure, anyone can still crank up a printing press, boot up a computer, print a homespun 'zine, loose a flood of E-mail, or even hand out pamphlets on the street corner. And yet the people who are really getting heard are the Big Boys and Big Girls of the major media. Believe it.

Consider these memorable lines, written by William Peter Hamilton in the *Wall Street Journal:* "A newspaper is a private enterprise owing nothing whatever to the public, which grants it no franchise. It is therefore affected with no public interest. It is emphatically the property of the owner, who is selling a manufactured product at his own risk."

That is steel-hard, tough, cold-iron fact, and it is far, far removed from the ephemeral mumblings, empirical dreamings, and dewy-eyed idealism of many in today's media. Never mind the public's right to know, the chilling effect, and sticking by a story. The media are big business, and all the hifalutin talk is tossed off not to protect democracy, but to protect a huge and profitable franchise.

In today's world, journalists and, yes, politicians behave in a way that makes Americans dangerously cynical. Politicians must speak more honestly about our own flaws and shortcomings, and the media must stop trying to inflate profits by attempting to turn news into entertainment. News is not entertainment. News is news. And covering the news means telling stories clearly so that the people will be informed and educated. "Commit that one to memory," as Miss Gertrude Smith used to say.

The media's right to free speech is, I think, much more vigorously protected than are the privacy rights of the public person. Even though the *Sullivan* decision dealt specifically with public figures, we have since seen the continuing erosion of the private rights of public people. This erosion affects the victim of rape or abuse who may choose not to speak, the person who was found not guilty of a crime, and the rights of any man or woman who would simply prefer to keep his or her own damn business private. People no longer have a consummate and unconditional right to be left alone, and out of the papers. Ask the mother of Justice Clarence Thomas about that. She did not nominate Clarence for the Supreme Court, nor did she ask for her own life and her son's life to be taken apart like an old car engine. Ask the former wife of Clarence Thomas; she went through the same thing. Ask Clarence Thomas, who said during his confirmation hearings, "I have never, in my life, felt such hurt, such pain, such agony." Ask his son. Ask his sister. Ask his father. Ask his former father-in-law. For that matter, ask Anita Hill, who endured her own brand of hell at the hands of the media. Ask her family. For the rest of their lives, Thomas and Hill will be stopped in airports and asked about things which are none of anyone's business. On this point, I must agree with Ayn Rand, who wrote in her epic novel *The Fountainhead:* "Civilization is the progress toward a society of privacy."

With *Sullivan* serving to gird them with the armor of righteousness, the media use the First Amendment as their sword to incise public officials through the gut—and twist it in others who are much less able than we are to defend themselves in the arena of life.

Of course, they twist it into the guts of politicians, too. I spoke on that subject one blustery evening at the Wyoming Press Association's annual convention in Casper. I had been invited to the meeting to give an after-dinner speech on the media and their duties and responsibilities. I told the gathered journalists they need always to be aware of their power in this nation and in Wyoming.

A great percentage of thinking citizens rely solely on the media for their information. Some of that information is pretty slim fare. My dear friend Daniel Boorstin, the distinguished author, historian, and former librarian of the Library of Congress, once noted, "We are surfeited with information—but we lack knowledge."

And then came the part of the speech that really got their attention. I mused that it is ironic that the media spend so much of their time, talent, treasure, and energy in impaling politicians—perhaps quite unaware that the targets of their ridicule are the same people they count on to protect them from any changes in law that might impinge on their beloved press freedoms. First they skewer you and cook you over a flame, and then they beseech you to please leave alone *New York Times* v. *Sullivan*. Funny, ain't it? I recall finishing up the speech to some generous applause. I stuck around after the talk to enjoy a drink with the troops. A pleasing number of the journalists expressed words of appreciation. One publisher—a man who had served as both vice president of the Wyoming Press Association and as vice chairman of the state Republican Party—said, "Gee, Al, we needed to hear that. Thanks for shaking us up."

Apparently it took time for my remarks to sink in after the shaking. Within a few days, several journalists wrote pieces decrying what they regarded as my "assault" on the First Amendment. These writers wondered, "Was Al Simpson talking in his disarming and clever way about 'blackmail'?" The word then spread across the high plains, mountains, and prairies of Wyoming that Al Simpson was out to kill the messengers. According to the rumors, if journalists didn't lay off politicians, Al Simpson was going to get some of his elected-official buddies together and take away some of their most cherished freedoms. Not true. I had merely commented on something I found most ironic. If anything, I was the one now being muzzled. Even the publisher who had complimented me after the speech later spun around and wrote me a letter of fiery indignation. That act and others gave me the strong sense that the media don't believe any politician should ever talk much about the First Amendment.

Too many journalists treat the First Amendment the way a

gaggle of spoiled kids might treat playground equipment. When they're using it to play their own little games, they're pretty happy. But if you come along and try to use it, too, they'll holler and hoot and maybe even conk you a good one over the head. Well, the First Amendment of the Constitution of the United States does not belong to the media alone. It belongs to all of us.

CHAPTER SIX

Saddam, Peter, and Me

My run-in with the Wyoming Press Association was nothing compared to the bare-knuckled fistfight I had in 1991 with the Cable News Network. That was the year I took a hard swipe at CNN correspondent Peter Arnett—and got my ears boxed pretty snappily in return.

This story had its beginnings in 1990. In April of that year, I went to the Middle East as part of a U.S. Senate delegation led by Bob Dole. With Communism crumbling in Eastern Europe and peace breaking out in many other places, Bob had decided that it was time for some senators to issue a plea for peace in the Middle East as well. The members of the delegation—Dole, Howard Metzenbaum of Ohio, Jim McClure of Idaho, Alaska's Frank Murkowski, and I—were scheduled to meet with President Mubarek of Egypt, King Hussein of Jordan, President Assad of Syria, and various officials of the Israeli government, which was then in transition.

The trip progressed nicely. Then, during a meeting in Cairo, Egyptian President Hosni Mubarek asked if we were thinking of

going to Iraq to meet with Saddam Hussein. Bob indicated that
we very much wanted to go, but had been wholly unsuccessful in
our attempts to arrange the visit. Mubarek exclaimed, "That is too
bad." Then he added, "I'll take care of it. Hand me that phone!"
We did, and he began furiously punching in numbers. Within
minutes, he had made all arrangements for us to meet with Saddam
Hussein. Don't worry, he told Hussein's nervous emissary on the
phone. "These people are not crazies." At that time, the United
States and Iraq were facing many serious and contentious issues.
With those issues firmly in mind, we looked forward to confront-
ing the man known as "the Butcher of Baghdad."

We were not allowed to enter Iraq from Egypt, so that night
we flew back to Jordan. From there, we would travel to Iraq. That
night, we also called President Bush from our hotel to ask what
he would like us to say to Saddam Hussein, and to tell him what
we intended to say. We wanted to be sure that we spoke with the
president's full consent and approval, and that the letter we had
drafted correctly reflected the priorities and goals of our government. We discussed all our many problems with Iraq. The president listened carefully, shared his thoughts, and wished us well,
saying he would be eager to hear our report when we got back.

Early the next morning, our U.S. military plane flew us to the
main airport in Baghdad, where we were met by our able ambas-
sador, April Glaspie. Our Iraqi greeting party included Foreign
Minister Tariq Aziz, who would soon become a familiar name to
Americans. For some time we cooled our heels in the airport's
opulent President's Lounge. Then we were told that we would be
whisked by Iraqi Airlines to the city of Mosul for our meeting with
the president. We didn't much care for the idea of leaving behind
our military plane. Howard Metzenbaum—the only person of
Jewish faith in our delegation—expressed some trepidation, and
not without reason; we were, after all, in a Muslim country which
had recently vowed to turn Israel into a "fireball." I remember
Howard saying with a great grin and a wink, "Just stick with me,
guys—I don't know where the hell that plane may set down." We
told Howard that we were aware of the risks—political and physical—of his traveling in that part of the world, and that we appre-

ciated his being there. I think we all had a surge of concern while trudging up the ramp into that Iraqi Airlines Boeing 737.

Thankfully, the flight was swift and sure. On the way to Mosul, our delegation had a ton of questions for our hosts; unfortunately, they had an ounce of answers. We disembarked at Mosul and traveled in two cars on a circuitous route through the countryside, with biblical names and places abounding. Finally, we were escorted to a hotel along the banks of the Tigris River, passing through heavy security all along the way. We were ushered through a maze of holding rooms and told, again, to wait. At long last, in strode Hussein, along with a dazzling array of aides, attendants, and lackeys.

Bob Dole personally delivered our letter to Hussein. It stated in part:

> We cannot stress too firmly our conviction that your efforts to develop a nuclear, chemical and biological capability seriously jeopardize—rather than enhance—your security, potentially threaten other nations of the region, and provoke dangerous tensions throughout the Middle East. Your recent statements threatening to use chemical weapons against Israel have created anxiety among nations throughout the world. In your own interest and in the interest of peace in the Middle East, we urge you to reconsider pursuit of these dangerous programs and provocative assertions.
>
> We must also express our profound distress at the alleged activities which led to the expulsion of an official of your diplomatic mission in the United States on charges that he was involved in a conspiracy to murder. We repeat: If our two nations are to have better relations, such activities as those alleged to have occurred must never happen again.

Bob also stated in the most clear and concise terms our concerns and anxiety regarding the current issues so seriously dividing our two countries.

Saddam reached forward and accepted the letter. It was then slowly interpreted and simultaneously read to him. He sat very still as he listened. The Butcher of Baghdad was nattily attired in a sharp business suit with silk foulard, yet he was very dour in demeanor. Obsequious and eager staff members seemed to be everywhere in the large room and adjoining open areas. The place was full of microphones and electrical cords; obviously, everything we said would be recorded, so we would have to watch ourselves carefully. We all knew we were on the record.

After listening to the text of our letter, Saddam pronounced some minor diplomatic niceties. With those out of the way, he launched into a lengthy dissertation on the eternal, devil-driven, monstrous conspiracies committed by the West against his courageous and powerful Iraq. I couldn't tell if he was trying to buffalo or bullshit us, or if he actually believed the stuff he was saying. But it did become clear that if we were going to get to the issues that concerned us, we would first have to discuss what he called his "perception problems" around the globe. He devoted much of his speech to bemoaning the power and bias of the Western media. He obviously didn't appreciate the way he was portrayed to the world. He seemed to think that the United States, England, and other Western countries could do something about the way their media wrote about him. After long minutes of his bombast, we were all wondering when we were going to get in our licks.

Finally he wound down. Bob then spoke powerfully on behalf of the delegation. When he finished, we went around the room in order of Senate seniority. At last it was my turn to speak. I felt impelled to tell him crisply that the Western media and the United States government are two distinct and separate entities, not bound together in any fashion, unlike the media and government in his country. Later, a transcript of that meeting was circulated far and wide. Be aware that this official transcript was tailored for the print media by the Iraqi government and then adjusted specifically for Iraqi radio. In the transcript, I am quoted as saying, "I believe that your problems lie with the Western media, and not with the U.S. government. As long as you are isolated from the media, the press—and it is a haughty and pampered press—they all consider themselves political geniuses. That is, the journalists do. They are very cynical. What I advise is that you invite them to come here and see for themselves."

That is close to what I said. But that was not all that I said. I began by assuring Saddam that there was no Western government conspiracy against him. If he felt he was being treated cruelly by the media, he should simply allow them into the country to look around. He kept saying during our meeting that he had nothing to hide. I said, pointing to a map, "If that facility is truly a pesticide factory, let them see it." I was challenging him—daring him—to let the world know, through the same media he decried, the real truth about what was going on in his country. But perhaps not surprisingly, my complete remarks did not make it into the Iraqi government transcript.

The transcript also omitted our strong and critical remarks about Iraq's gassing of the Kurds, the hanging of a British journalist, the "big cannon" oil pipe, the possession of those nuclear triggering devices, and so on. Indeed, the transcript issued by the embassy of the Republic of Iraq in Washington is highly suspect, for it was only fifteen pages long. Fifteen pages of transcript from a meeting that lasted three hours and fifteen minutes? That doesn't make any sense. One U.S. senator sitting alone in a room can generate more talk than that in a fraction of the time. At the time of the meeting, though, we were not concerned about transcripts. That would come later. For the time being, we cared only about making our nation's position clear, and we left Iraq feeling we had done that damn well.

Apparently, Saddam Hussein was not cowed or intimidated by our words. In August 1990, just four months after our meeting, he ordered his army to invade neighboring Kuwait, which it then did with violent zeal. According to Amnesty International, the Iraqis brutally crushed an undefended population, committing atrocities against men, women, and children. President Bush then forged an international alliance. Working closely with the United Nations, he vowed that the invasion of Kuwait "would not stand." At the president's urging, the UN imposed tough economic sanctions on Iraq and demanded that Kuwait be returned to its previous form of governance. A United Nations peacekeeping force was swiftly formed, with the United States taking the firm lead. Dick Cheney, my old pal and for ten years my Wyoming congressional sidekick, was the secretary of defense at the time. No finer man could we have had in the post. Early on, Cheney visited with officials of the Saudi government and discussed our plan with them. The American military was mobilized. The president issued an ultimatum: If Saddam Hussein did not withdraw his forces from Kuwait, American military fighting men and women would go to war.

It was in this highly emotional context that the American public first learned of our meeting, four months earlier, with Saddam Hussein. The first brief mention was in *U.S. News & World Report.* Then, late in August, Jack Anderson published portions of the doctored Iraqi transcript in his column. Many in the Fourth Estate saw my comments—and hammered me hard for them. Some members of the press stupidly reported that the conversation between our delegation and Hussein had been "secretly taped." This gave the (no doubt intended) impression that the Iraqi transcript was indeed accurate, and that I had indeed commiserated with Saddam. On August 28, the *Wyoming Tribune-Eagle* published an editorial headlined "Simpson and Saddam Share Common Enemy." Here, in part, is the text—and remember, the author of this editorial is gleefully taking words uttered at a more benign time in April and applying them to September's hideous, vicious, and barbaric circumstances.

> The revelation in Jack Anderson's syndicated column Monday that Sen. Alan Simpson of Wyoming isn't fond of members of the Fourth Estate hardly came as a surprise to us. He's been whining about reporters and editors for years, even though he has never failed to get favorable media coverage even among the wild pack of Eastern liberals back in D.C.
>
> But we have to wonder what in the world our state's junior senator was thinking when he met with Iraq's Saddam Hussein last April. . . . Simpson told Saddam that all

of the Iraqi leader's problems "lie with the Western media and not with the U.S. government."

Is this the same Al Simpson who branded Saddam a madman comparable to Adolf Hitler during a press conference in Cheyenne last week? "He's nuts and bears watching with great, great care," Simpson told reporters here. . . .

We doubt that if Al had been in the bunker with Adolf and Eva he would have suggested they talk to *Life* magazine and clear up their image problems. Why, when he had the opportunity to hit Saddam with some tough questions about his threats against Israel and his penchant for chemical warfare, did Simpson start acting like his public relations agent?

It's relatively easy to sit in Cheyenne and call Saddam a madman who must be stopped. Simpson handled that just fine, but when he had the rare opportunity for a face-to-face meeting with Saddam, he chose to talk about their common enemy instead. That was not only a stupid decision on his part, but a shameful one.

Later, the Washington paper *Roll Call* said in its Press Gallery section that I find it "hard to resist dumping on the press." Well, well. As I often do, I cranked up my dictating machinery and let loose a response. Here's an excerpt:

The other day I heard someone relate that the human skin weighs about six pounds. The factoid of the day! Surely that must represent the total skin weight right here in our nation's capital, where thin skin seems more like an official uniform. . . .

. . . I have come to one vivid conclusion: Reporters wear a thin skin, too. They love to peer through the microscope at the makers of public policy, but blanch quickly when they see a challenging eye looking back.

Roll Call charges that I find it "hard to resist dumping on the press." How curious. I've been beat on the old

bald dome by some of the best editorial writers in the
country (and by a few reporters who characterized their
blitz as "news") and have even come to enjoy the give
and take of those exchanges. But when I cocked the old
blunderbuss and fired a few rounds at the few members of
the media who deserve it, even those not targeted began
to bleed. . . .

The crux of the *Roll Call* article would indicate that I
sat down with Saddam Hussein last April to note that he
was a pretty good guy and that his "image problem" was a
result of a ghastly relationship with the world media. What
a goofy and dull-witted conclusion. . . .

It was quite correctly reported that I . . . told Hussein I
felt that some members of the media indeed seem
haughty, cynical and pampered. I do feel that. They are a
minority but they surely exist.

Did representatives of the executive and legislative
branches of our government misjudge Hussein's character
and intentions before he invaded Kuwait? Indeed. He is
one clever cat and has now proved to be a clear danger to
the entire world.

Was I critical of some elements of the media in a portion of my conversation with him? Indeed. But the char-
acterization of that conversation as two chums hacking
away at the media because of their own woes is just stupid
and irresponsible. And the fact that this hackneyed old
story is still making the rounds five months later further
illustrates my point about a thin-skinned media.

Then I referred to the letter we had hand-delivered to Saddam—the letter that outlined our vivid objections to his nuclear
and chemical weapons programs, and so forth. I quoted from the
letter: "If our two nations are to have better relations, such activities as those alleged to have occurred must never happen again."

I ended my letter to *Roll Call* with these words: "Where is the
repeated coverage of that tough statement we carried with us and

hand-delivered? What's good for the goose is good for the gander—or some such old saw! See you around the campus."

I never got a satisfactory answer to that last question: Why were the media so much more interested in my remarks about reporters than they were in our strong message to Saddam? Yes, I do believe that some members of our media are pampered, cynical, and haughty. And nothing proved that better than the hypersensitive, childish reaction of some writers. Sadly, there were few in the press who were willing to admit how thin-skinned some of them can be. As I see it, those who can't make honest distinctions between the lightweights and the heavyweights in journalism cannot ever honestly evaluate their own profession.

A lot of the criticism of my remarks was offered after Saddam had revealed himself to be the personification of evil. Yes, I wish we in government had seen that more clearly. As a nation, we were too kind to him. If journalists were to go back through the letters, speeches, and public papers of legislators whose states depend heavily on exports, they would find a ream of nice little thank-you notes to Saddam—notes expressing gratitude and pleasure that he was buying their wheat, rice, corn, vehicles, equipment, or whatever. Saddam had money. He had power. He put the screws to Iran. We all liked that. We liked it so much that we were willing to overlook things we should not have overlooked.

But characterizing my meeting with Saddam as a pity party was downright unfair. To say we were chopping away at the media because we shared a common hatred of journalists is stupid and scornful. It just stinks. And yet my run-ins with the press over Iraq had only just begun.

Months passed, and eventually I voted with the majority in Congress to authorize the use of force to liberate Kuwait. That was a tight and difficult vote—52–47. I cast my vote with a deep sense of personal responsibility, aware that many young Americans would surely shed their blood in the cause. I served in the infantry at the end of the Army of Occupation in Germany but never heard a live shell whistle past my ear. Still, my military service gave me a deep sense of patriotism. Also, I could recall some of America's past successful wars—wars in which we had a clear sense of duty and mission—and felt again that we were on the side of right.

The January 15, 1991, deadline for Saddam to get out of Kuwait came and went. The next day, a massive array of Coalition air forces—with Americans leading the charge—began a punishing, pummeling, powerful attack on Iraq. I'll hunch most Americans could tell you exactly where they were when the news broke that the air war had begun. Americans offered up a common prayer that this action might be swift and decisive, and that our fighting men and women would come home soon, and whole.

Most also remember the early television and radio reports coming from Washington, Riyadh, Saudi Arabia, and Israel. News of what was happening in Baghdad was harder to come by. When the war started, Saddam Hussein pulled the plug on the media and tossed out virtually every single Western news reporter. One who was allowed to stay—Peter Arnett of CNN.

Peter, Peter, Peter. Day and night during those first few shocking days of war, I watched with increasing alarm—and then plain irritation—as Peter Arnett broadcast from somewhere in downtown Baghdad. I was ten years old when World War II began, and could vividly remember how totally united we were against the hated enemy. Now, during the Gulf War, I just could not for the life of me understand how an American journalist could justify reporting on a war from inside the enemy's capital city. (Arnett is a native of New Zealand who has adopted the United States as his home.) American soldiers were getting killed, and this reporter was being pampered, protected, fed, and given a comfy place to sleep, all courtesy of the enemy government. All Peter Arnett and CNN had to do in exchange for this was submit their stories to Iraqi censors before airing them. In other words, all they had to do was surrender their last shred of journalistic credibility. Unbelievable.

In the Gulf War, Peter Arnett's viewers saw nothing more or less than what the Iraqi government wanted them to see. Period. When the fighting started, the Iraqis hand-picked members of the media and told them they could report from Baghdad only under certain conditions—conditions that clearly compromised their

ability to report anything fully and objectively. Any reporter allowed to remain in Baghdad was cloistered in a downtown hotel
until an official Iraqi host arrived to take him out on location.
Then the media people were finally allowed to tape and file stories
which, by God and Allah, damn well had to be favorable to Iraq
and Saddam Hussein. No reporter was to offend or criticize Hussein in any way. Journalists and their crews were permitted to stay
in Iraq as long as they agreed to be censored and as long as their
reports served Iraq's—not America's—national interests.

My question was: What the hell was CNN doing there? Most
journalists will tell you—whether you ask them or not—that a free
and vigorous press requires that journalists be able to report the
facts uncensored, in an atmosphere of openness and freedom. That
atmosphere clearly was not present in Baghdad. So what should
Peter Arnett have done? When an ethical reporter finds himself or
herself being used as a pawn in a giant propaganda war put on by
a brutal bastard, what should he or she do? The answer is clear:
The reporter should take a hike—get the hell out of there. Journalists who allow themselves to be used in this way sell their reputations and credibility down the river and forfeit any hope of
honestly and objectively reporting the truth. That's where I come
from.

The hard-driving moguls and business types who run the news
business (or is it the entertainment industry?—the two seem to
have blended together) swiftly and deftly tried to explain this obvious ethical breach. They pointed out that every Peter Arnett
dispatch was broadcast with a disclaimer at the bottom—a few
words explaining that the story had been approved by the Iraqi
authorities. Surely, these executives said, the American people
were smart enough to read between the lines of what Arnett was
saying. The truth would emerge despite the censorship. What
tripe! And what a precedent to set for the reporting of news! According to that logic, it is fine to report propaganda as long as you
tell people that's what it is. The code of ethics of the Society of
Professional Journalists—yes, that damn thing again—states,
"Journalists who use their professional status as representatives of
the public for selfish or other unworthy motives violate a high

trust." Those are journalists' words, not mine. And if CNN was not compromising its journalistic role for higher ratings, then I have a full head of flowing golden hair. When Peter Arnett returned to his adopted land after finishing his guided (and therefore not too informative) tour of Baghdad, he commented that he was being hailed as a hero across the globe.

Then he took a leave of absence and set about the writing of his book, for which he got a hefty advance. This guy was no hero. He was a tool. In my naive Wyoming mind, it is simply plain wrong for a journalist to act as spokesman for another country when his or her own country is at war. Those who dispense, report, broadcast, or otherwise disseminate the enemy's propaganda become thus aligned with the enemy. That's how I feel, and nobody will rock me off that opinion.

While Peter Arnett was happily accepting the Iraqi government's conditions—and its food and lodging—petulant, pushy, and indignant members of the stateside media were complaining about "the conditions" placed on their own reporting by the United States government. The media thought they should be able to go everywhere and know everything. It was then that Secretary of Defense Dick Cheney and Pentagon spokesman Pete Williams—a couple of fine, bright, sensible, home-grown Wyoming products—really let the media have it. As dear Pop used to say, "They told 'em to go to hell in a way they looked forward to the trip." The media felt the U.S. government was censoring them in the same way that Iraq was censoring Peter Arnett. How arrogant, idiotic, and self-serving. Quite unlike Iraq, the United States was not engaged in a full propaganda campaign. The rules for American reporters had but two motives and objectives—to safeguard and protect human life by imposing reasonable restrictions, and to protect the security and secrecy of our military operations. Reporters were free to criticize, carp, and bitch all they wanted about the war effort—and many surely did. That was fine. Peter Arnett had no such freedom. He was a kept man.

I can surely understand the reluctance of some members of the press to accept the government's statements during wartime. The United States lost a lot of credibility by constantly telling lies during the Vietnam war. The government's relationships with the media and with the public have never been the same. Certainly Dick Cheney and General Colin Powell felt that. They had a hard time gaining the trust of the press and the people. Still, they had to be somewhat secretive. They were not out to trick the media or deny them information they should rightfully have. Some information—how many troops were being moved at a given time, what missions were planned—was necessarily kept secret, even from the American people. The safety, the very lives, of American troops depended on it.

I had the sinking and appalling feeling that some reporters could not—or didn't want to—distinguish between their own country and the enemy. I could not stray from my simple belief that journalists are citizens first and reporters second. What a green pea I was! Somehow, these people had managed to exempt themselves from any shared sense of national purpose or good in that war. Was I—am I—could I be—questioning their patriotism? Yes. Our country was doing its best to protect our fighting men and women. The other country, Iraq, was airing propaganda on CNN, lobbing scud missiles into Israeli neighborhoods, displaying tortured Americans on Iraqi television (tortured against all provisions of the Geneva Convention), and creating an environmental disaster by setting fire to some of the world's largest oil fields. Can't you see the difference between those two countries? I can. Journalists apparently couldn't.

Watching Peter Arnett's continuing reports from the heart of Baghdad only served to heighten my sense of outrage. With those feelings so close to the surface, I traveled back to Casper, Wyoming, for yet another press convention. This time, I was supposed to debate columnist Jack Anderson about the role of the media in America. This was the same Jack Anderson who had misreported my meeting with Saddam. Boy, I wanted a piece of him! Well, he didn't show. He felt that developments in the Persian Gulf required him to remain in Washington, so he appeared on the program by satellite. I knew damn well he wasn't needed in Washington—if I wasn't, he sure as hell wasn't—but if he wasn't willing to take me on in person, there wasn't much I could do about it.

I really slung it to Jack Anderson in that debate. I could see the shocked look on his televised face as I whirled a wet sock full of sludge around my head and let it fly. When the forum was over, I didn't feel too good about myself. I had been irrational and shrill. Jack and I would later patch things up, but at that moment, in Casper, I was feeling pretty steamed—and low.

I was still at the meeting hall in Casper when I was approached by a journalist I had known for many years. This was a highly respected person who had covered many dramatic national and international incidents for a major media company. I considered this individual a real friend, and a real pro, and a lot of others did too. We visited for a while. During our chat, this person shared certain information with me which I found both startling and offensive. The information was about Peter Arnett. As you know, my friend said, Peter Arnett covered the Vietnam War for the Associated Press. What you may not know, he went on, is that Arnett married a Vietnamese woman who had ties to the Communist Party. As a result, he was able to move freely and easily in Communist circles. Indeed, he was granted many accommodations by the Viet Cong, my friend continued. And it was a matter of public record that Arnett was among a small group of international journalists who were granted permission by the Communist government to continue reporting from Vietnam after the fall of Saigon.

I listened intently, eager to take on more high-octane fuel with which to start my engines on Peter Arnett. Not long after that, I got my chance. In February 1991, I attended a meeting of what is known as the Off the Record Club. At this regularly scheduled event, first-term Republican legislators lunch with Washington reporters, columnists, and bureau chiefs in hopes that we'll all become better acquainted. The funny thing is, everything said at the Off the Record Club is on the record. Reporters may ask any question they wish, so long as they take no more than two minutes to phrase it. The legislator must answer in the same amount of time. That's not easy for some senators and reporters, but we had fun trying.

The luncheon that day was held at the Monocle Restaurant on

Capitol Hill. I was hosting it along with Newt Gingrich, then the House assistant minority leader. Newt adroitly handled an array of questions and was then called to the House floor for a vote. I stuck around. I shouldn't have. Soon, somebody asked how I felt about the reporting of Peter Arnett on CNN. That was like asking a mother hen how she feels about foxes.

"Now I am going to get my size-fifteen shoe right into my mouth," I said, and then stuck the shoe down the gullet. "He was active in the Vietnam War and he won a Pulitzer Prize largely because of his antigovernment material. He was married to a Vietnamese whose brother was active in the Viet Cong." I should have stopped there. I didn't. I went on to call Peter Arnett about the worst thing you can call someone in time of war. I called him a "sympathizer."

Yes, I said that—boy, did I say it! It's on tape. I reddened. I wished I could snatch the words back, wad them into a ball, chew them up for a while, and then swallow them. But wishing wasn't going to help me now, for I had insulted one of the media's own, a person who was and is popular among his peers. I was in for serious trouble.

The trouble began in the next day's *Washington Post*, in an article by—there's that name again—Howard Kurtz. The headline was "Sen. Simpson calls Arnett 'Sympathizer.' " The subheadline said, "CNN Reporter Blasted for Iraq Coverage." Here's part of the text:

> Sen. Alan Simpson (R–Wyo.) charged yesterday that CNN correspondent Peter Arnett is "a sympathizer" with Iraq, that his reporting during the Vietnam War was biased and that he has a brother-in-law who was "active in the Viet Cong."
>
> At a Capitol Hill luncheon with reporters, the Senate minority whip assailed Arnett for his censored television reports from Baghdad. He said the reporter is "what we used to call a sympathizer. . . ."
>
> An Arnett family member, who asked not to be identified, said the Viet Cong allegation is "completely untrue."

The family member said Arnett's wife, Nina, from whom he has been separated for several years, had two brothers— a heart doctor who was forced into early retirement by the Viet Cong and died in the 1960s, and a math professor in Hanoi who was not politically active during the war and who has not been allowed to leave the country.

Friends and colleagues of Arnett reacted angrily to Simpson's remarks. . . .

Asked if he felt it was proper to make such an allegation public without attempting to verify it, Simpson said, "I find a lot of those [kinds of allegations] used in your line of work. . . . They slap guys like me around day and night [with such charges]."

"This is what I was told by a source I consider to be reputable. . . . To me, it has not been refuted." . . .

Author David Halberstam, who also won a Pulitzer for his Vietnam coverage, said yesterday he was "stunned by the ugliness" of Simpson's remarks about Arnett.

"I like Alan Simpson. I think he's smart as hell, funny as hell," Halberstam said. "But the ugliness of him even mentioning someone like Nina, and connecting Peter's extraordinary coverage, as if that made him a sympathizer to the other side. . . . He's dead wrong. I know the family and that charge is particularly painful for them."

Terry Smith, a CBS News reporter who was the *New York Times* Saigon bureau chief, said, "It is ludicrous to suggest[Arnett] is a sympathizer with Saddam Hussein, or that he was in any way sympathetic to either the North Vietnamese or the Viet Cong. He makes crystal clear in every report that he was taken to this or that site on a guided tour by the Iraqi government.

"People are intelligent enough to hear that and understand exactly what he is telling them. I just find this sort of personal attack outrageous," Smith said.

Other friends and colleagues of Arnett read the *Post* story and other accounts of what I had said, and they also rallied passionately and defiantly to his defense. The talk-show talking heads reacted with horror. Other journalists were simply incredulous. Rollie Evans, who was then writing a column with Bob Novak, called and said, "Would you please tell me why you did this?"

My friend Al Hunt, bureau chief of the *Wall Street Journal* and a regular on *The Capital Gang,* phoned and said, "I just can't believe what you said and did, Al. Why?" He saw nothing wrong with Arnett's reporting from a cozy suite in Baghdad. Indeed, he said he could see no difference between Iraq's censorship of Arnett and the limitations placed on American journalists by Dick Cheney. So I told him the difference—for full attribution. I said I could not understand how the hell someone could not tell the moral difference between the United States government and an Iraqi enemy whose leader had sworn to drown our finest in a "sea of blood." Al was alarmed. He really punched my lights out in his next few talk shows and columns.

The *Washington Post* then published a savage editorial, right smack at the top of the page. The *Post* said I had been "bootlicky and obsequious with Saddam Hussein" during the April meeting. The editorial further trumpeted that Peter Arnett was doing a "respectable, forthright job under what must be hideous circumstances. . . . Nevertheless, he has become an object of hysterical hatred to a lot of people who, so far as we know, never made the mildest objection to the kowtowing to Saddam that went on in the Republican Administration before August 1 or to the performance of the famous traveling troupe of senators in April.

"Peter Arnett is standing up straight over there in Baghdad. Here at home Alan Simpson has dipped into the slime," the *Post* succinctly concluded. I read that one at Dulles Airport while rushing for a plane to Wyoming for my daughter Susie's wedding. That editorial really hit me low and hard, like the toe of a cowboy boot to the groin.

Then, boys and girls, the criticism came in waves. I was drawn and quartered by journalists in every medium—television, radio, print. I was the object of derision, rejection, ridicule, and plain old searing hostility. I had taken on one of their own, and therefore I would pay. Valery N. Soyfer, a George Mason University professor who knew Arnett during their days in Moscow, insisted in an op-ed piece in the *Post* that Arnett was in Iraq "doing what he's always done: working courageously to convey the truth as best he can." David Webster, a former director of the BBC, wrote a piece saying it was no big deal for CNN to broadcast censored reports. "Do we think the American public is so dumb that only the egregious Sen. Alan Simpson is aware of this Iraqi control?" Only William F. Buckley, Jr, seemed to come to my defense. Again in the *Post,* he wrote a piece headlined "Criticism of Arnett Is Not Ridiculous." In it, he also pointed out that we knew for a fact that the United States was doing its best to limit civilian casualties in Iraq. "If we really didn't care about civilian casualties, we could end the war tomorrow by simply nuclearizing Baghdad," he said.

Buckley continued: "But here is Peter Arnett, day after day, retailing the Iraqi line that we are hitting innocent civilians intentionally. . . . It is simply true that X number of people will believe that, indeed, we are conducting ourselves inhumanely. And these misconceptions should not be taken too lightly."

Buckley was a rarity. Most writers nuclearized me. I must say I considered that ironic. These journalists criticized me personally—calling me "egregious" stung me—because I had assailed Peter Arnett's estranged wife and her family. I should not have done that. And yet those who criticized me for getting personal had often gotten extremely personal themselves when writing about people in the public eye. Many of these were the same journalists who ripped into the Kennedy clan, Richard Nixon's brother and his wife, Lyndon and Lady Bird Johnson and their families, Jimmy Carter's family, Geraldine Ferraro's husband and son, and George Bush's son Neil. When they savaged people, they were fulfilling the public's sacred right to know. When I made a comment about someone in their extended journalistic family, I was "egregious" and much more. This same posse would later ride out to harass Clarence Thomas's mother and his ex-wife. The journalism profession utterly shattered the lives and privacy of both of those fine women, all because Thomas had been nominated to the United States Supreme Court. Is it any wonder that the American people can't stomach the way some journalists do things?

Just when I thought the Peter Arnett flap couldn't get worse, it got worse. I made my comments about Arnett at noon on February 7. Two days later—the day the *Post* editorial appeared—I flew to Wyoming to fulfill various commitments in Cheyenne, Casper, and Sheridan. Susie's wedding to a dear young man named John Gallagher was set for February 16 in Jackson Hole. I would be joined there by Ann, my mother, Lorna, Ann's mother, Pansy, our two sons, Bill and Colin, daughter-in-law Debbie, and granddaughter Elizabeth.

It was a horrible time to be so busy. That week, a number of daily and weekend news shows called and asked me to be on. Many reporters also called asking for interviews. I had to turn everybody down. I knew from my talks with Rollie Evans and Al Hunt that my words could not be placed in their proper context during any five-minute phoner. Besides, I was not going to let anything take precedence over Susie's wedding. And so it seemed a thousand articles came out saying I could not be reached for comment— which most readers take to mean that I was hiding out somewhere. I had violated my first rule of dealing with the media: When they're after your ass, answer the phone. How I wished I could have! If I had been able to do interviews, I could have played down what I had said about Arnett's Vietnam experience and played up my very solid objection to the reporting he was doing in Iraq. But since I was unable to do long interviews, the story remained fixed on one regrettable word: "sympathizer." I should add that my failure to respond was my fault, not the media's. They wanted me to explain myself; I just couldn't get it done.

Days and weeks passed. Coalition forces were scoring a decisive victory over Saddam Hussein's army, air force, and propaganda machine. America continued to celebrate, though cautiously, the miraculously low number of casualties while also grieving for the families who had lost sons or daughters. In short, the American-led forces were winning—and doing it with skill, power, pride, and precision.

The media remained intent—it seemed to poor, thin-skinned me—on beating up on one Alan K. Simpson. *Time* magazine carried a piece called "Shooting the Messenger." *Time* writer Stanley

Cloud wrote with wounded passion, "In recent weeks the halls of Congress have been fouled by superpatriot blast." He went on to imply that I was criticizing Peter Arnett simply for "telling the truth," as if the crap that Iraq was feeding to Arnett bore any resemblance to the truth.

Soon after that piece appeared, C-SPAN aired a program about how the editors produce an issue of—you got it—*Time* magazine. In one scene, the editors were shown meeting to discuss that week's issue. The assembled journalists agreed that the only effective weapon Saddam Hussein had left in his vast arsenal was "the propaganda weapon." These otherwise bright and thoughtful journalists somehow did not seem to see the connection between the "propaganda weapon" and the journalist they had just finished lionizing in their pages. What better propaganda tool did Saddam ever have than Peter Arnett, whom *Time* had just described as the victim of those ugly superpatriots in Congress? The folks in that staff meeting also agreed that "most people" would describe Arnett's reports as "news." How terribly deceptive. How slickly distorted. How sick.

Many Americans still recall the story, televised by CNN, of the distraught Iraqi woman mourning the destruction of "civilian life and buildings." In near-perfect English, this woman condemned America for its transgressions against the innocent people of Iraq. What Peter Arnett and CNN never reported was that the same Iraqi woman gave the same performance in near-perfect French for the benefit of French television. The whole thing was a setup. And yet Arnett reported the woman's outburst as if it were a wholly spontaneous event. This was the sort of crap *Time* magazine was calling news.

The Iraqis staged many other events for the Western media. In one story, we were shown a badly damaged building. We were informed that the structure had been mercilessly bombed by Coalition forces. Peter Arnett's voice was then heard saying that the building "was the only source of infant formula food for children one year and younger in Iraq." The signboard at the entrance of the building said "Baby Milk Factory" in both English and Arabic. The puzzling use of the English language on the sign was never explained. Was this really a baby milk factory? No, it was not. Our government had identified the place as a biological weapons factory disguised as a baby formula plant. A *Washington Post* reporter toured the site after the bombing and wrote, "The plant is surrounded by barbed wire, with at least three observation towers, perhaps 10 feet off the ground, at intervals along the perimeter. [A] plant official, asked to explain the purpose of the observation posts, said that it is 'the usual practice' to surround every factory with barbed wire and towers." Barbed wire? At a baby formula factory? Come on. Peter Arnett had fallen for the Iraqis' ruse. Were the American people really "smart enough" to figure out the truth in that case? For most people, I'm sure, seeing was believing.

To this day, Arnett maintains that American bombs "took out a baby milk facility." He reported the story just as his duplicitous hosts hoped he would. He did what he was told, saw what he was allowed to see, and went where he was supposed to go. And his towering ego and new fame hindered his ability to hear or see the obvious. He failed us. I think he failed himself.

Another time, Arnett told us that American bombs had killed hundreds of civilians at one location. In this case, Arnett's hosts apparently roused him from his sleep and hustled him to the scene, where once again he reported exactly what the Iraqis wanted the world to believe. But should we have believed it? The bombed structure was clearly a military bunker. This was confirmed by all who examined the photos taken before and after the shelling. Yes, the bunker looked at first glance to be a civilian building, but the furniture and other trappings were only a front. Our intelligence described the bunker as a military command and control center, built expressly and solely for that purpose. But Arnett never looked into that angle of the story. Instead, he used his camera crew to focus on scenes of carnage. He did not investigate. Didn't ask any tough questions. Couldn't. Didn't probe. Did not seek to find out who, what, when, where, and why. He didn't do his job.

The general impression viewers got from Peter Arnett's reporting was that American bombs were killing large numbers of civilians and leveling civilian neighborhoods. Certainly it was true that some innocent civilians were killed. War is hell. But it was also true that many Iraqis were placed in harm's way by a neurotic and callous leader who wanted to hurl their dead bodies as weapons in his propaganda war. Indeed, journalists who entered Iraq after the war reported the truth about the facility where hundreds of "civilians" were killed—it was a bunker. Arnett has yet to acknowledge that.

I soon again had reason to question the patriotism of some journalists. In February 1991, I was invited to participate in a discussion of the media role in the Gulf War. The forum was to be called "The Agony of Decision," with the affable and energetic Fred Friendly of CBS as moderator. Other panelists included James Schlesinger, Jeane Kirkpatrick, ace journalist David Halberstam, Pentagon spokesman Pete Williams, Bruce van Voorst of *Time*, Congressman Bill Gray, and Michael Gartner, then president of NBC News.

Gartner was asked during the forum if he believed American journalists should remain completely impartial when covering a war involving their own country. His answer, in short, was yes. He said that the media's role is simply "to inform . . . to try to tell as much as you know as clearly, as thoroughly, as accurately, as carefully as it is possible to do."

His remarks startled me. I couldn't believe he would say that journalists have no obligation to side with their own country in a time of war. I don't buy that argument, and I sure as hell don't think Ernie Pyle or Edward R. Murrow—legendary war correspondents—would, either.

Later, Gartner resigned as NBC's president after it was revealed that he had allowed the airing of a *Dateline* segment in which the fiery explosion of a General Motors truck had been rigged for the cameras. So maybe my sense of his sophistication as a journalist was right on target.

The destruction our military caused in Iraq was brutal and tragic. Still, we did what we had to do. We did it with precision, power, and potency. Soon it was over. And soon Peter Arnett was back on American soil. On March 13, 1991, Peter Arnett's son Andrew wrote a piece for the *New York Times* in defense of his father and of his father's work. Andrew said he had purposely remained silent during the war but now felt that there were "some personal issues that deserve attention." He went on to say that while I had not said much about his father recently, "the damage had already been done." He was justifiably upset by my accusation that his mother had ties to the Viet Cong. He then described the death of her brothers living in North Vietnam and said she still mourned them.

"This pain has been compounded by Mr. Simpson's unsubstantiated allegations. There are others beyond my family who have been hurt by Senator Simpson's words," he said. "Are we to be told by our leaders to refrain from expressing ideas at odds with their own? In smearing my father, Mr. Simpson used guilt by association—tactics more in keeping with a dictatorship than a democracy."

I felt terribly sad when I read that piece—sad about the way I was being portrayed, yes, but also sad because I had hurt Peter Arnett's son and his family. As I read the piece, I recalled all the times that my own children rallied behind me when I was under attack for something I had said or done. At such times, one of the children invariably called me late at night, or sent a yellow rose and a tender greeting card, or just gave me a hug and a kiss. As I read Andrew Arnett's essay, I couldn't help thinking that any one of my three kids would have written the same kind of article in my defense if I had been wronged. I felt that Andrew Arnett's piece deserved a thoughtful and honest response. In a letter published in the *New York Times* of March 20, 1991, I issued an apology.

> While I still strongly criticize [Peter Arnett] for his reporting from Baghdad during the Persian Gulf War, I do feel the deep personal need to apologize for repeating the rumors about Mr. Arnett's family connection to the Viet Cong. I said from the outset that if it couldn't be proven, I would apologize. In the absence of concrete evidence to corroborate the family situation, I wish to do so now. I greatly regret any hurt, pain or anguish that I have caused his family. Furthermore I admonish all who have engaged

in this item of gossip over Mr. Arnett's past to put up or shut up. I regret being part of it. Just as Operation Desert Storm has healed many wounds left from Vietnam, it is also time to allow that wound to heal. So I direct this expression particularly to Peter Arnett's son, Andrew, who wrote so eloquently and poignantly in "The Truth About My Family."

I concluded: "My choice of the word 'sympathizer' was not a good one. I wish I could have snatched it back and rephrased my remarks. The word 'dupe' or 'tool' of the Iraqi government would have been more in context with my original comments. However, I do know when I am wrong and stubborn—and for that I apologize. I would also hope the news media might acknowledge their share of serious mistakes on the coverage of the Gulf War from Baghdad. But I sure won't hold my breath on that one."

Once again, Howard Kurtz at the *Washington Post* was right on top of the story. In an article headlined "Sen. Simpson's Print Apology to CNN's Arnett," he quoted Arnett as saying he was struck by the "audacity" of a "public figure of his stature . . . bringing up unsubstantiated charges" against a reporter's family. According to Kurtz, Arnett called me "an impetuous man."

Maybe so. But some people appreciated the apology more than Arnett apparently did. The morning my letter appeared, a nationally known television journalist called my office and said, "I wish I had the guts to do that. I've made some doozies of mistakes in my time, but never had the courage to admit to them. I commend you for it." That call meant a great deal to me not only because of the stature of the man who said it, but because I knew of the controversy that often surrounded him as a media type.

Some reporters took my letter to be a cleansing admission that I now regretted ever opening a discussion of journalistic standards during wartime. I felt no such regret. My intention in writing the letter was to apologize for mentioning Peter Arnett's family and for using the word "sympathizer"—and that was all. Having done that, I hoped that we might continue to debate whether it was appropriate for a reporter to work under the conditions Arnett had accepted. My sense was that the media wanted me to come to them with hat in hand, nervously fingering and rotating the tattered brim, to say that I had learned my lesson and would never speak ill of them again. But that ain't my nature. I was, and am, ornery and steadfast in my belief that many in the media behaved shamefully and stupidly during the war—and that Peter Arnett committed a gross disservice to his country and to his chosen profession.

The toughest lesson and tragic irony of the whole Peter Arnett episode was that I had done exactly what I often criticized the media for doing: I had taken the outrageous claims of an anonymous source and published them without first checking their veracity. I firmly believed that my source was telling me the truth, but in such matters, faith is not enough; by going ahead with the accusations, I had fallen into the trap that snares so many journalists. For that I am sorry, and am still embarrassed.

But even after my apology was printed, journalists continued to come after me, and hard. Some of the people attacking me were journalists I had once considered friends. These were folks with whom I had dined many times, sometimes in my home and sometimes in theirs. Some really stuck it to me. And then I would see them somewhere, and they would avert their eyes and utter a muffled greeting. That was tough for me to take. Ann would say, "You can't change them. Just toss it off. Forget it. Ignore it." If only it were that easy. Most of us politicians know why we get hammered from time to time—we bring it on ourselves! But I was still hurt and saddened to see the apparent glee with which some of these media "friends" stuck it in my gazoo.

Every day's newspaper seemed to bring a new attack. Ann and I were still asleep early one morning that March when the phone rang. I answered. A familiar voice said, "Did I get you up?"

"Oh, hell, no, I had to get up to answer the phone anyway," I said.

President George Bush said, "Well, I'm sorry to wake you. I take it you haven't read today's *Washington Post*, then?"

"No, not yet," I said.

"Well," he said with a gentle chuckle, "they did a little number on you there—but it could have been worse!"

Later, when I read the paper, I wasn't sure I agreed. Here are some excerpts from Lois Romano's piece:

> When Alan Simpson arrived in Washington some 12 years ago, he captured the hearts and minds of the manicured political set with his effortless earthy cowboy humor, his startling characterizations and his erudite full-bore attacks on adversaries. Indeed, this conservative Republican with the abortion rights stand appeared to be, refreshingly, his own man.
>
> But as the senator from Wyoming is the first to tell you, Washington's spotlight of approval is fleeting. And these days, it seems to be shifting away from him. His humor, some now say, is beginning to sound like a Borscht belt comedian's overused shtick. His intellectual bite, it is said, stopped being entertaining when it started getting personal. And his pattern of attacking first and apologizing later, partisan opponents say, has worn thin.
>
> What is now surfacing in Washington's back rooms is a concern that Simpson's often unchallenged stridence is getting out of hand. Detractors say that under the guise of humor and openness and collegiality, Simpson operates as though he can say just about anything about anyone.
>
> And sometimes that's a bit too much.

So much for the idea that I was a "Western Breeze Through Stuffy Senate," as the *Post* had called me years earlier. Romano went on to say that I seemed "to hold [the media] in extremely low regard—which some armchair analysts think comes from his inability to always control the final product."

At the risk of sounding thin-skinned (again!)—and certainly the piece wounded me—let me take a moment to deconstruct this story. According to Romano, "some" said I was not funny and "it [was] said" that my intellectual approach was not appreciated.

Furthermore, "partisan opponents" didn't like me and there was a concern "in Washington's back rooms" that I was out of control. But who exactly was saying those things? Who were these "armchair analysts"? Nobody she quoted. Lois Romano quoted eight people other than me. Two were my friends. Two were people with whom I had had run-ins in Wyoming. (One of the run-ins had taken place more than nine years earlier, the other five years before.) And who were Lois Romano's four other sources? Journalists. Years before all four were journalists. So where were all these detractors, all these partisan opponents, all these mysterious Washington back-roomers? In Lois Romano's imagination, maybe? Could be? No wonder George Bush was calling to give fair warning.

Toward the end of our conversation, George asked if Ann and I would join him and Barbara at Camp David for the weekend. He said two other couples would be coming along—our friends and theirs Fred and Martha Zeder and Jack and Bobbie Fitch. I said excitedly that we just might just be able to rearrange our schedules! He said, "Great, I'll get back with the details."

On the appointed day, we headed for the White House, for the quick flight to Camp David. As it happened, this was the very day that George Bush's national approval rating reached 93 percent, the highest rating ever achieved by a president while in office. I was so damned proud of him, this friend I had known for thirty years. When we arrived at 1600 Pennsylvania Avenue, Ann and I were ushered into the small room off the Oval Office. Barbara was sitting on a lovely old couch, doing needlepoint and chatting with George. The president was reading letters, then signing them with that loopy, left-handed flourish. The four of us visited. I told a couple of suitably shaggy stories. George told a couple of his own. Then I realized that the walk from that room to the helicopter would mean passing by a gauntlet of reporters. On this, his most glorious day as president, I didn't think George should have to be seen with inglorious, tarnished me. On that day he was famous; I was infamous.

I said, "Look, this is your big moment. You're at the peak of

your game. Let Ann and me get on the chopper through the back
door—or somewhere—and you come out on the lawn to the roar
of the crowd."

George Bush responded with that slim chin jutted forward,
head cocked, and eyes twinkling. "Now you two just sit tight. I'm
running this show," he said. When the time came to board Marine
One, he said, "Now here's the way we'll do it. Barbara, you and
Ann walk out together first, and Al and I will be a few steps behind
you. Let's go!"

Barbara and Ann stepped out smartly, walking arm in arm across
the expanse of the south lawn. George and I followed. On our left
were White House staff members and friends waving signs reading
"Ninety-three percent," "We love you George and Barbara," and
"You make us proud." To our right were the journalists—television, print, and radio people. As I waved to the White House
staffers, George said, "Don't just wave over there. Turn around
and wave to all your fans in the media." He was already facing
them, waving both arms. I dutifully turned to them and gave a
halfhearted wave. Then George gave me a big, showy, friendly
thwack on the back. He had deliberately done this so the media
could see, and I knew it.

We finished our brief walk across the still-green expanse of
lawn and were ready to board the chopper. George Bush raised a
final friendly wave and said to me, "Duck your head, big fella, and
get in there." Soon we were floating above the Ellipse, looking
down on that magnificently planned city and all its treasures—the
Washington Monument, the Capitol, the Jefferson Memorial, the
Mall, the Lincoln Memorial. Barbara and Ann sat talking. George
went to work reading staff memos, news briefs, and the latest intelligence reports. I had something to say to my friend, but this
was not the time to say it.

After settling into our generously appointed "cottage" at Camp
David, we undertook the program of always intense physical activity that George Bush thinks of as rest. We played horseshoes.
We shot skeet. We bowled. We jogged. We rode bicycles. We
told tall tales and terrible stories. We played wally ball—a game

played with a volley ball on a handball court, with a volleyball net strung across the center. When you run out of bounds in that game, you bust your ass and your brains on solid concrete. Ann and I played every set for two days and couldn't walk for five more.

The morning after we arrived, George was reading a stack of morning newspapers at the breakfast table when he suddenly said, "There we are, Al! That's the way I hoped they'd cover it." He pointed to some front-page pictures in a few of the nation's papers. One showed him shepherding me along, arm around my back. He jabbed at it with a big grin and said again, "Yep, just the way I would have wanted it!" I knew again what I wanted to say—but there were too many people around now for me to feel comfortable saying it.

Later in the day, we were relaxing buck naked in the sauna, just the two of us. I finally had the chance to thank this man, my friend. I said, dead seriously too, "I want to tell you something very important to me, George. I am not at all unmindful of what you are doing for us, and for me, this weekend. You are rehabilitating and restoring energy and good spirit to your old beaten-up, smashed-in, crapped-on friend. Oh, sure, I've felt sorry for myself. But I know what this is all about—and don't think I don't richly and deeply appreciate it. It is truly an act of genuine friendship extended to me and to Ann. I thank you, my friend!"

George Bush doesn't handle comments like that very well. They embarrass the hell out of him. He smiled kindly and almost shyly and said, "It was something Barbara and I wanted very much to do."

Several weeks later, I attended one of those Washington dinners where people just can't help telling secrets. Someone there told me that two of George's top aides had tried to persuade him not to invite me to Camp David. After all, he was at the peak of his popularity and I was at my nadir, and sucking up a little canal water besides. He ignored them. That should tell you something about George and Barbara Bush—family and friends always come first. Those closest to them know it, and know it well.

When Ann and I returned from Camp David, I resumed my battle with the nation's media. That same month, Richard Cohen of the *Washington Post* wrote a column about my meeting with Saddam Hussein—a meeting that had taken place a full year earlier, mind you. I wrote a letter to the editor calling Cohen's column "pungent" and accusing him of "raking me over the coals." I also called him "a pretty cynical and haughty reporter. And a pretty lazy one too." As I said earlier, somebody once advised me never to pick a fight with somebody who buys ink by the barrel. Well, the *Washington Post* buys it by the vat. Soon, Cohen took yet another crack at me. I was flustered and irritated as hell.

Indeed, I was at a slow burn that whole spring. My war with the media had turned me into a testy and sometimes angry man. I had become willful and obstinate and touchy as hell. This was hurting me—and certainly it was hurting Ann. As I was leaving the house one morning she said so in the clearest possible terms.

"Al, turn and look at me," she said, touching my arm. "If you choose to continue to do this thing of yours with the media you are only going to be known as a loser."

"I know what I'm doing!" I snapped, jerking my arm away from her. I had never done that before.

"No, I mean it," she said. "You'll be a loser. I have a thought for you. I mean it, too. Why don't you just shut up?"

In our thirty-seven years of marriage to that day she had never used those words with me. We had exchanged some harsh words during our long marriage, as most couples sometimes do, but until then Ann had never, ever said anything so piercing and direct. I was dumbfounded.

"What the hell are you saying?" I said, looking hard at her.

"I'm saying you are a wonderful person and it's crazy to see what you are doing to yourself," she said. "You seem obsessed with this issue of Peter Arnett and the media—and you can't win. When are you going to admit for the first time in your life that you cannot win? And since you can't win, why don't you just shut up?"

Shut up? Quit? How was I supposed to quit? I had never quit anything. As a young kid I was big, fat, knock-kneed, and hopelessly uncoordinated, and yet through my own determination I had turned myself into a respectable high school basketball and college football player. I struggled in my first year of law school, but was so determined to become a lawyer that I told the dean that I would eventually get a law degree even if I had to go to Panhandle A&M to get it. I had run for public office many times, in some tough races, and never lost. And I had always said whatever I damn well pleased, whether about the media or anything else. And now I was supposed to shut up?

But Ann was so right. What she was trying to help me understand was this: One can never, ever win a battle against the media. No matter how many interviews I gave or letters I wrote to editors, no matter how many angry or disgusted phone calls I made to TV producers, I would never get anyone in the media to admit that there are problems in the profession. Instead, some wiseass reporter or columnist would always be out there, ready to write a cutesy column undermining whatever I was trying to say. What Ann was telling me was that I would never get the last word, so I might as well quit blathering. I might as well shut up.

I love her. I took her advice. I eased up. Oh, I still took the occasional opportunity to criticize the press; I love a good argument too much ever to stop doing that. But I finally understood that I would never win the war. I would never mount the heads of journalists on the walls of my cabin near Cody. These days, when I give a speech whacking the media, I generally wind up by saying, "You can bet that the media will now take one more big Jurassic Park–size chunk out of my ass, and the greatest thing is I won't mind it that much anymore. It was only when I damn well honestly and truly thought I could win that I really minded it."

By the way, I finally got a chance to visit with Peter Arnett. The opportunity came in March 1992, more than a year after our blowup, at the White House Correspondents Dinner.

The room that night was full of journalists and political types, most of whom serve as the anonymous sources for what the journalists write. Very cozy. When I arrived at my table, I checked my program and saw Peter's name. Then I found where he was sitting and ambled over to his table. He had just seated himself. When he saw me coming, he slid back, rose, and gave me a cheerful greeting. I returned it in kind.

I told Peter, "I'm sorry about the heavy comments I made about your family." Then, explaining that I was sorry to have caused such pain to his son, I said, "I hope you saw my apology in the *New York Times*."

"I did," he said. "Thank you."

I then said I was not prepared to take back any of the things I had said about his reporting from Iraq. I felt I would not have been honest if I did not say that.

"No, I didn't think you would be amending your comments," he said. "But I did want to correct an inaccuracy in your published remarks about me. You said in an interview you and I had never talked before."

I looked at him curiously and said, "Have we?"

Then Peter told me of an interview he had had with me in my office while I was working on illegal immigration reform some years back. He reminded me that we had shared some great jokes about being bald—we both qualify—and had told a few other good stories too. Then I remembered. We shared a laugh about those times.

As we stood there, quite resplendent in tux and black tie, both looking forward to a long night of jousting and joviality among media folk and political junkies, I felt I needed to say one more thing about our run-in. So I told him, "Judging by the reaction to my remarks about you, I'd say you have more friends in this town than I have."

Peter probably could have taken a few shots at me right then— he could have said something ringy about politicians who shoot off—but he did not. I appreciated that. He's a pretty good egg. I think we both understood that we would continue to disagree about some things, but we also knew that disagreeing is part of life—like air or water—in Washington. Peter Arnett has since given many a speech telling his side of the Iraq story, and has also published his book. He has had his say, and now, for the first time in any depth, I'm having mine. That is as it should be. No, I will never win the war of words with the media. But I will always enjoy the scrap.

CHAPTER SEVEN

And You Can Quote Me

I f you read a newspaper this morning, you joined with millions of Americans in being manipulated. You were manipulated by journalists, who were in turn manipulated by people whose identities—and, more important, biases—were never revealed to you. This web of manipulation was presented to you as unbiased reporting, pure as snow. In fact, many of the stories in your morning paper probably did to the truth what a funhouse mirror does to a person's appearance—warped and twisted it way out of shape. How did this happen? Through journalists' use of anonymous sources. Asking unnamed people to comment, Greek-chorus-like, on the day's events is a common, universally accepted practice in the media. It is also lazy, dishonest, and downright dangerous. The anonymous source is introduced to you as the bearer of truth. In fact, he or she is the enemy of truth.

And just who are these anonymous sources? They most often are people with deeply held biases and hidden agendas who are nonetheless given an extraordinary gift—the ultimate shield of protection for what they say. Journalists generally are eager to label their on-the-record sources as conservative (meaning suspect) or liberal (meaning very good) or as members of a public interest group (meaning very good, true saints). But they will rarely identify their anonymous sources with such a label. Off-the-record types generally escape any kind of definition that would help the public to understand what their biases and beliefs are. Instead, they are referred to only as a "top elected official," "someone close to the investigation," or "a source who fiercely requested anonymity." Go back and take a peek again at your morning paper. Cast your peepers through the front-page articles—especially in those national publications such as the *Washington Post*, the *New York Times*, and the *Los Angeles Times*. You'll find these anonymous sources in virtually every article. You're simply supposed to trust them, even though you don't know them one whit.

It is very easy to see why some people refuse to go on the record with what they say. By staying off the record, they can affect public opinion—and often public policy—without taking responsibility for it. But why would journalists allow them to do that? The answer is simple. Reporters use anonymous sources to get their own ideas and opinions into circulation while seeming to do the noble, honorable, distinguished job of journalism. Journalists can't always brazenly publish their own strident views in the middle of a news article. But they certainly can call someone who shares their views and quote him or her anonymously, thereby accomplishing the same thing. If you can't slant an article yourself, you can always get someone to do it for you—especially if you promise not to put the source's name in black and white. Besides, can't you just see the reporter sitting in front of the doubting editor and saying, "I know this is juicy stuff, but I can't reveal my source"? And can't you just hear the editor excitedly saying, "Tell me more!"?

Not long ago, while chatting with a group of journalists, I quite intentionally said something totally outrageous about something that was happening in Washington. One of the reporters said, "Where did you hear that?"

"Why, from an anonymous source!"

One of them said, "Who? Come on, who?"

I said, "Oh, no, I'd go to jail before I would ever reveal the name of that person!"

At first they laughed. Then they thought about what I had said and some were embarrassed. Each one of them was in the habit of publishing unkind and untrue things about people, and then refusing to reveal the source. But only when I did the same with them did they see how stupid it sounds in these times. I hope I made my point, at least with that small band.

Unfortunately, the larger profession continues to use the anonymous source with relish and regularity. They do this most often—and with consistently deadly effects—in profiles of the nation's celebrities, athletes, rascals, and politicians. The personality profile is a prime refuge for the cowardly writer. Too often in these pieces, unnamed individuals are allowed to savage another person's character and integrity under the cloak of anonymity, frequently for an audience of hundreds of thousands, or even millions. I know it well because that very thing has happened to me.

In the late fall of 1990, the editors of *The New Yorker* asked distinguished writer John Newhouse to begin work on a personality profile of your loyal scrivener. I felt quite delighted and honored they would choose me as a subject, as I had read and enjoyed a long piece Newhouse had done about a man I admire greatly, Congressman and former Speaker of the House Tom Foley. I thought the piece about Tom was balanced, and sometimes even downright friendly. I knew well that *The New Yorker* had pioneered the craft of personality journalism and had published some of the finest personality profiles seen anywhere. Being selected as the subject of one of those long, gray analyses was like being asked to pose for a portrait by Whistler. Well, almost.

I must say I was surprised at *The New Yorker*'s choice, because I did not have an especially well known persona at the time. At that juncture I had not yet sallied forth to wage war against CNN and Peter Arnett. The confirmation hearings on the nomination of Clarence Thomas to the Supreme Court were not even a glimmer on the horizon. I had at that point never even heard of Anita Hill, whose name would one day be associated with mine, and with the names of my colleagues on the Judiciary Committee. Oh yes, I had engaged the media in one or two skirmishes, but I had done little to generate the kind of controversy that in turn generates *New Yorker* profiles. At the time I was still seen by most of the press as "Western Breeze Through Stuffy Senate," to use the *Washington Post*'s phrase.

Still, Ann and I welcomed Newhouse and his *New Yorker* project, just as we had done with others who had done profiles in the past. John was and is a genuinely pleasant and delightful man. I talked with him at great length. He visited my friends from all around Wyoming and Washington. He talked with members of my family. The days turned to weeks, and weeks to months. And still, for whatever reason, he did not finish the piece. At one point he said it would run in March 1991, but it didn't. I was still waiting for the piece to appear when I had my little episode with Peter Arnett. A few months after that, Newhouse called and said, "Now what has happened to you here? What is going on with you and Arnett?" I could see I had flunked at least one of his tests. I had taken on one of his brethren and was about to pay the price. Or so I hunched. But still more time went by and the article did not appear. I truly hoped it had ended up in the dumper somewhere.

Enter Clarence Thomas and Anita Hill and my earnest and vigorous participation in that high Washington drama. After those well-documented Senate hearings came another visit from Newhouse, this time with a more intense and focused series of questions: "What in the world has happened here? Why did you do this? What was driving you?" I guessed right then I was going to take a beating. I sensed that John was by now pretty fed up, disappointed, and bewildered. Boy, was I right.

The piece came out in *The New Yorker* in March 1992—some eighteen months after Newhouse conducted his first interview. I had a granny knot in my gut as I read the lead paragraph:

Not long ago, Alan K. Simpson, the Assistant Republican Leader, or Whip, and junior United States Senator from Wyoming, was envied by colleagues for what he lacked: serious vulnerabilities and critics who mattered. Stylistically, Simpson is, or was, the Senate's most arresting and exceptional figure. Besides being its tallest member, at six feet seven inches, he was its funniest and earthiest—benignly mixing the profane with the scatological—and no one in the chamber had demonstrated more spontaneous charm. Simpson was also known as one of the Senate's most effective speakers, one of its hardest workers, and one of its most skillful legislators. Moreover, he was, and still is, President George Bush's closest friend in Congress—probably his closest in Washington after Secretary of State James Baker. Simpson and his wife, Ann, belonged to a social circle built largely around the town's movers and shakers. At home in Wyoming Simpson was the State's most popular figure in modern memory—possibly ever—and many Democrats saw little reason to finance campaigns against him. In short, Simpson struck everyone as being unassailable politically. He isn't now, and the magic is gone.

The magic is gone? Wow! And that was just for starters. One friend thought she was reading my obituary. At the time, I thought the article was little more than an attempt to dig a big hole, shove me in it, throw the dirt on top, and tamp it down.

The piece was long—too long, really. It covered some nineteen ponderous pages, more than most people are willing to read about anybody, much less a bald-headed, half-glassed (some would say half-assed) politician from Wyoming. But after I got over the sting of the first paragraph, I began to appreciate some of the work Newhouse had done. I didn't agree with everything people told him about me, but I was most grateful to those who at least had the courage to speak their minds on the record. What bothered me then and continues to rankle me now were the extremely harsh comments offered under the veil of anonymity, all of which I suspect Newhouse gathered and used to paint the picture he had already sketched out in his head. The theme of the profile was that I was once beloved, later became nasty, was now reviled, and was about to be tossed out on my ass in the snow. And yet only the nice parts could be attributed to any specific person.

In his story Newhouse reported, ". . . I did speak with three veteran Republican Senators about the effects of the Arnett and Hill episodes on Simpson's [leadership] position and, more specifically, on whether his role as whip could be undermined. Two of these Senators expressed strong support for Simpson."

And here he quoted two of my colleagues on the record:

"Arlen Specter said, 'Al maintains high marks as a leader. Yes, he does speak his mind, and that is very refreshing especially in a calculating world. As for Simpson's whip job, I think he's alive and well, notwithstanding. I've heard no talk of anyone challenging him. And no one is maneuvering Al into that position."

Then Newhouse quoted Missouri's John Danforth:

"He isn't the creation of some image-maker. He is Al Simpson. That is why they love him. He is quintessentially one of us . . . This will have no effect on his role as leader. All of us here have ups and downs and we all know that about one another. We all have spats and temper tantrums and flareups."

Then came the views of the phantom third colleague. This fellow was given the cloak of anonymity, and he hunkered behind it while taking a potshot. He was asked about the Peter Arnett and Anita Hill episodes. "I don't think he will ever be elected to another leadership position," this person said. "This has hurt him that much, I think."

That's strong stuff. This person—whoever he or she was—was saying, basically, that I was persona non grata in my own party and that my days of influence were near their end. Newhouse apparently asked most of his sources—real or imagined, alive or dead— "What about Simpson's role as whip? Is he finished?" Those willing to speak on the record said I was not finished, but Newhouse didn't quit until he got some anonymous colleague to say I was. I found that galling, and still do. In public life, image can all too quickly become reality. I think that process is speeded up dramatically whenever anonymous sources are used. Readers, I think, are very likely to believe what is said by anonymous sources; they feel these people are telling them important—and utterly true—

secrets that those named in the article were too timid or anxious to reveal. Furthermore, there is no question that Newhouse's use of tough anonymous quotations gave courage to other critics in the media. The profile in *The New Yorker* came at what was inarguably the low point in my relationship with the national press corps. Plenty of journalists were happy to read an unflattering piece in *The New Yorker*. As my old friend Jack Danforth said, "This is 'Let's attack Al Simpson' season."

If Newhouse had updated his article a few months later, he would have had to report that I did stand for reelection to the position of assistant Republican leader, also known as minority whip, in the Senate in December of 1992. I was pleased and honored to win that election against a very able colleague by vote of 25 to 14—with three of my friends who had pledged their support to me being unable to attend the voting. Those twenty-five votes were more than I had received when first elected to the leadership in 1984. Newhouse's source, then, was not only cowardly and unkind, but also dead wrong, which is usually the case with anonymous sources.

I wonder if Newhouse was disappointed when he read the news of that reelection. It's funny. I have seen him since the article appeared, but have never really talked to him about it in depth. Once in a while, one of his friends will come up to me (at John's urging, I sometimes think) and say, "How did you feel about the article John did on you?" (They always use that phrase—"on you.") I usually say, "Well, I think he is a delightful guy and a pleasant fellow and I enjoyed meeting him and his wife. We had many nice hours of conversation. But I could easily see that once I started talking about Peter Arnett and Anita Hill, he completely forgot about any redeeming features he might once have thought I had." I also say that I think John took some pretty hard shots at me, and that his think piece turned into a shrink piece, a guided tour of my psyche led by an unlicensed psychojournalist. Beyond that, I always mention a few things that deeply disappointed me. One, he had placed a quote in the mouth of my father that included the "F" word. Pop had supposedly used the word in front of a large group of people. Well, I heard Pop use that word a few times in my life, but certainly never in public. Another disappointment was John's use of harsh, cruel, and nasty comments about my fine friend and senior colleague Malcolm Wallop. They needn't have even been part of the article. They were nothing more than gratuitous chops to the groin.

And of course, I was sorry that a man as capable as John Newhouse and a publication as fine as *The New Yorker* had resorted to the use of anonymous sources to discredit and embarrass. I do understand that most of the personality profiles that appear in the press are long on criticism and short on praise. Controversy sells; journalists and the publications they work for do not prosper by simply detailing the mundane, painstaking, and dry work that public figures often do. And while I sure as hell don't appreciate some of the shots fired at me, I do richly understand that eternal press scrutiny is part of the political process. And yet if one is going to have critics in life, one would certainly like to know who they are. What galls me is that the media resolutely provide a vast, open forum for rhetorical terrorists, cowards who lob the verbal equivalent of a Molotov cocktail and then run off and hide. Anonymity generally is granted only to those who would demean, diminish, and denigrate their fellow man or woman. Those who are fair and reasonable don't need their identities protected, for the simple reason that what they say is defensible. Is it good journalism to quote someone without telling the reader who is speaking and whether that person has an ax to grind? Not in my book. Strong, conscientious reporters abhor anonymous sources. Weak ones love them. The same goes for politicians who fall for it, too.

Thus, if I may paraphrase a great Missouri philosopher, the reports of my political death were greatly exaggerated—by anonymous sources. And the sooner we see the death of anonymous sources in journalism, the better off we'll all be.

But don't hold your breath. Anonymous sources continue to form the shaky, sandy foundation of many a mean-spirited article. I see stories all the time that make my *New Yorker* profile look like a puff piece.

An unfortunate example was an August 4, 1992, *Washington Post* piece about the senior senator from South Carolina, Strom

Thurmond, an extraordinary, disciplined man of the highest integrity. The headline was "Thurmond & the Girl from Edgefield," and the subheadline was "Old Stories Have Reemerged About the Senator and His Longtime Ties with a Black Woman." According to the story, this white senator years before had fathered the child of a black woman. His illegitimate daughter was supposedly still alive and well, and in occasional contact with the legislator. This was all pretty juicy stuff, considering Thurmond was once a segregationist who drew at least part of his support from those who believed in the permanent separation of the races. It was the kind of story one might expect to read in the *National Enquirer*—although perhaps the *Enquirer* might have had high enough standards not to print it.

And how did this remarkable story "reemerge"? It reemerged when the author of the piece—supposedly a journalist, a seeker of truth—got frustrated after years of chasing a nonstory and finally decided to go ahead and publish something based solely on innuendo. Just listen to the introduction to the piece written by Marilyn W. Thompson, ace investigative journalist: "The story has long been a whispered part of southern political folklore. Over the years various journalists, including this one, have tried to piece together the parts. I have interviewed dozens of people, some as long ago as ten years when I worked as a South Carolina reporter, some as recently as last week. Those interviews and documents from Thurmond's gubernatorial papers show clear ties. But both Thurmond and the supposed daughter have denied that he is her father, and no one has provided evidence that he is."

Having made that pathetically weak disclaimer, Thompson and someone named Bridget Roeber—identified as Metro Resource Director of the *Post*—devoted more than a full page and a half of that day's Style section to the story. The article tried to establish a relationship between Strom and the "daughter," then in her sixties. The evidence was thin gruel at best. One written note from the woman to Strom acknowledges receipt of a loan "with thanks" on October 25, 1947. The article said, "In several interviews she has denied that he is her father, calling him a 'close friend of my family—a wonderful man who has helped a lot of people.' She said he provided her with some financial help 'but not a lot.'

" 'He visited me one time [at South Carolina State]. One time, that's all!' said the woman . . . in a telephone interview from her Los Angeles home last week. 'He was on campus on other business, and knowing me and knowing my family, he asked to see me. That is all there was to it.' [The woman] declined to discuss her parentage."

And who can blame her? Why the hell should she discuss her parentage with some panting, prejudiced reporter from the *Washington Post*? So much for the right of privacy so praised in the journalists' code of professional ethics. What was worse, this article then quoted three dead people. That's the best way to get information that no one can ever refute—talk to the dead. This anecdote calls to mind a one-liner that went around town after the *Post*'s Bob Woodward wrote a book in which he said that William Casey had implicated himself in a deathbed interview. It was wryly bandied about that "Woodward was the last person to interview Casey after his death."

The article on Strom also relied heavily on information supplied by at least one well-known adversary of the senator, namely W. W. Mims, the Edgefield, South Carolina, newspaper publisher who first printed the scurrilous allegation in 1972. For years, Mims worked feverishly to prove that Strom was this woman's father. He failed. But that didn't stop him from pretending it was so when the *Washington Post* rang his phone. He told the *Post*, "This conspiracy by the mass media has protected Thurmond all these years, but it is my strong opinion that we, as journalists, have a duty to expose this. It is a shame that now, as an old man, he will have to suffer the consequences. It is a story that should have been told long ago." But it *had* been told long ago, and nobody had believed it then, either.

Mims spoke of a "conspiracy" on the part of the media to "protect" Thurmond—and yet here was one of the giants of American journalism, the *Washington Post,* resurrecting this long-dead and rotten old tale. The appearance of Mims's quotation in a major national newspaper disproved his point. As for the consequences Strom was supposed to suffer, well, I don't know what Mims had in mind. Strom was well into his eighties by the time the *Post* article appeared. If you ask me, any man who has lived so vitally into his ninth decade doesn't have much left to fear. In any case, precisely nothing happened to Strom Thurmond as a result of the article, save for his being crudely embarrassed one more time by a careless, stupid, and thoughtless story. Strom simply continued to be an active, respected, vigorous participating member of the United States Senate.

At one point too in the story, the *Post* finally quoted the alleged daughter. The *Post* reported that she had "been living the quiet life of a school teacher until her peace was interrupted weeks ago by reporters seeking a new line on an old story." How sad for her, and for the people who read this worthless piece of junk. And what did this woman have to say? Here's what: " 'That is just not true,' she said, again and again." " 'They are making up lies about me. I wish they would leave me alone.' " But that was the last thing they were going to do. Never mind her right to privacy, the one articulated on the bronze plaque outside the National Press Club. Well, you say, at least the *Post* quoted her denial. And so it did, but not near the top of the story. No, her words were placed at the very end of over one hundred column inches of turgid sludge.

We politicians know—and mostly accept—that when we go into public service, much of our private lives become public. But in all my years in politics, I've still never seen the media go quite as far to try to humiliate someone as the *Washington Post* did in this dippy and insipid story on Strom. What the *Post* did was glorify what the paper itself acknowledged was nothing more than a vicious old rumor (the headline on the second page was "Senator Thurmond and the Rumor"). I think that single article stands as an example of all that is wrong with journalism. Most sources were either unnamed or dead. One, publisher Mims, had a long-acknowledged burning disdain for Strom. Those who spoke on the record rejected the story, and thus were given minimal coverage. Yes, that was some piece—a piece of crap.

Allow me to offer a few facts about Strom Thurmond. He devoted almost his whole long life to public service, at great personal sacrifice. He served with extraordinary distinction in the United States Senate beginning in 1954 and continuing to the day I write this in the mid-1990s. He had top seniority on the Armed Services, Judiciary, and Veterans' Affairs committees and served as president pro tem of the Senate from 1981 through 1986. He practiced law and served his community in South Carolina as city attorney, county attorney, and state senator. During World War II, Strom Thurmond was in the Army glider landing in Normandy with the 82nd Airborne Division on D-Day, June 6, 1944. He was decorated for his valor and courage, receiving some of the highest military honors this country can confer. At the time this *Post* article was printed, Strom Thurmond was the proud father of four children. A senseless tragedy would take away the life of his beloved oldest daughter many months later. Nancy Moore Thurmond was killed by a drunken driver while in the prime of her life, and a fine and dear man grieved.

Yes, in the 1940s—fifty years past—Strom and most other Southern politicians embraced segregation. He had long since altered his views on the subject, proving it every day in his deeds and in his Senate votes. Still, his supposed fathering of a black woman's child was too good a story for the *Washington Post* to resist. There was just one basic and fundamental problem, a problem the *Post* never acknowledged.

The story was not true.

The day the story ran in the *Post*, several senators visited with Strom and shared our loathing of it all. Strom, his head held high, just raised both hands and said, "The rumor is still out there after sixty-six years and there is nothing new there. It has been brought up in every campaign I've ever been in." Then, referring to the people who wrote and edited the story, he said, "What kind of people are they?" Damn good question. Really it is.

Beyond the lazy, sloppy, and banal use of anonymous sources, the media allow an equally subtle—and only slightly less reprehensible—form of manipulation to saturate the news pages. First, they bring to a story a whole set of their own biases and prejudices.

Then they select certain special interest groups who share their views to become their main sources. Happens all the time.

To illustrate, let's talk about the media coverage of the federal budget agreement that was worked out in the fall of 1990. This was a stressful time, a time when Democrats and Republicans alike were having to make some tough decisions in an effort to reduce the national debt. And it was happening at the halfway point in the Bush administration, just weeks before a national election. President Bush was determined—perhaps much more determined than any of his advisers were—to make a dent in the budget deficit. Seeing that the economy was still growing at an acceptable pace, he decided to press Congress for a bold yet realistic deficit reduction plan. That was clearly a sensible thing to do. The deficit was monumental; estimates placed the figure anywhere from $128 billion to $200 billion. The Democratic leadership in both the House and the Senate then set the hook. Democrats were adamant that the talks not begin until President Bush renounced his famous pledge of his 1988 presidential campaign: "Read my lips—no new taxes." If Bush did that, the Democrats would work with the president on a budget. If he did not, they promised he would never get the country any closer to a balanced budget. George Bush was, to use the vernacular, screwed.

And in a way he probably only blamed himself. He likely should not have issued the "no new taxes" pledge, but politically he had little choice. Four years earlier, Walter Mondale had said candidly that he would have to raise taxes if he became president. And what happened? Ronald Reagan wiped him off the face of the political earth. President Bush did not want that to happen to him. Besides, I think he hoped to honor the pledge, and might have been able to do so if he had received more help from Congress in cutting spending. But when he had to choose between the convention vow and hurting America by continuing to run up an uncontrollable deficit, it was no choice at all. He broke the vow, and sealed his political fate. Telling America to read his lips may have been most unwise. But I think laying himself on the line for the good of the country in 1990 was a statesmanlike thing to do.

In reporting on the budget summit, the media all took virtually the same approach to the story: Bush "breaks 'no new taxes' pledge." Only if you read very, very deep into these stories did you discover that congressional Democrats simply refused to negotiate or move forward until he did so.

For example, a *Washington Post* story of June 27, 1990, reported, "President Bush yesterday jettisoned the 'no new taxes' pledge that was at the center of his 1988 Presidential campaign, saying that 'tax revenue increases' must be included in an overall package to reduce the federal budget deficit . . . Bush's statement marked the most significant policy reversal of his presidency and represents a political gamble by the President, who has been warned repeatedly that Republicans will lose their most effective campaign weapon if he agrees to new taxes as part of a budget deal." This approach made it seem as if the president simply woke up one morning and decided to go back on his word. Readers who were not otherwise well informed never would have known that the Congress was holding a gun—cocked and loaded—to the president's head.

The *New York Times* deserves credit for being more objective than the *Post*. The Times's headline yelled, "BUSH NOW CONCEDES A NEED FOR 'TAX REVENUE INCREASES' TO REDUCE DEFICIT IN BUDGET, BREAK WITH PLEDGE. President also calls for cuts in military and civilian programs." The *Times* lead paragraph said, "With negotiations on cutting the budget deficit stalled, President Bush today broke with his vow to oppose new taxes and said any agreement with Congress would require 'tax revenue increases.'" At least this version of events acknowledged that Bush was under powerful pressure from Congressional Democrats, though even this article didn't spell things out the way it should have. Of course, the decision by the president was far too delicious a story for the press to resist. The mainstream media were absolutely salivating, snarling, baying at the moon. The broken-promise angle was far more exciting to reporters—and to the partisan players at the budget table—than any other possible angle on the story. For the first time in recent memory, a president in the midst of a titanic budget struggle was willing to sweep aside partisan and political advantage in service of the national interest.

Now, please—I'm not saying that George Bush did not issue

the no new taxes pledge partly for political advantage. Sure he did. But I believe it is also true that he changed his mind because he knew this country needed some new revenue after all, as distasteful as the idea was. The only angle that got real play in the media was the first one. When given a choice between an angle that reflects well on someone (especially a Republican politician) and one that reflects poorly, the media always, always, always choose the latter. Guaranteed.

By trumpeting the negative angle, the media downplayed such an important part of the story. This, by the way, is one of the many negative consequences of biased reporting: You cheat people of half the story. In exchange for the president's admittedly dramatic statement, Congress had agreed that there would be a serious, sensible slowing of the rate of increase in certain federal programs. Yes, the president had given up something, but he had also gained something—an opportunity to get a firm grip on spending when it mattered most. And yet, that part of the story received little coverage, if any. Apparently the only news that was fit to print had to do with the president's lips, and nothing much more.

By early fall 1990, the budget negotiators had overcome a number of extraordinary hurdles previously described by administration officials and politicians as being insurmountable. Still, there was a hell of a lot of hard work ahead. In the final throes of the negotiations, members of Congress and representatives of the Bush administration (usually referred to in the press merely as "officials") attempted to get the job done by closeting themselves away at Andrews Air Force Base south of Washington. This was done in order to eliminate the persistent intrusions of both reporters and lobbyists. By the end of September, everything was high drama. The talks would lurch forward and then crumple back—but always with some evidence of progress.

In my role as assistant leader of the Senate Republicans, I was often briefed by our fine leader, Bob Dole, who sat through many a ponderous session at Andrews. Bob would often say the negotiators were close, but just could not seem to deal with the "hot-button issues." Among them were Social Security COLA (cost-of-living allowances), federal retirement, Medicare, and Medicaid. Bob would tell me the two sides would never agree, and then later he would report tiny progress. I remember how hard he worked and how—as a true leader—he knew that we had to embrace what the president would do, had done, and could do. No one was more loyal to George Bush than Bob Dole during the whole tour of George's duty. No one.

Finally, the negotiators reduced their ranks to just eight participants. The administration was represented by my old tried-and-true friend Treasury Secretary Nicholas "Nick" Brady, brilliant and acerbic White House Chief of Staff John Sununu, and Director of the Office of Management and Budget Richard Darman, a brusque and driven man with tremendous institutional memory. House negotiators included Speaker Tom Foley, Majority Leader Richard Gephardt, and Minority Leader Bob Michel. The Senate was represented by Majority Leader George Mitchell and our leader, Bob Dole.

On September 30—known as "drop dead day" because it was the last day of the fiscal year—an agreement was announced that would reduce the deficit by $40 billion in the first year and $500 billion over five years. The Congress was also to pass a stopgap spending bill to keep the government functioning for a few more days. On October 1, fiscal year 1991 began. On October 2, in a nationally televised address, President Bush appealed to all Americans to support what he called a "tough" deficit-reduction package. Bush knew full well that he and Congress couldn't do anything unless the people were behind it.

This was where all the special interests came in. Before the agreement had even been announced, representatives of the most powerful senior citizens' lobby let out their whooping cries of anguish. These lobbyists—paid and unpaid—wailed long and hard about the agreement's rumored cuts in Medicare. But were there any cuts? Certainly the negotiators took a hard, long, responsible look at the recent outrageous increases in Medicare and Medicaid spending. Nobody was suggesting cutting the amount presently being spent on the health and welfare of the elderly. The idea was simply to slow the increase in the growth of the programs to a safe, healthy, responsible rate. The idea was never to cut, but merely to slow that unsustainable rate of growth.

Still, in its coverage of this issue, the media allowed themselves to be thoroughly manipulated. Here's how. First, spokesmen for the nation's most selfish old fogies managed to sell the mainstream media on the idea that the negotiators' reasonable increase in Medicare was in fact a "cut." Reporters should have known better, but they fell for it. Having done so, they pulled on their overcoats, turned up their collars, and hit the streets in an effort to humanize the story. Just about every day, it seemed, a TV crew would approach some older denizens with mikes extended and cameras cranking. These pathetic seniors, the correspondent would say, are being tossed out onto the concrete by a heartless and indifferent Congress. The camera would then zoom in on some dissolute and ragtag chap and the reporter would say, "What will happen to you sir, now that your medical care will be cut?" The correspondent would always get a dramatic response: "I'll never make it"; "I can't understand how they coulda done it"; or, if the reporter was really lucky, "Well, I'll probably just die." The crew would usually stick around, its camera continuing to roll, until the subject would cry, or take a good, tough, nasty shot at Bush or his or her elected representative. The correspondent would then close the story with a knowing look and these words: "Thank you. This is So-and-so reporting for Underground Cable News about this tragedy unfolding in our country." Or some such crap.

Oh, those lobbyists for some of us old farts are so good. And some farts aren't even that old. I never thought of myself as a senior citizen until I received an application for membership in the American Association of Retired Persons when I was fifty-five. But I guess I was pretty old, and on my way out to pasture, because the AARP said I was. Well, its membership is now open to those who have reached the doddering, drooling, incontinent age of fifty. They don't miss a trick, these AARP people. They understand that the way to build power is through numbers, and they have accomplished that. I got a good whiff of their firepower when they took the press for a ride on the "cutting" of Medicare in 1990.

The special interest groups—including the AARP, the Committee for the Preservation of Social Security and Medicare, and the Gray Panthers—got what they wanted. Seeing the press's irresponsible and brainless reporting on the issue, our constituents started knocking us down like bowling pins. Phones in the Capitol rocked off the hook. The budget agreement was killed before it could ever be thoughtfully and honestly explained to the American public. The fogies' lobbyists all pounded their chests and probably immediately sent out new fund-raising letters asserting that they had saved the poor old seniors from having their shriveled buns bounced out in the snowdrifts.

This was so similar to what happened when Congress repealed catastrophic health care. The AARP wasn't officially active in that legislation, but their members throughout America sure rattled the cages of the politicians. Remember when that deceptively frail group of seniors jumped up on Danny Rostenkowski's car in his Illinois district? Of course, that story got some great coverage through the land.

With the death of the budget agreement, the nation was at a standstill. The White House said it might have no choice but to close down the government. I remember creeping into my office during the weekend the government was closed. I felt like a fugitive from justice and hoped I wouldn't be recognized.

With government closed down, the negotiators went back to the drawing board. After a short time, they reached an agreement similar to the first one, the difference being that Medicare would not be "cut," if you'll pardon the expression. This agreement passed easily. But was there any reason to rejoice? A huge increase in Medicare, a program wholly out of control, was allowed to go right through. Some were satisfied with that. I was not. As far as I was concerned, the press had allowed interest groups to dominate the discussion to a point where reasonable and responsible voices simply could no longer be heard at all. By doing so, the media had deprived the American people of the information they so badly needed.

Of course, the politics of an election year had a lot to do with what happened that fall. I sure as hell knew that—I was running for reelection in November. Here I was, a historically outspoken critic of the interest groups that the media were portraying as the very Mother Teresas of the lobbying world. Naturally people began to turn against me. My own campaign polls showed I dropped seventeen points between October 1 and the time I went home to campaign. I made it back to Wyoming with only two weeks to go before election day, and boy, were the voters waiting for me! They were loaded for bear.

And why wouldn't they be disgusted? First the press had portrayed us as a bunch of simpering incompetent boobs, incapable of making tough decisions on the budget deficit. Then—after the difficult budget negotiations were complete—the media cast us as mean-spirited poops, ready to dump all of America's fine senior citizens into the compost pile. If you had to be portrayed as gutless or heartless, which might you prefer?

My Democratic opponent in the Wyoming Senate campaign was a thirty-two-year-old woman named Kathy Helling. This was a bright woman, a wife, mother, and part-time Casper College student who felt very strongly about the drift of government and those in it. She also embraced a very strong anti-abortion position—unusual among most Democrats, maybe, but still heartfelt and sincere.

I am pro-choice. I believe that a woman who decides—after consulting with her partner (if she has one), her spiritual adviser (if she has one), and her doctor—that she wants to have an abortion should be able to get it. This legal medical procedure should be available to her, plain and simple. I have taken this position on this emotional issue through all my years in public life. In Wyoming, there is a solid percentage of citizens who would never politically support a person with my views. I understand that, and respect their feelings. I do not attempt to impose my position on others. Still, I knew Kathy Helling was going to point out this and other differences between my thinking and that of some people in my state. Because of the abortion issue, and because of the budget mess, I was going to be vulnerable.

All during the shortened campaign, I kept answering the same questions: "Why would you vote to cut Medicare?" "What are you doing to the veterans?" "What did you do to Social Security?" Those questions can be all asked within the space of a thirty-second sound bite, but they sure as hell take longer than thirty seconds to answer. So I went plowing around the state and told my side. But I was defensive and restive, and those who have known me for a long time knew damn well it was so. Yes, I was angry and testy with the press. I was also burned at some House Republicans who had refused to support the original budget agreement. Here their own president had jumped off a political cliff for the good of our country, and they turned their backs on him when it came time for the tough vote, and they got a helluva lot less deficit reduction the second time around. Shameful, I felt.

I worked with high energy in those final two weeks, ultimately winning with 64 percent of the vote in a year when many incumbents across the country went down to defeat. I felt pretty good about that margin; it was a hair more than the 63 percent I had received during my first campaign in '78, yet less than the 78 percent in 1984. Still, when I think about what that victory cost me in funding, I am not so impressed with myself. I had raised more than $1 million for my Senate campaign and spent more than $800,000 in both the primary and general. That was a fortune, considering my opponent was virtually unknown in the state and was not able to scrape up even the $5,000 needed to trigger her first campaign report to the Federal Elections Campaign. For Kathy, garnering 36 percent of the vote under those circumstances was a clear moral victory. I think she would agree with me that she received fair and significant press coverage, and that she got the attention of the anti-abortion movement and of those who were fed up with Congress. She did very well, and I did less well than I should have. Plenty of media folk in Wyoming made sure I knew it. Hey, they didn't need to tell me that. I have always understood what the voters were saying. And I have always lived by this simple motto: "Get out before they throw you out!" In that year of the underdog, I was pleased to have won by any margin.

I certainly didn't get any help from Wyoming's largest newspaper. Remember that old saying that I mentioned earlier: Don't pick fights with people who buy ink by the barrel? Well, by the time the 1990 campaign started, I had been in a six-year OK Corral gunfight with the *Casper Star-Tribune*, and the people there bought more ink than anybody else in the state. That paper loved to strafe me at every opportunity, mostly on the editorial pages and in the letters to the editor. I would fire back almost every time, on the old theory that an attack unanswered is an attack believed. No matter what the insult, I tried hard not to hold a grudge. My dear pop used to say, "I'm too busy loving to hate." I can't say I always lived that philosophy during my tangles with the *Star-Tribune*.

I can remember one thing the newspaper did that was simply disgusting. During the campaign, the paper's cartoonist drew a caricature of me wearing a campaign button reading, "Never give a Hispanic an even break!" That was a low blow. No one who ever worked with me on immigration legislation would ever have suggested that such an ugly position was mine. The cartoon was crude and unfair. This cheap shot came from a newspaper that had a virtually all-white staff and whose philosophy on immigration matters could be summed up thusly: "Open the borders. Send us everybody you've got—we'll put them to work for next to nothing, and when we're through with them we'll throw them out of the fields and call the Immigration and Naturalization Service." This is what I call the *Wall Street Journal* theory of immigration reform.

The *Casper Star-Tribune* cartooned me as a bigot for a simple reason: because using labels to describe people is much easier than finding out the truth about them and reporting it. Reducing people to labels is the lazy journalist's easy way out. Well, I have always been hell on lazy journalists. I have flunked damn near every litmus test that was ever administered in politics. Let me explain again. I am a conservative—but not as far as the Christian Coalition is concerned, because I am pro-choice. I think of myself as an environmentalist, because I worked hard on conservation issues when I was in the Wyoming legislature. And yet I am a true believer in the multiple use of the public lands, something the real tree huggers will never support. I am committed to the Social Security program and protection of our deserving senior citizen population—but I flunk out because I don't think all wealthy seniors deserve an automatic cost-of-living increase, and because I think we should start assigning benefits according to actual need. I am a veteran and I believe strongly in veterans' benefits. And yet some people say I am anti-veteran because I don't think people who were not in a combat theater or who suffer injuries wholly unrelated to their armed forces service should be entitled to the same benefits as the combat veteran. Now, think: If you were to draw a cartoon caption trying to sum me up in one phrase, what would it say? Good luck.

The downside of being unpredictable is that I often get skewered by liberals and conservatives alike. My run-in with the *American Spectator*, a conservative magazine, is another good example of what the media can do to you when you think for yourself.

In February 1986, I was the subject of a hatchet job by *Spectator* writer Tom Bethell. Bethell's piece was prompted by something that happened in New Orleans. This was a strange story. One day, a Soviet sailor jumped ship in the New Orleans harbor. He was promptly rescued and interviewed by American officials. Was he trying to defect? Did he want to be granted asylum? Nope. The Americans interviewed him all night long, let him rest and fed him, and he never once uttered the word "asylum." Never even grunted or mumbled it. A lot of American conservatives thought he should be granted asylum anyway, on the theory that even if he didn't ask for it, he probably wanted it. "Oh, heavens, don't let him go back to that hideous country, the Soviet Union. If he does, he'll be killed immediately," they said.

I thought that was absurd, and I said so. If the man did not want to leave his own country, he shouldn't have to. A lot of people considered my position outrageous. To understand why, you have to recall the context in which this incident happened. When the Soviet sailor jumped ship, Ronald Reagan was halfway through his second term as president. Much had been accomplished during the Reagan Revolution. And yet the more rabid conservatives still had not achieved their goal of overhauling the nation's entire social structure. Women continued to have this abominable right to choose an abortion; sensible sex education was still being taught in the schools (perfectly acceptable in my view); many other issues had not yet gone—the double meaning is intended here—"the right way." I was thus among the moderate Senate Republicans who often found themselves under attack by the extreme right-wingers because we were not supporting their full—sometimes radical—social agenda. By the time I stated my position on the swimming Soviet, a lot of the far right was already het up after me. Much, much later, we all learned that the sailor went back to the Ukraine, got married, and enrolled in what we would call community college. But at the time, some conservatives figured I was downright disloyal, if not actually pro-Soviet.

Bethell may have been one of them. His article dragged on for six pages, and yet not once did he quote someone who would go on the record with a criticism of me. That's right—once again I was the unwilling subject of anonymous quotes. Bethell's sources, if they ever existed (who knows?), put words in my mouth that I never said, and insisted that I had thoughts I had never had. It was obvious to me that I was being criticized because I refused to exist inside the confines of the conservatives' little box. I was supposed to be a tried-and-true Reagan Republican, and in so many ways I sure was. I genuinely supported the president and what he was trying to do. But when I stepped out of line, the *American Spectator* let me have it.

As is my wont, I rocked back and returned fire. To the editors' credit, the *American Spectator* printed every single word of my response. I opined:

> Tom Bethell is a complete mystery to me. His grim visage and furtive shadow have never darkened my doorstep. He has never at any time attempted to communicate with me personally in any way—not by letter, phone call, or personal meeting. Damned if I've ever seen the guy. His deep-seated personal aversion to me must then be based on what he has read and heard second, third, or even maybe fourth hand. Is that journalism? It doesn't seem so to me.
>
> It's easy to be a critic—any fool can qualify. I often

flunk the many litmus tests that are administered in this
fascinating village by single-issue groups . . . so I doubt
very seriously if there is anything I could ever do or ever
say that might change that. Although I would still enjoy a
personal visit.

With regard to whether I had the proper conservative credentials, I noted:

I have consistently and sincerely stated my concerns over
the so-called "social issues." They always have the real potential to be emotional and very divisive—and the clearest
and most real part of it all is that you can debate those issues for literally days on end, and you won't change a single vote. For instance, I have always supported school
prayer. I differ with some conservatives on abortion. I've
supported sensible anti-business legislation—but once we
have had the full and fair Senate debate, then let's move
on with our work.

Then I took sharper aim and blasted away at Bethell's anonymous sources:

Apparently to substantiate the pungency of his article,
Washington correspondent Bethell cites the omnipresent
"unnamed Senate aide"—the unelected and most often
unelectable person with no mandate from the people, but
sometimes simply a hidden agenda all his or her own. I
know some of those fine young people. Some are absolute
zealots. To paraphrase Santayana, a zealot is someone who,
having forgotten his purpose, redoubles his efforts. Lord
spare me the opinions of zealots—and share with me always the opinions of those who are down there in the
arena sweating, those who have to vote "yes" or "no"
and not "maybe," those who came here to work with
those other fine staffers and fine colleagues, and my constituents.

I concluded by suggesting Bethell and I might even get together—noting we could then personally review one another's imperfections in a more spirited and sociable fashion.

You may be aware that few journalistic publications will ever let you get in the last word. Believe it. The worse the media look, the harder they'll hit back. Thus, just below my published letter, Bethell was given space to take a few new potshots at me. Great was his indignation. And indefensible was his argument. He began:

> One issue the Senator raises is worth exploring. He says that I never contacted him or his office. True, but I just don't agree that journalists are obliged to abide by such rules of decorum. . . . No one has to read what we write or take any notice.
>
> Had I spent an hour with Simpson, I wonder if I would have written anything at all. I disagreed with him, and still do . . . but I wonder how inclined I would have been to voice my disagreement after a friendly chat—perhaps even lunch. The Senator has a reputation for geniality, which I am sure is well deserved. Human nature (mine anyway) is such that the interaction of personalities is likely to prevail over misgivings about policy. The resulting article might have pleased the Senator and his immediate family, but it would have been bland and I'm not sure that many others would have found it worth reading.

Hoo, boy! Old Tom couldn't see the point in observing that fussy old rule of decorum known as getting both sides of the story. Why, if he had called me or come to visit, anything could have happened! He might have wound up liking me—or worse, agreeing with me! This intrepid one wasn't going to let those things happen. There is an ironic old saying in America's newsrooms: Too much reporting can ruin a good story. In other words, if learning the truth will ruin your preconceived story, don't bother. A journalist who thinks it is simply not necessary to get both sides of the story shouldn't even be writing obituaries for the *Butthorn*

Daily Bugle-Clarion, never mind covering Washington for the *American Spectator.*

Now, now, I'm perfectly aware that the editors and writers who work for such magazines will argue it is their right to present commentary and opinion, and they are correct. But even though a magazine may have a specific philosophical bias—as the *Spectator* does—I feel it still must adhere to the same ethical standards of supposedly objective and nonpartisan publications.

Years later, in 1989, I had the opportunity to have lunch with Tom Bethell. It was a decidedly pleasant experience. He is an articulate, well-educated, and witty man with a love of his craft and great enthusiasm for the conservative cause. I don't know what he'll write about me in the future, if anything. It doesn't matter. But I'll bet that next time he'll call me for a quote. And I'm hopeful that he won't rely so heavily on anonymous sources, though again, I'm not counting on it.

I think most thoughtful journalists have to admit that the practice of using unnamed sources raises some serious ethical questions. Remember, these sources are anonymous only to the reader, not to the writer who quotes them. What the writer is saying when he uses an anonymous quote is, essentially, "Trust me. This information comes from a reliable and honest person." But careful readers don't read the newspaper with the same sense of faith they bring to the reading of the Bible; they want hard information, and they want to know who the hell is giving it to them. The writer who relies on anonymous sources is asking his or her source to do a hell of a lot of trusting as well. You know how that relationship works: The source dishes out the dirt in exchange for a promise that he or she will remain forever anonymous. The writer then gets the old juices flowing and tells the story, blind quotes and all.

But should journalists even be trusted to guard their sources? If a journalist promises you anonymity for all the days of your life, will you get it? Maybe. Maybe not. A story that unfolded in Minnesota in 1982 is a darn good example of what happens when the veil of secrecy is lifted. The whole smelly, petty little episode raises a multitude of questions about the way in which the media cover politics.

It seems that in 1982 there was a pretty hot race in Minnesota for lieutenant governor. The Republican candidate had a loyal supporter named Dan Cohen. As sometimes happens in this cut-throat game of politics, Cohen had gathered some pretty good dirt on the opposition—something about the Democrat candidate having a criminal record. So, as anonymous sources often do, he shopped the information around to various news outlets. The *Minneapolis Star Tribune* and the *St. Paul Pioneer Press Dispatch* listened to his story, jotted it in their notebooks, and promised him the anonymity he sought. The papers received Dan Cohen's little pile of refuse in their eager, cupped hands.

Apparently the story about the Democrat's criminal record wasn't quite tawdry enough for the editors of the two newspapers. So they reneged on their promise and did the unheard-of—they wrote a story focusing on Dan Cohen's efforts to smear the candidate. And they named the poor rascal! The editors of these publications decided that the criminal record Cohen exposed was not newsworthy, but that Cohen's efforts to spread the story were. How could this guy Cohen do such an awful thing? these newspapers seemed to say. Never mind that American newspapers use anonymous sources every day to discredit and humiliate people. The big, powerful Minnesota papers, suddenly seizing the high ground, weren't going to let it happen this time, by God—even if they had to deceive Dan Cohen to make their point.

Cohen was stunned and appalled. So was his employer, who summarily fired him when the story was published. His cunning and sneakiness coldly exposed, Cohen sued. He rightfully claimed that the news organizations had broken their promise of confidentiality, thereby costing him his job and his reputation. Cohen wanted big money damages. Now, maybe you won't sympathize much with old Dan Cohen. Probably shouldn't. He's a bit like the kid who kills his parents and then asks the judge to grant him leniency because he's an orphan. In other words, Dan got himself into that mess by trying to slime his man's opponent. But the newspapers never should have promised him anonymity and then unilaterally taken it away, either. Two wrongs never make a right, right?

Predictably, the newspapers stirringly defended themselves by asserting their First Amendment right to free speech. Of course they did—that's standard operating procedure when a newspaper is caught doing something unseemly. Unfortunately, the Minnesota supreme court bought their argument, saying that the First Amendment protections did apply. The dogged Cohen took his claim on to the United States Supreme Court.

Fiercely, righteously, and vigorously, the big business of journalism closed ranks around the Minnesota newspapers. The amicus briefs they filed with the Supreme Court were based on a most arrogant premise—that a promise of anonymity might bind a person ethically or morally, but not legally. They gravely asserted that the First Amendment gave them the right to print whatever they wanted to—no matter what promises they had made.

Well, these errant and arrogant newspapers found out that journalists are subject to the same laws as other citizens. In a wire-thin, 5 to 4 decision, the U.S. Supreme Court ruled that a promise is a promise is a promise, the First Amendment notwithstanding. Writing for the Court majority, the ever-thoughtful Associate Justice Byron White stated that the First Amendment "does not confer on the press a constitutional right to disregard promises that would otherwise be enforced under state law."

The media's behavior in this case was unspeakable. Normally, newspapers will fight to the death to protect their sources of information. No matter how compelling the public interest in a certain piece of information, journalists will always, always, always say their sources should be inviolate. Not this time. This time, the newspapers glibly promised anonymity to someone, then broke the promise because they thought doing so would make for a pretty good story. Having broken the promise, the newspapers— and many of their powerful friends—argued that it didn't matter what they promised; all that mattered was their right to free speech. That, to me, is a perfect expression of the Grand Canyon–like difference in thinking between the media and the average American. To most of us, a promise made is supposed to be a promise kept. To the media, a promise made is a promise kept unless it becomes expedient or profitable to break it. Too many practitioners of the craft want only and always to do exactly as they damn well please with no constraint, restraint, or remorse, all under sublime cover of the First Amendment.

As I've said, I don't think Dan Cohen may have had any damn business calling the media in an effort to embarrass his opponent anonymously. I have no use whatever for people who smear others anonymously, for in doing so they only pander to journalism's base lust for gossip, innuendo, and negativism. I have never allowed any of my supporters or campaign people to do such a thing during any one of my races. But journalists need to understand that they created the Dan Cohens of the world. I would bet there are some far more unsavory characters than the unfortunate Mr. Cohen in the anonymous information business. But we will never know who they are because the press protects them. The solution is not to promise them anonymity and then expose them, as the Minnesota papers did. The solution is to find people who will speak on the record, so that readers (or listeners or viewers) can honestly assess their credibility for themselves.

In one recent and embarrassing case, a journalist's actions raised questions about his own credibility. This happened while President Clinton was trying, again and again, to find a suitable nominee for attorney general of the United States. Zoe E. Baird's name had been withdrawn when it was revealed that her family had not paid the Social Security taxes of their domestic employees. A sad tale. She deserved better. The administration then floated the name of federal judge Kimba Wood as a possible nominee. While waiting for a reaction, the administration asked Wood and her husband to provide a full accounting of their financial lives. Both the nominee and her spouse were happy to oblige. Before long, the media began quoting anonymous sources in support of Wood, on whom the administration was staking what was left of its credibility.

During this time, Howard Kurtz, the fine media reporter for the *Washington Post,* published a story that blew the lid off what we might as well call Kimbagate. As Kurtz pointed out, it has become standard practice in Washington to float trial balloons on everything from presidential nominations to tax proposals to the health of presidents. This is always done anonymously, of course.

Floating trial balloons is a way for politicians and political operatives to test an idea without getting their hands soiled. If the public
approves of the idea, the person who floated it usually can't resist
coming forward to claim the credit. If not, the anonymous source
simply retreats back into his or her cave, and no one is ever the
wiser. That, to me, is a purely phony business. But it was happening here.

In this case, Kimba Wood's name was floated as the probable
nominee, and almost instantaneously certain news outlets had a
wealth of information, all of it coming from an anonymous source.
According to Howard Kurtz, the source was . . . the nominee's
husband, Michael Kramer, who also happened to be a top political
reporter for *Time* magazine! Even *Time* itself had used information
supplied by Kramer, though readers were never told where the
supportive comments about Wood were coming from. Kramer's
quotations were said to be spoken by "Wood's supporters" and
"Wood's sympathizers"—which, when you're talking about a
woman's husband, is a serious understatement.

Is there anyone who would not have been asking questions
about Kramer's objectivity as a reporter during this process? Seriously, how could he cover politics on one hand and secretly campaign for a cabinet-level nominee on the other? And is there
anyone who would not have asked some hard questions about
what the rest of the media did with the information Kramer provided? Of course not. Hell no. Now, I have no objection to a
husband's defending his wife's reputation, or a wife's defending
her husband's. I can only imagine the anguish Kramer felt as
Wood's good name was turned into hamburger in the cold, steely
meat grinder that we call the nominating process. And yet I cannot
condone what Kramer did in an effort to manipulate the media.
If the public has a right to know the story, it also has a right to
know where the story is coming from.

Even now, I have to ask myself: What if the nominee in question had been Clarence Thomas, and it was revealed that his wife
was being used to provide "background"? Using Ginni Thomas
as a source would not be as objectionable as using Michael Kramer,
because nobody would expect her to be objective. Still, I wonder:

Would the media have guarded her identity as carefully as they guarded Michael Kramer's? If you can find an answer different from the one I'm thinking of, the drinks are on me.

It seems certain to me that if the use of anonymous sources continues or even grows, the entire media profession will end up biting itself in the ass. None of us is naive enough to believe that American journalists will actually stop using anonymous sources, but they sure as hell ought to hold themselves and their colleagues to higher standards. The public is sick and tired of being kept in the dark or just plain deceived. The media must begin to confront the bias with which they choose sources, anonymous and other-wise. People who say critical, nasty, or simply vicious things under the shroud of anonymity get lots of coverage without accepting any responsibility. And that is wrong. When reporters quote people anonymously, they leave out an important part of the story. They deprive their audience of important information. Maybe just as bad, they censor themselves, ironically doing to themselves the very thing that they are always trying to prevent others from doing. What a damn shame for a damn fine profession in a damn fine country.

CHAPTER EIGHT

The Hunters
and the Hunted

ypocrisy is Washington's most widespread original sin. The number of people in that town who say one thing and do the opposite can be frightening. No doubt you have read articles or seen television reports about hypocritical politicians. Journalists are good at exposing such people, as they should be. But probably you have read or seen much less about hypocrisy among journalists themselves. What follows is a story about hypocrisy in journalism.

For many years, members of Congress were allowed to accept honoraria for giving speeches to various civic and trade organizations. A lot of politicians made a lot of money for doing what they did best—flexing their jaws. In the 1970s, Congress voted to set a $2,000 limit on the amount that could be received for each speech. Under the new rules, lawmakers were also required to disclose how much money they received and who paid it. Congress later placed a limit on the number of honoraria a member could receive in a given year. No longer could a politician amass unlimited sums by giving an unlimited number of speeches. Still later, Congress

voted to make it illegal for members to keep any of the money
they received for giving speeches. The old gravy train was finally
derailed. The phrase "free speech" took on new meaning in Congress.

These reforms were instituted largely because of the carping of
the news media. For years and years, journalists had been roundly
and gravely denouncing politicians for accepting honoraria. Media
people believed—no, insisted—that if a member of Congress ever
took money for making a speech, he or she would be forever
indebted to the group that paid the fee. Therefore, if the National
Grommet Association paid one of the worthies a fee to give a
speech, the lawmaker would simply have to cast pro-grommet
votes forevermore. No question about it. According to the nation's
journalists (those ethical paragons), interest groups were buying
votes, or just plain buying politicians. The practice had to be
stopped.

I can understand that perception. Indeed, I'm sure some of the
interest groups believed they could purchase us like packages of
hot dogs. A few years back, when it was still legal for politicians
to accept honoraria, some people from a national retail organization asked me to fly to Florida to give a speech at their national
convention. They said they would give me two plane tickets, pay
all my expenses, and write me a $2,000 check besides. Ann and I
accepted the invitation. During our weekend in Florida, we were
wined, dined, and generally treated royally. But as the end of the
convention neared, I still had not given my speech. A bunch of us
were all sitting around the bar in casual garb on the last day when
I asked one of the group's leaders, "So when do I give this speech?"

"Ah, don't worry about it," he said. "You don't have to do
that. Just have a good time here, and remember us when we come
to Washington."

"Now wait a minute," I said. "You paid me to come down
here and give a speech, and I'm going to give a speech whether
you want one or not."

The guy looked kind of startled. "Uh, okay," he said. Then he
shouted to all the people at barside and poolside, "Hey, everybody,

come on over! The senator's going to give a speech!" Somebody propped a podium on the bar and I gave my speech right then and there.

A few weeks later, a leader of that group showed up in my office and asked to see me about a piece of legislation of interest to his organization. I remembered him, so I invited him in. So I'm sure you could say that his organization gained access to me by paying me for a speech. In the days when I accepted honoraria as personal income for speeches, I knew that the money was paid with the understanding that the donor would get some access. Seven out of ten of the groups that hired me on would later ask to pay a "social call" to talk about a piece of legislation. But so what? Paying an honorarium never bought a decision or changed a vote, at least not in my office. Even if money had influenced one of my decisions, everybody would have known it full well, because the names of the donors and the amounts of money received were always fully disclosed to the public. If you thought I was being influenced by groups that had paid for speeches, all you had to do was check the public record. Was I consistently supporting the legislation of groups that had paid me? It was all right there—I was not. And I don't think most other members of Congress were either.

Still, I supported each of the honoraria reforms as they came along. The press had successfully created the impression that politicians could be bought for the price of a speech, so the changes simply had to be made. When the law required me to disclose all speaking fees and the organizations that paid them, I gladly did so. In most cases, I donated the honoraria to charities in Wyoming, or to worthy causes in Washington or elsewhere in the country. I also supported the later reforms, including the ban on keeping honoraria for personal use. In my last years in Congress, I often received $50,000 or more a year for making speeches, all of which I gave to charity.

The media had much to do with getting those reforms passed, as I have said. And yet, as often happens, a lot of journalists were not practicing what they preached. Throughout the evolution of

the laws on honoraria, one thing remained constant: Many journalists covering the issue were giving speeches to civic and trade
organizations—and receiving large sums of money for doing so.

Over the years, I have participated in many discussion panels
organized by business groups, or perhaps by consortia of businesses.
Often, a big-name journalist would also be invited to take part.
Remember now, the most I could ever take—and ever did take—
for those appearances was $2,000. Many of those events took place
when I was banned from receiving any personal jack for my appearance. But the media heavyweight sitting there with me on the
platform often received as much as $25,000 for his or her sage
comments. What's wrong with this picture? Certainly both of us—
the journalist and I—had some ability to influence public opinion
and public policy, and yet one of us had to report all of his speechifying income and the other did not. One could take a pittance
and the other could accept a fortune. I'd say one of us had a conflict—and it sure as hell was not me.

Once, the insurance industry sponsored a forum featuring me
and my impish friend Bob Novak, the columnist. I received the
usual $2,000 and gave it to charity. Bob got $20,000. That is not
a misprint. Now, wasn't it possible that Bob might someday have
to comment on something of importance to the insurance industry? Yes, of course it was possible. And yet his gentle readers and
viewers would never know the depth and breadth of his gratitude
to the industry.

I don't mean to single out Bob Novak. Many, many well-
known journalists receive big money for giving speeches. There is
no shortage of opportunities. The busy-bee village of Washington
is swarming with trade groups representing bankers and broadcasters, morticians and metal fabricators, arts advocates and airlines.
Some of these groups hold their annual meetings in some of the
most delightful and luxurious resorts in the nation. And generally
they like to have a Washington insider present to tell stories and
loosen people up. Frequently, the Washington insider is a media
type—sometimes one who covers, or could someday cover, the
group that has hired him. But remember, this supposedly totally
unbiased, unflinching journalist pockets a big speaking fee, plus all

meals, greens fee, and all expenses. With a hearty wave and a call of "Just charge it to the room," these journalists live it up, all the while expecting us to agree that their private lives are none of our damned business. Remember, too, that these are the same people who harangued us politicians for years about the appearance of impropriety that was created when we took money from groups that might someday try to influence legislation.

The extent of these journalists' hypocrisy has not been widely publicized, but we're getting there. A few years back, *The New Yorker* did a good piece on the subject, and the journalism trade magazines have also looked into it. But if you're waiting to see a piece on *60 Minutes* or *Dateline*—if you're waiting for the big-time media to say something about themselves that will make the public really furious—keep waiting. Journalists' double standard on this issue is appalling.

The issue is not going to go away. Anyone who seeks to gain the public trust—and journalists say they do—are duty-bound to honor that trust. The reading, listening, and viewing public damn certainly has a right to know if a journalist covering the savings and loan debacle ever received money to speak to a member savings and loan association. Should anyone who is fortunate enough to pick up $20,000 or $25,000 for speaking to a gathered industry group be obligated never to write about the industry again, and be further obligated to disclose the fee? The Big Question.

I am not the first to suggest that journalists disclose their outside income. In Congress, the House and Senate periodical galleries do the necessary business of issuing credentials to the working press— newspapers, magazines, and print publications of all kinds. The galleries have a board of directors made up of journalists. To their credit, some of the board members once decided that it was unseemly for journalists to receive big money to speak to groups they might be covering. These board members suggested a new rule: Henceforth, anyone applying for press credentials must disclose any and all sources of outside income, including honoraria accepted for making speeches and fees accepted for freelance writing. The reaction was unsurprising. Washington press people refused to follow the rule. In doing so, they repeated the old, hackneyed argument that they are public citizens, not elected officials, and therefore do not legally have to disclose anything. Well, no, not legally. But what about the moral and ethical obligation of journalists to be open and honest about their potential conflicts of interest? That question did not occur to them, I would guess. Indeed, they became so angry and indignant that they booted out the board members who suggested the rule in the first place.

Some sensible members of the profession say that the press galleries may not be the most appropriate place to require journalists to disclose outside income. They may be right. But if the press galleries are not the place, then what is? In fairness to the readers and viewers they try to inform and in some cases try to influence, journalists must find a way to acknowledge and publicize these potential conflicts. Just as I have acknowledged that I felt taking honoraria for speeches obligated me to grant access later, journalists must realize that trade groups who hire them for speeches are also buying a kind of access—access to the public. The similarities between politicians and media folk become ever more recognizable here.

There are many subtle ways in which journalists get caught in ethical traps, but you don't hear too much about most of them. These days, the trendiest of trends is for journalists to appear on television and radio to provide commentary on the issues of the day. Certainly, some of these folks are columnists, people who are paid to publish opinion pieces. But some are supposedly objective reporters, people who are supposed to leave their opinions out of what they write or broadcast. Well, they don't do that, and they don't conceal their opinions on television, either. Some shows even draw battle lines between liberal and conservative reporters, as if it were all right for reporters to identify themselves according to political ideology. Cokie Roberts, of National Public Radio and ABC News, is a good example of an able reporter who may tell you an "objective" story on the radio one morning and then offer "analysis" of the same story that weekend on one of the talk shows. "Analysis" is a word that the *New York Times* smartly began using years ago when it really meant "opinion." Now everybody who spouts opinion calls it analysis. What Cokie Roberts and other supposedly impartial journalists do on these talk shows is quite preposterous. I grew up listening to and watching Edward R. Murrow, and I simply can't envision him participating in some forms of the spectacles we know today.

Here's another overripe example of an ethical conflict for journalists. Recall again when Bill Clinton withdrew his nomination of Zoe E. Baird for attorney general after the media disclosed that she had not paid the Social Security taxes of someone who was caring for her child. But I can tell you that some of the women journalists who reported that story with such zeal were themselves not following the law with regard to their own nannies. That was a well-known fact around town. Obviously none of those reporters stood to become the highest law enforcement officer in the land, as Baird did. Still, if one of them was chiding Baird for breaking the law while breaking the same law himself or herself, wouldn't you have wanted to know it? Wouldn't you have been interested? Of course. But the media will never tell you those interesting and important truths about themselves. They never see themselves as part of the problem, or even as part of us.

That needs to change. Any elected official is a holder of the public trust. Journalists are too. Certainly there are laws that apply to lawmakers and other elected officials that would not normally apply to journalists. That is good. That is as it should be. But while public officials and journalists are not always bound by the same laws, they certainly share similar ethical and moral obligations. The hunters of the media—as the daughter of my Wyoming friends chillingly called them—ought to be looking ever more closely at themselves. And the rest of society should be watching them more closely, too.

Alas, the hunting metaphor is all too appropriate. Today's journalists do not merely report; they go for the kill. At the first scent of blood, they unleash themselves like bloodhounds upon all those panting, stumbling public figures. Yes, I know—many politicians bring the hunt on themselves by doing dumb or even criminal things. And yet very few people deserve the kind of torture that is routinely inflicted by the media today. And again, the media are much better at dishing it out than they are at taking it. Many of today's star reporters are known well enough to qualify as public figures. And yet when hunting season starts, they try always to remain among those who wear the orange caps and carry shotguns. Never would they want to be among those of us whose asses have been continually plinked with the buckshot. The hunters like to be in control.

But often they go out of control. One of the more sweeping, prolonged, and memorable news hunts of my tenure in politics took place in the late 1980s and early 1990s—the interminable coverage of the Iran-contra episode. What a weird and unsteady walk down the primrose path we all took on that one. The media spent years covering that sordid story, and yet nobody in the press ever laid a glove on the real prey—Ronald Reagan and George Bush. Investigations by Congress and by special prosecutor Lawrence Walsh ate up millions of dollars, with similar results. And yet nothing could persuade the media that this was not another Watergate. The media kept creating crisis after crisis—"Once a crisis, always a crisis" would be a good media motto—to the delight of partisans hoping for political advantage. But nobody ever found that elusive smoking gun. All we ever got was smoking gums, overheated words from the mouths of talk-show hosts and the usual Sunday pundits. Some in the media are still plenty angry that they couldn't find anything. Others are still looking—and looking stupid.

The whole hunt might have been amusing to watch if it had not had such grave consequences for the country. Official Washington was well nigh immobilized by the Iran-contra issue. While the rest of the country was hoping and praying for action on any number of issues—the budget deficit, the ecomony, the environment—everyone in town was trying to put out a fire that the media had created, and would not let die. As I said earlier, President Reagan tried to get the Congress and the country to move ahead with his agenda, but Iran-contra kept getting in the way. Reagan compounded the problem by refusing to hold a press conference for weeks and weeks. Instead of simply answering the media's questions and moving on, he remained quiet, which allowed the press to continue assuming the worst, and continue relentlessly digging.

Still, I could not forgive the way the media were abusing the president. And so, on that beautiful March morning in 1987, I made that ugly face at the White House press corps and introduced the word "gazoo" into the Washington lexicon. God, that felt good. Weeks after that, I was in New York when a guy from Brooklyn approached me to discuss the gazoo episode. He couldn't understand why the press did not know what a gazoo really was. He said, "Isn't a gazoo the same thing in Wyoming it is in Brooklyn?" I assured him that it was. We both laughed to beat hell. Apparently that guy went to the same kind of grade school I did.

The day after my gazoo remark at the White House, Ronald Reagan finally held a press conference. The networks billed it as a major event. And so it was. The media people pitched question after question, and to their dismay and exasperation, Reagan hit each one out of the park, as he often did. The media were not able to hurt him. Some reporters would later complain that the press conference had "strayed off the subject," which I'm sure they felt was Iran-contra. Allow me to say here that I felt the event stuck to the real issues concerning the country—the economy, trade, defense, and so on.

A headline in the next day's *Washington Post* said, "Showdown in the East Room: Reagan at the ready." Tom Shales's review of the television coverage was headlined "The President: Clear eyes, in command." Most of the stories I read about that news conference conveyed the idea that Ronald Reagan was indeed in command and in control, contrary to what the media had been suggesting throughout their Iran-contra coverage. Their responsibility and honesty in covering the press conference was long in coming.

A *Post* story by Eleanor Randolph, "The Press: 'Simpsonized' and Subdued," focused on the behavior of the media. It began, "Under the crystal chandeliers of the East Room last night, the White House press corps seemed to be on its Sunday best behavior.

"Facing the President for the first time in four months, even the television reporters seemed to lower their booming voices to ask questions that in many cases were a lot tougher than they sounded." Later, Randolph wrote, "Afterward, as reporters streamed out of the White House and back to their offices, a number said they thought the press had been 'Simpsonized' as one put it. . . . Several reporters said they detected a self-consciousness that may have come not simply from their own concern that they not appear to badger Reagan but also from Simpson's surprising outburst."

At one point that evening, television reporter Chris Wallace seemed to suggest that my comments to the press had been orchestrated—that the president, or somebody, had told me to make the gazoo remark. He noted that President Reagan said mysteriously, "I'll leave the falsehood to others." Said Wallace, "Was that the press he was talking about? [The president's comments] may have been spur-of-the-moment and they may have been in coordination with Simpson, for all we know."

Wallace's cynical remarks say an awful lot about how journalists' minds work. They assume that everything public officials say and do is part of some devilish and carefully contrived plot, some devious scheme to trick the American people. How ludicrous. Look, the average group of political operatives can't agree on what toppings to put on their pizza, much less plan that kind of sophisticated media manipulation. Besides, I am not the sort of person ever to follow such a plan. My "outburst," as Randolph called it, was pure Al Simpson, and could not have been conceived by anyone but me. I said what I said because I was plain damn fed up, not because somebody wanted me to say it.

Remember, I made the gazoo remark right after the White House press people had tried to rattle Reagan by shouting questions at him during a photo opportunity. They do this all the time, and it is terrible to watch. Put the news media within hollering distance of the president, any president, and they loose their inane questions in full-throated cry. You can't imagine the cacophony of hard voices, the discourtesy, the crudeness. I am often surprised at the press's behavior, because by and large the White House

media are top-of-the-line, talented, and highly experienced professionals. Many are quite erudite and interesting to know. The
trouble is, they get tied in knots every day because they cannot
get access to the president, whoever it is. They have to write something about this person every day, and yet they rarely get a chance
to talk to him, and may never, in their entire careers, be granted
an in-depth, one-on-one interview. Their jobs are tough; they
truly are. Still, there is no excuse for the way they sometimes
behave. When you hear the shouting, the bickering, and the whining, you can only feel disappointed in them.

The president is not the only one who is treated unkindly.
Often his visitors are too. On one occasion, President Reagan
received a visit from His Eminence Geron Iakovos, leader of the
Greek Orthodox Archdiocese of North and South America. This
gentle man, who had led the Greek Orthodox faithful for almost
thirty years at that time, was leaving the White House when he
was hailed by the media. Reporters asked a couple of fair, responsible questions, then quickly began making obscure, inane, and
irreverent inquiries. One journalist said, "Your Eminence, did the
president use three-by-five cards?" Another asked, "Was the president asleep?" If the questions were supposed to be funny, they
did not seem that way to the archbishop. And I cannot possibly
imagine that the public really had a right, or a need, to know
whether the president used notes in a meeting with a visitor.

The Iran-contra story was still festering as Washington and the
rest of the nation prepared for the end of Ronald Reagan's second
term, and with it the election of a new president. For the Democratic presidential aspirants, the Iran-contra story created a real
opportunity. Instead of acknowledging that Reagan and Bush had
ushered in the longest run of sustained economic growth in America's history, they could attempt to distract the voters with accusations about Iran-contra. Many of my congressional colleagues—
Gary Hart, Al Gore, Richard Gephardt, Al Cranston, John Glenn,
Sam Nunn, and Dale Bumpers among them—were mentioned as
possible Democratic nominees. But perhaps the most star-crossed
candidate was my companion and colleague during the Three Mile

Island episode, Senator Gary Hart of Colorado. He had run a rather cerebral campaign for the presidential nomination in 1984, and by spring of 1987, he was considered by many to be his party's front-runner. He was the young, New Age candidate, full of ideas and promise.

His candidacy did not last long. It effectively came to an end on Monday, May 5, 1987, when the *Miami Herald* reported that he had spent the weekend with a woman who was not his wife. A crafty, dedicated, and curious crew from the *Herald* had followed Donna Rice to Washington, then staked out Hart's townhouse to see what he and Donna were up to. When Gary and the young woman emerged, the reporters confronted them and asked—somewhat rhetorically, I'm sure—what was going on. In the most lurid and titillating tradition of America's trashiest pulp tabloids, they got their man. And woman. The *National Enquirer* or the *Globe* could not have dreamed up a better or more salable story, for this one had a handsome, persistent candidate for president, a sexy blond aspiring actress, and an anguished and regrettably absent wife. You could almost hear the chortling coming from the *Herald* building down on Biscayne Bay. Hart tried desperately to reconstruct his image, but in the end was forced from the race.

In the days after the story appeared, many of the TV pundits and commentators argued that the marital fidelity—or lack thereof—of a presidential candidate was not proper fodder for newspaper stories. I disagree. Fidelity in marriage is some indicator of character, and I think the character of the man or woman to be entrusted with safety, security, and social structure of the United States is indeed an issue. What Gary Hart and Donna Rice did was highly newsworthy. I did not object to the facts, but rather to the way they were gathered. Every person has a right to a reasonable level of privacy—a right to go into or out of his or her own home or apartment without having *Miami Herald* reporters watching. At least one columnist accused the *Herald*'s reporters of hiding in the bushes to get the story. That wasn't so. But what the reporters did was almost as bad. They tailed Donna Rice like amateur gumshoes, including on her flight to D.C., then hung around outside Gary Hart's private home until, alas, he and Donna went for a stroll.

That was going too far. Now, some will argue that reporters could not report on the important issue of character without following people at least once in a while. Hogwash. If reporters talk to enough people, they will get the story. These things never remain a secret for long—nor, in the case of presidential candidates, should they.

After the *Herald* story broke, the rest of America's media played catch-up—or, rather, piled on. Again and again, we viewed the videotape, made just weeks earlier, in which Gary Hart had told reporters that he had been a faithful husband, and had urged them to "follow me" if they did not believe it. We also watched as the media intruded vacuously and viciously on the lives of Donna Rice and her family and friends. We saw pictures of her parents, pictures of her friends, pictures of her relatives, pictures of everyone, no matter how obscure. Once the mainstream media created this sensation, some of Donna's "friends" began selling their stories—and pictures. The late-night comedians had a field day; what would they ever do without the news media to give them material?

Throughout the spectacle, my thoughts and prayers went out to my friend Gary and his wife, Lee, who were in the whirling center of the storm. Yes, I know what you're thinking—he had it coming; he brought it on himself. Certainly Gary made a grave mistake. And yes, he should have been aware that Washington is a tough town; one week you're on the cover of *Time* and the next week you're doing time. But I'm not sure Gary did anything to bring down the kind of heartless and intrusive "coverage" he and Lee got. After the *Herald* story came out, Gary's and Lee's (when they could find her) every private moment, every tear, and every sigh was analyzed, rehashed, and recounted in the media. Was that fair? And at probably the worst moment of her life, Lee could not leave her Colorado home without hearing the thwacking of news helicopters hovering overhead. What had she ever done to deserve that?

On the Wednesday after the Hart story hit, I was at the National Press Club to give a speech about illegal immigration reform. I was honored to be invited, and so I presented my handwritten speech with great gusto. Then, in keeping with the format, I took questions from reporters. Some asked about immigration, others about the budget. Most of the questions were routine. The last question—and we politicians know it is always the last question that holds the most peril for us—was not. I was asked to state my personal views regarding the news about Gary Hart.

I said I knew Gary Hart well and regarded him as a pretty fair legislator and as a nice friend. I related my strong belief that the media should consider the human toll when they tell such stories. Then I said, "While you're having a high old time with this, how do you think Lee Hart feels? Any of you think of her? She's out there digging out of the rubble of it all." Though I felt Gary had made a mistake, I cautioned the press about being too judgmental. I said there was no such thing as perfection in any human life. I went on to say that, as a Christian, I believe we are all sinners, no better and no worse than Gary Hart.

Fine so far. It was the next portion of my rambling answer that got me into trouble.

"Let's look at the life of Christ as chronicled in the Bible," I said. "Where was he from the age of twelve when he left the temple until the scribes picked him up again when he was about thirty? There's not one single thing reported on him in that span of time. Why? Likely because he was doing all the things we ever did. When they came to writing the chronicles of that life they said, 'Whew, boy, better leave that part out. I mean, we're writing about the perfect life.' So there's no such thing as perfection," I said. I concluded by saying that Washington is quite a town: "There are organizations in this town that protect every living thing—bats, trees, sharks, whales—but give them another human being to trash and they'll chew him to shreds!"

When the luncheon ended, Mary Kay Hill, my press secretary, warned me that some folks would very likely misinterpret my remarks about Christ. She asked me what I was trying to say, and I explained. She told me she did not think people would understand. She was right. By the time we were back in the office, my phones were ringing with complaints from some who had seen and heard my remarks on C-SPAN. In making an effort to show why basic

Christian principles of forgiveness, tolerance, and charity should apply to Lee and Gary Hart, I apparently had gone too far and offended some people on that subject of perfection.

In an attempt to minimize the damage, Mary Kay and I quickly drafted a statement. It said:

> There are surely few things more intimate and personal than one's own deeply held religious belief. My church and my personal God are the very foundations of my life—faith is my anchor and my rock—especially in this fascinating profession that the people of Wyoming have allowed me to pursue. News accounts of certain comments I made recently on the life of Jesus Christ have caused concern to some.
>
> In response to a question posed at the National Press Club recently about the press stakeout of former presidential candidate Gary Hart, I reflected that this is a funny kind of town, where there are myriad organizations organized to protect every living thing—bird, bee, tree of the field, whale, snail darter. But give them another human being to gnaw on and they shred him. I also said that underneath all the rubble were two very pained and bruised human beings—Gary and Lee Hart. I then reflected that the public seems to expect perfection in their elected representatives and even more specially when they don't have it in their own lives. In an effort to dramatically note the human aspects of such expectations I referred to the chronicling of the most perfect life as we yet know one— that of our Lord and Savior Jesus Christ. I did not try to desecrate Jesus Christ. Please surely know that I meant no offense. I was simply relating one aspect of Christ's life that brings me ever closer to the faith that I firmly hold.
>
> I do believe that during the unrecorded time of Christ's life he was fulfilling his Father's mission—to live life on earth as a human being—and that only deepens and enriches my own faith. For I believe during that time

he was striving, searching, making mistakes, growing, stumbling, succeeding, erring, facing temptation, loving, judging and misjudging others—indeed living a human life. That belief of mine about his remarkable human life is what led me to the full acceptance of Christianity. That is the promise of the cross—that he died for our sins and he asked forgiveness for his own and ours. That teaches me ever much more about my own failures and enables me to better cope with my own often errant human life.

It was only through a belief in God that I long ago learned where to turn when I didn't know where to turn. It is not corny to say that one never really gets it all together until one puts one's life in the hands of that Higher Being. My religion does not need any credential checking. I have always felt that it would be arrogant or ignorant of me to presume to ever judge the type or quality or depth of another's religious faith or beliefs. I have never been comfortable watching others try to perform those tests of religious purity or piety on their fellow beings.

No possible extension of my remarks could be seen to equate Jesus to Gary Hart. I do not condone, nor do I know, what actually happened. Suffice it to say that if I had been asked that blockbuster question about my personal life as Gary Hart was—the answer would have just been no.

I sent a letter containing those ideas to every person who contacted me. I also sent my statement to Wyoming newspapers in the form of a letter to the editor, and most were gracious enough to print it in its entirety. I found that many critics did come to appreciate and better understand what I was trying to say. Those who still would not forgive apparently were the kind who would never forgive much of anything. Many of my colleagues in Congress appreciated my words about the media's—and the public's—unjust expectation of perfection in the lives of public people. That pleased me. Warmed me.

Gary Hart was among those who thanked me. He called from

his ranch in Lonesome Gulch, Colorado, and said, "Al, I did appreciate that. All of this makes you wonder where your friends really are. You surely find out who they are, too."

I still stubbornly maintain—almost a decade later as I write this—that if the people staking out Hart's residence had been FBI agents instead of reporters, the media never would have stopped shrieking, grieving, and braying about the heinous and unjustified infringement on Hart's sacred right to privacy. We would have seen an Iran-contra-size investigation of the matter; the press would not have quit until the FBI director's head had been served on a shiny platter. And of course, if the Republican National Committee or any of its minions had been lurking in the bushes outside that townhouse, every Woodward or Bernstein wannabe in Washington would have been on the story. We would have been treated to televised hearings, muckraking profiles of the culprits, and God knows what else. The nation would have been in an uproar; the media would have made sure of it.

In fairness to the profession, there were some in the media who were critical of the way the *Miami Herald* got that story—the way it got Gary Hart. Speaking on the *Today* show, Sara Fritz of the *Los Angeles Times* called the stakeout a "dumb stunt." She had it right. It is a pity that her thoughtful words were not met with universal agreement. But as I have said, you can always count on most members of the Fourth Estate to protect their own, and you can almost never count on them to admit a serious mistake, especially a mistake in judgment.

It is time, I think, for reporters—the hunters—to truly take the time and effort to examine the way they do things, and to think about their place in the democracy. And I believe that the public is now insisting that they do so. The American people have grown disgusted with the hunters as they draw back their bows or flick the safety off on their blunderbusses. Americans may even feel a bit sorry for the public figures who have great big concentric-circle targets painted on their backs, for they understand that the arrows fired by the Fourth Estate enter the body in precisely that place—the back. A true hunter, a sportsman, is fair to the hunted; he or she gives the prey a fighting chance.

The same cannot always be said for the media. They are furtive, clever, industrious, and creative. Taking steady aim can mean big trophies, including the Pulitzer Prize. The promise of such an award will always justify the hunt to them, even if the prey is the most unpopular, most private, shyest, or most vulnerable creature alive. Gary Hart, one of the hunted, is as tough as leather, and yet you can still see his wounds. Most are not as tough as he.

CHAPTER NINE

Borked and Thomased

O n Friday June 26, 1987, Justice Lewis Powell announced his resignation from the Supreme Court of the United States. The resignation of such a genteel, genial, and impressive man from the nation's highest court would have been a major story at any time. But Powell's announcement was especially newsworthy because it was heralded as the end of decades of liberal domination of the Supreme Court. Powell had been regarded either as a liberal who backed the social agenda of the Court's judicial activists or as a thoughtful moderate who often provided the swing vote in some of its most troublesome and contentious cases. Either way, his retirement offered an opportunity for President Ronald Reagan to nudge the Court to the right—right where he wanted it. The nation's liberal interest groups—and its powerful news media—were going to do everything they possibly could to stop him.

Within hours of Powell's announcement, people representing every left-wing cause in America were mobilizing in a frenzied effort to influence the next appointment. These activists came from consumer groups, civil rights groups, women's groups, environmental groups, and so many more. Perhaps the best-known and most cleverly manipulative liberal who became involved was Ralph Neas, executive director of the Leadership Conference on Civil Rights. Neas knew immediately that he desperately needed the media on his side—not that it would take much coaxing to bring the Washington press around to his point of view. Fearing that a strong, forceful conservative would be nominated to fill the Powell vacancy, he and his supporters began brokering the idea that such a right-winger would destroy the "ideological balance" on the Court. That was an absurd claim; presidents have never nominated judges to the Court in an effort to preserve balance. They want justices who are on their side. Still, the press repeated Neas's claim as if it were incontrovertible fact. No doubt the media were also hoping and praying for a liberal—or at least not some archconservative—nominee.

The frantic efforts of the liberal groups and the liberal media did not pay off. President Reagan remained determined to send up the name of a solid conservative with a strong philosophy of judicial restraint. Reagan was looking for an individual who would not appear to make new law, as many felt the Warren Court had done, but rather someone who would stick to the Constitution.

One day, a few of us senators were sitting around talking of possible Supreme Court nominees with Howard Baker, our fine former senate majority leader who was then serving as Reagan's chief of staff. Someone mentioned Robert Bork's name. Bork was a truly distinguished conservative jurist with a well-deserved reputation for putting liberals in their place. Five and a half years earlier, the Senate had confirmed him for a seat on the District of Columbia Court of Appeals, a breeding ground for future Supreme Court justices. Baker and I and the others agreed that it was critically important to nominate a strong scholar with a track record for making sensible decisions, and Bork clearly met both qualifications.

"I do like Bork," I told Baker. "Send him up and we'll do our damnedest to get him confirmed."

Obviously I was not Bork's only strong supporter, because the president soon sent his name to the Senate for confirmation. The wretched and disgusting events that followed would forever change the judicial selection process. They would tarnish what once had been the highest honor that could be conferred on a judge—nomination to the U.S. Supreme Court. And, in my view, they would also do serious damage to future civil political discourse in America.

Within minutes of Robert Bork's nomination—and I underscore the word "minutes"—my old liberal friend Ted Kennedy took the Senate floor to viciously and cruelly denounce Bork as a person whose philosophy was outside the mainstream of American judicial thought. He said, "Robert Bork's America is a land in which women would be forced into back-alley abortions, blacks would sit at segregated lunch counters, rogue police could break down citizens' doors in midnight raids, schoolchildren could not be taught about evolution, writers and artists could be censored at the whim of the government, and the doors of the federal courts would be shut on the fingers of millions of citizens for whom the judiciary is often the only protector of the individual rights that are the heart of our democracy." Kennedy—who, remember now, had not opposed Bork's nomination to the D.C. Court of Appeals—went on to condemn many of the decisions Bork wrote for that court. He also criticized many articles Bork had written during his tenure. Clearly Ted's speech had been prepared well in advance; he could not have said all those things unless he had been ready for Bork's nomination, and ready to oppose it. The liberal interest groups had been all lathered up to go after Bork long before the president had decided to nominate him. Much later, Michael Pertschuk and Wendy Schaetzel published the book *The People Rising,* describing the hows and whys of the liberal interest groups' sabotaging of Bork's nomination. The book now serves as a sort of bible for people who are trying to "bork" other people.

Ten weeks passed between the announcement of Bork's nomination and the opening day of the dramatic Senate confirmation hearings. During that time, liberal interest groups continued their shrill, unwarranted, untrue, and almost deafening crusade against the nominee. Never before in the history of our country had a Supreme Court nominee been subject to such extremism, and to such distortion of his or her professional record. People for the American Way—a group whose leaders talk a good, fair game while smiling sweetly and sharpening their teeth with a No. 10 file—helped fund a $2 million advertising campaign against Robert Bork. In one of these ads, the respected actor Gregory Peck claimed that Bork "has a strange idea of what justice is. He defended poll taxes and literacy tests which kept many Americans from voting. He opposed the civil rights law that ended 'whites only' signs at lunch counters." After peddling these outrageous mutations of Bork's record, Peck went on to say that Bork's views were outside the mainstream and threatening to our Constitution.

Really? During that quarter century, Robert Bork had twice faced confirmation votes in a Democratic-controlled Senate, and had been confirmed handily both times—first as solicitor general under President Gerald Ford, and then as a judge on the D.C. court. Where the hell was People for the American Way when he was under consideration for those jobs? And why weren't the media pointing out the hypocrisy of People for the American Way now? I can answer that second one. The media were not criticizing the cunning Ralph Neas and his liberal friends because they damn sure wanted the liberal side to win this one.

Neas did a stunning job of making sure that every liberal legislator did as he or she was told. Several weeks before the hearing, Judiciary Committee chairman Joe Biden, the Delaware Democrat, had said he disagreed with Bork's judicial philosophy but nonetheless believed he was qualified to serve on the Supreme Court. The liberal groups quickly disabused my old pal Joey of his fair and reasonable viewpoint. By the time the hearings began, one of Biden's top aides—an anonymous source, of course—told the *Washington Post,* "The Democratic opponents of the nomination plan a broad assault on Bork's overall judicial philosophy."

The aide was quoted as saying that the hearings would focus on "the broad-ranging constitutional philosophy of Bork that does not reflect the American people." Again, the source of this quotation was not named. As a member of the Judiciary Committee, I gamely still thought the focus of the hearings would be Bork's qualifications, or lack thereof, and not his ideology or philosophy.

And yet the chairman of the committee and his staff were now saying that the point of the whole spectacle was to show that Robert Bork was somehow out of the mainstream.

Look what the *Post* did in that story. By quoting Biden's aide anonymously, it gave the liberal side a free opportunity to build public opposition to the nomination. The *Post* was only too happy to provide such a forum to the liberal side because the paper wanted to see Bork pulled down.

The *Washington Post*'s coverage of the first day of the hearings demonstrated how the liberal special interests had set the agenda for the process. One article published that day appeared to give equal weight to the efforts of Bork and his opponents, noting, "Liberal and conservative groups went into high gear yesterday in their bitter and expensive battle over the nomination, holding news conferences to rebut each other's arguments and announce more studies of Bork's record."

The story was misleading because only one side had waged an "expensive battle." Bork's supporters had not spent a fortune; only his detractors had. And yet the *Post* coverage, like much of the national media coverage, had the gentle reader believing that this was an even struggle between right and wrong, that both sides were equally girded for the fight. This simply was not so. President Reagan handled the nomination of Bork in the traditional, time-worn way: He introduced the nominee, made a generous speech about him in order to gain public support, and then asked members of the Senate for a quick and decisive nomination. The opposition, on the other hand, was buying up advertisements and courting the press in a well-orchestrated effort to defeat the nominee—and humiliate the president.

The courting of the press paid off richly. Many media people published articles or broadcast stories about articles and speeches Bork had written and rendered in which he disagreed with previous Supreme Court rulings. The implication of these stories was that Bork would cause a heap of trouble for this country by bringing about the reversal of many Supreme Court precedents. The NAACP Legal Defense Fund went so far as to estimate that thirty-one decisions would be jeopardized by Bork's confirmation to the

Court. Though Bork spoke forcefully of his respect for Court precedents, this twisting of facts proved to be one of the keys to his undoing.

The media's liberal bias can clearly be seen here. Several years later, President Bill Clinton nominated the highly qualified Ruth Bader Ginsburg for the Supreme Court. Like Robert Bork, Ginsburg had criticized certain previous conclusions of the Court. For example, she said in one speech that the Court might have gone too far in its *Roe v. Wade* decision legalizing abortion. She felt that perhaps the country really had not been ready for such a far-reaching decision. If a Republican nominee had said such a thing, the press would have torn him or her to shreds. But because these honest reflections had been offered by someone who supported abortion rights—someone who, like most of the media, was left of center—the press and the women's rights groups merely smiled and clucked. The reaction was much the same when Ginsburg conceded that she had hired no minorities as law clerks. The media and the interest groups let that one slide by, too, because they saw her as one of them.

The fiery debate over Robert Bork's nomination was burning out of control when the *Washington Post* decided to throw more gasoline on the fire. One day, the paper listed the names of the twenty-six previous Supreme Court nominees who had been rejected by the Senate for one reason or another. The *Post* seemed to be saying, "It's all right to reject this guy; in fact, rejection is part of our nation's cherished history." By publishing those names, the *Post* gave further legitimacy to Bork's opponents, and subtly suggested that rejecting his nomination was the right and necessary thing for the Senate to do.

If the media had wanted to report fairly and evenhandedly about Robert Bork's nomination, they would have focused on the over one hundred opinions he had written as an appellate judge. Not a single one of those opinions was ever overruled by the United States Supreme Court—and six of his dissents had been crafted by the justices to become majority opinions of the high court. But fairness was not the order of the day. Instead of discussing Bork's considerable intellectual achievements, the media slavishly devoted themselves to a few salacious items. One was Bork's participation in the infamous Saturday Night Massacre, one of the low lights of the whole sordid Watergate story. On that day, President Richard Nixon ordered the firing of Watergate special prosecutor Archibald Cox—and then dismissed Attorney General Elliot Richardson and Deputy Attorney General William Ruckelshaus when they refused to carry out Nixon's order. The number three man at the Justice Department then was none other than Robert Bork. Clearly, the simplest thing for him to do would have been to resign. Indeed, he was fully prepared to refuse the president's order to fire Cox. But he feared that if he were to quit, Cox would be dismissed and the Justice Department would never properly investigate Watergate. So he dismissed Cox, but stayed doggedly on to make certain that the truth eventually came out. Bork would later explain, "My moral and professional lives were on the line if something happened to those investigations."

The media did not care much for Bork's explanation. Even today, journalists regard the *Washington Post*'s work on Watergate as among the best moments in the history of the profession. I do not question the proven value of the reporting done by Bob Woodward and Carl Bernstein. The trouble is that many of today's journalists are more interested in becoming wealthy media stars than they are in conveying the truth. The *Post*'s Watergate coverage inspired a generation of young people to become journalists, but it also instilled a belief that everyone serving in government is corrupt. When Robert Bork's name again became associated with Watergate, he did not stand a chance with the salivating media. It did not matter a whit what he had accomplished in the intervening years.

I can understand why one would want to scrutinize Bork's actions during Watergate. I don't agree with the conclusions of his critics, but I can understand why they were on the prod. There was much about the press's coverage of the Bork story that I could not understand. In one childish effort at journalism, a reporter from the *City Paper,* an alternative rag, obtained from a Washington video store a list of the movies Robert Bork and his family had rented. The wire services gleefully picked up the story, and within

days all of America knew all about the Bork family's taste in movies. How idiotic. Nobody ever explained what Robert Bork's
video rental habits had to do with his qualifications for the Supreme Court of the United States—possibly because the article
was inexplicable and indefensible. When Bork accepted a nomination to the Supreme Court, he did not in any way relinquish his
right to a private life. No one does. You could never have convinced the media of that. I consider it ironic that so many of Bork's
detractors in the media criticized him for his views on issues of
privacy, never stopping to consider the cruel ways in which they
were depriving him of *his* privacy. What hypocrisy. What arrogance. What chilling gall.

Later, I cosponsored legislation that made it illegal for the media
to make public a person's video rental records. The legislation
passed overwhelmingly in both the House and Senate. The reporter who did the video-rental story responded with an essay in
which he maintained that Bork was just another public official and
thus there was nothing wrong in printing which videos he had
rented. Again, a member of the press was setting a different standard for the media than he would set for public officials, political
parties, or even law enforcement. What if it became known that
the FBI inquired into the video rental habits of a reporter it had
under surveillance? What if the Reagan campaign had tried to find
out what kind of movies Fritz Mondale liked to watch at home
with his wife, Joan? These invasions of privacy—for surely they
would be appalling invasions of privacy—would be reported in
haughty and disbelieving tones. Is it any wonder we wonder about
the media?

But even as I was thinking unkind things about the media, some
journalists were writing some good things about me. For example,
my participation in Bork's confirmation hearings drew the attention of the *Washington Post,* which assigned reporter Charles Trueheart to do a story. The resulting piece was titled "In Bork's
Corner, Alan Simpson's Angry Defense." The subtitle was "Wyoming Senator Frustrated, but Making Points at the Hearings." I
felt that the article was a fair attempt to describe the frustrations of
those on my side of the debate. I appreciated that fairness. I told

Trueheart that really good people would no longer be willing to go into public service after seeing what had happened to Bork.

Trueheart wrote, "From here on out, [Simpson] says, nominees will have unexceptional records, and therefore unexceptional minds. Take 'Jerome P. Sturdly,' a fellow Simpson invented during the hearings. Sturdly 'has quite extensive experience on the bench and at the bar,' according to Simpson's portrait, but he 'has said very little, has written very little that was either thoughtful, challenging or provocative.' Such nominees will be 'sterilized before they get to us,' he says, sadly."

Trueheart went on, "[Simpson] is known as his own man, nobody's lap dog, a politician of catholic convictions and healthy disengagement from the self-important follies of Capitol Hill, someone with brains and manners—and a formidable sense of humor.

"So when he loses his temper, as he has many times since Robert Bork was nominated, his colleagues on both sides of the aisle tend to notice."

The article concluded, "To judge him by results, Simpson is among the most effective politicians in the Senate. . . . Simpson is regarded as something of an intellectual in the Senate. . . . Simpson gets very good press, yet he does little to pander to the needs of the news media other than deliver witty lines. . . ."

The article also quoted friends, observers, and detractors—all by name, mind you. All in all, that story was very positive. I liked it. Who the hell wouldn't?

Trueheart's colleague the television critic Tom Shales was not quite so kind. In an article about Bork's televised confirmation hearings, Shales asked, ". . . who really needs opponents when one has allies like . . . Alan Simpson, who reprised his pained posturing about the brutalities and ruthlessness of life on the Hill; oh how can we be so beastly to this dear little man, why must we sully and pillory such a distinguished jurist, have we at long last no decency, and so on. You'd think Simpson had been suffering through 40 years of bloody congressional skirmishes instead of a mere nine."

After lengthy, moving, and intense debate on the Senate floor, each member of that body stood at his or her desk and voted on

Robert Bork's nomination to the United States Supreme Court. We conducted a roll call vote because the nominee and his supporters asked us to. It was important to him—and to me—that the American people see democracy at work. Those of us who supported him were all too happy to have the people know exactly which senators did not support him. When the voting was ended, Bork's nomination had gone down in defeat. This result was expected. With the help of a willing press, the liberal special interest groups had succeeded in totally distorting the life of this fine human being, and thus had won their victory.

But oh, so much was lost. As a nation, we lost a man who would have made a great contribution to jurisprudence in our country. We lost our sense that even a vigorously conservative intellectual can have a place in our democracy. And we lost our belief that a nomination to high office in this country was a great honor, something to be accepted with gratitude and openness. There was a time in America when a president could nominate someone for such an office with the expectation that the Senate would conduct a fair, reasonable discussion of the person's qualifications, and then hold a fair, sensible vote for or against confirmation. This assumption usually held true even when a president chose someone whose political leanings were different from those in the majority party of the Senate. I had always respected that tradition. In my view, the president had a right to appoint the Supreme Court justices he wanted, so long as they were qualified to do the work. I vote that way. The tradition I speak of was extinguished with the sabotaging of Robert Bork. Thereafter, the confirmation process became a stage for petty partisan bickering. After Bork came Senator John Tower, Zoe E. Baird, Lani Guinier, and on and on. What a sad thing for our country.

As for me, I lost faith in some media people whom I had previously thought to be fair and decent. And I lost much of whatever patience I still had left. I thought, Dammit, the First Amendment belongs to me too! I became more determined than ever to critique the work of journalists. After the roll call vote, I visited with a saddened but still dignified Robert Bork and with his courageous wife, Mary Ellen. From that moment forward, I felt a deep and powerful determination to speak out more forcefully against what I felt to be the excesses of the media, and against those who so cleverly and cynically manipulate public opinion with the media's help. That kind of determination can get a guy in a heap of trouble. And so it came to pass.

After Bork's nomination was rejected, President Reagan decided on Anthony Kennedy, a solid and studious man with a most pleasing and genuine demeanor. The liberal groups had decided to let Kennedy slide, and the Senate confirmed him easily. The left-wing interest groups remained generally subdued when President Bush nominated the quiet, delightful, thoughtful, and taciturn David Souter to a seat on the Court. But then came another nomination fight, one perhaps worse than the one we had waged over Robert Bork.

One night during Ronald Reagan's presidency, I was privileged to be seated next to Justice Thurgood Marshall at a big Washington gala. I knew him and liked him. He wasn't feeling well—his legs were bandaged and he was hurting. Still, he was his charming, curmudgeonly, effervescent self. His doctor had advised him to abstain from the wine, get home early, and stay out of the cigar smoke, and Thurgood was ignoring every bit of that advice. If he had to attend this damn fool event, by God, he was going to have a good time. I was the beneficiary. We told ribald stories, had a few laughs, and did some grousing about the national political scene. All in all, it was a great evening with a great spirit.

Somewhere around the third or fourth course, a rather obsequious gentleman approached us at the head table.

"Oh, Justice Marshall, you are the most wonderful justice we have ever had," he said. "You made the world a better place. I hope you never leave the court. But if you were ever to think of retiring, when would you do it?"

Thurgood slouched in his chair, peeked over his glasses, and growled, "When that son of a bitch Ronald Reagan leaves here!"

After the astonished visitor returned to his seat, I said, "Well, you seemed to get that off your chest pretty well, didn't you?"

He chuckled, "Yeah, I loved it! Sure startled that guy, too!"

Obviously Thurgood Marshall made no secret of his disdain for

Reagan, and later for George Bush. This pioneering civil rights
lawyer had played an integral part on the liberal Warren Court,
and therefore had little use for any conservatives whom Reagan
and Bush would appoint as justices. The night he and I dined
together, I think he still hoped that he could keep working until
a Democratic president was elected, thus increasing the odds that
a liberal would succeed him on the Court. But in 1991, he finally
gave in. George Bush was riding a wave of popularity and seemed
likely to be reelected. Marshall, his health failing quickly now,
announced his retirement, saying in his inimitable gruff way, "I'm
old. I'm falling apart." He died in 1993.

Now the Court needed a replacement. Within hours after Marshall announced his retirement, liberal special interest groups began
speechifying about George Bush's "obligation" to appoint someone who would carry on Marshall's work on the Court. According
to the liberal establishment, the appointment "belonged" to a minority.

Actually, it belonged to George Bush. Our Constitution gives
the president the awesome responsibility of filling Supreme Court
vacancies. In 1992, George Bush had become president by an
overwhelming vote; thus he would have the privilege and the
responsibility of replacing Marshall (not that such a man could ever
truly be replaced). And he was not going to be influenced by
anybody else's ideas. The president made it clear that race and
gender would not be the principal considerations in making his
choice. George Bush would appoint an individual of highest character who believed in the firm bedrock of the Constitution and in
the concept of judicial restraint.

As usual, the media speculated wildly about whom the president
would select. In making an endless stream of guesses, they quoted
every "reliable," "credible," "high-ranking"—and incorrect—
source they knew. For weeks, they tried to report the news before
it was made. They did not succeed. So they were all deeply surprised and, yes, even visibly chagrined when the president introduced Clarence Thomas to America while standing outside the
Bush home in Kennebunkport, Maine.

Thomas was a young, bright, articulate, well-regarded judge

sitting on the District of Columbia Court of Appeals—the same court that had produced Robert Bork. Thomas was, or should have been, a great story. Having overcome abject poverty and cruel discrimination, he now stood near the pinnacle of the legal profession. As a young black conservative, he was indeed something of a novelty. A graduate of Yale Law School, he had worked as an aide to my dear colleague Senator John Danforth of Missouri, and also had served as head of the Equal Employment Opportunity Commission. His legal credentials were superb. Though the media would soon try to make sure the nation forgot it, Clarence Thomas had sailed blithely through five previous FBI background checks and three previous confirmations by the Senate Judiciary Committee and the full Senate. He had received near-unanimous approval at each and every turn along the way by a Democratically controlled Congress.

Alarmingly, all kinds of people quickly started ganging up on Clarence Thomas. Some African-Americans didn't trust him because he was a Republican; they felt only a liberal could be considered a "real" supporter of their cause. The media made the same assumption. They seemed to have the twisted fantasy that any man who had grown up black and poor would obviously want to be a Democrat. And if he wasn't one, why wasn't he? What was wrong with this guy?

The special interest groups again cranked up and went on the attack. The same people who had insisted that the nominee be a minority now insisted that Thomas was but a token. What bullshit! What hypocrisy! The feminists attacked him because he was too conservative. The abortion-rights people—and remember, I'm one of them—attacked him because he opposed abortion. One disgruntled, venal, pea-brained outfit ran national advertisements asking for individuals to come forward with any dirt on Clarence Thomas—and supplied an address and an 800 number. And a member of a radical feminist group said, "We'll bork him!" How's that for fairness?

Sheeplike, the media played along. Having already concluded that Thomas was wrong for the job, they began trying to justify the conclusion. Anyone expressing opposition to the nominee was given prompt and prominent coverage. And reporters from virtually every media outlet began snooping into the personal life of Clarence Thomas. The press unmercifully and arrogantly hounded Clarence Thomas, his mother, his sister, his son, his father, and his ex-wife. The media so harassed the ex-wife, a quiet, religious woman, that her own father—Thomas's former father-in-law—found it necessary to come forward and say publicly that Clarence Thomas was a good, honest, and decent man. Had anyone else—the FBI, the CIA, anybody—hounded a Supreme Court nominee and his family in that way, the mainstream press would have raised a great hue and cry. But in this landmark case, anything went, because the target of this form of harassment—and I use that word quite intentionally—was a conservative black man. The media were not interested in the public's right to know. They were simply abusing and belittling the precious First Amendment.

And they kept right on doing it. Many overeager and obnoxious members of the Fourth Estate camped out at the Thomas home. They became suspicious about many things, including the fact that Thomas drove a Corvette. What could it possibly mean? One media outlet reported that Thomas attended a church where some people spoke in tongues. Heavens! This was nothing more than another bigoted attempt to marginalize the nominee. Thomas attended an Episcopal church with a large charismatic and evangelical following. Many Americans have been showing their belief in God in demonstrative ways for years and years. There is nothing new, strange, or sinister about those forms of worship.

But that sure wasn't the last church story we would see. Oh, no. A headline in the July 11 edition of the *Los Angeles Times* said, "Thomas' church a center of anti-abortion activity." So? I'm not aware of too many churches that promote abortion as a first option for pregnant women. Most either oppose abortion altogether or believe it is one of the last options a woman should consider. What was the point of that story? Were we supposed to know how Clarence Thomas would rule on individual abortion cases based on where he went to church? If so, we would have to assume that Senator Ted Kennedy opposes abortion, because he attends a Ro-

man Catholic church. Please. Spare me. The media were biased
against Thomas from the start.

Rank speculation wasn't good enough for some in the media.
This provided an excellent opportunity for certain bloodhounds
of the press. In his statement to the Judiciary Committee at the
beginning of the Anita Hill hearings, Clarence Thomas spoke of
"reporters sneaking into my garage to examine books that I read."
Apparently the reporters brazenly barged into the garage and began
rifling through a stack of books stored there. Were they seeking a
little relaxation between deadlines? Or were they following the
example of Mark Twain, who opened a letter addressed to someone else, read it, and then scribbled on the envelope, "Opened by
mistake to see what was inside"? No, this was the thought police
breaking in to see what Clarence was reading. Where I come from,
out in the Wild West, that's called trespassing, and you can get
your ass shot off for it.

For 103 days, things just like this happened to Clarence Thomas. The media plagued him like the hounds of hell. No person
should have to endure such sadistic abuse. And yet the journalists
who trampled his rights always said they did it in service of another
right—the public's right to know.

With all this coverage of irrelevant parts of Thomas's personal
life, it would have seemed only fair to note those aspects of his
remarkable life that made him well qualified to sit on the Supreme
Court. Here was a man who had overcome terrible early circumstances through sheer guts, self-esteem, and plain damn hard work.
Indeed, Clarence Thomas would bring to the court a range of life
experiences unmatched by any other sitting justice. The American
Bar Association had declared him qualified for the job. His presence on the court would seem to provide it with a renewed sensitivity to the struggles of those born to dire poverty. But that was
not the angle the media played up. Instead, this man who had
worked so hard to make himself a success was alleged to have
completely forgotten and abandoned others less fortunate.

But never mind, for a moment, what Thomas's life experience
would add to the Supreme Court. All that truly mattered was

whether he was qualified for the job—and he was. George Bush's nominee had extensive legal experience. He had worked as an assistant attorney general in Missouri, as a corporate attorney for the Monsanto Company, as a staffer for Senator John Danforth, as an assistant secretary for civil rights in the U.S. Department of Education, as chairman of the agency enforcing our nation's civil rights laws (the Equal Employment Opportunity Commission), and finally as a judge on the U.S. Court of Appeals for the District of Columbia. Clarence Thomas's résumé left nothing to be desired. Indeed, some of the most distinguished and influential justices in our nation's history had less courtroom experience when they took the job than Judge Thomas had when he was nominated. Some had none. Thomas had spent eighteen months on the federal bench and had written eighteen smart, readable opinions. Former chief justice Earl Warren is a good contrast. While he had gained extensive law enforcement experience as attorney general of California, he never sat as a judge in any courtroom in the land before being elevated to chief justice. When confronted with these facts, Thomas's opponents would become surly and indignant. Clarence Thomas, they would say, "is no Earl Warren." True. If Clarence Thomas's judicial philosophy was half as liberal as Warren's, George Bush would have nominated someone else.

Which is precisely my point. If Clarence Thomas had been more liberal, the media and the left-wing groups would have loved him. But the cold, hard truth was that the well-financed, well-drilled, elitist defenders of the public weal would have opposed almost any nominee sent up by a Republican president. This nominee was particularly offensive to them because he was bright, articulate, powerful in his own political philosophy, and unconcerned with certain narrow-minded people's biases about race and ideology.

In his testimony before the Senate Judiciary Committee, Thomas presented himself as a thoughtful, forceful, and intelligent nominee. Like all the prospective justices confirmed in recent years, he refused to answer specific questions about hot-button issues which would surely come before the Court. It has always been deemed highly inappropriate for any nominee to say how he or she would vote on a given issue. To venture such a comment in advance would rightly be seen as being prejudicial. Thomas understood that. Still, at least one member of the Judiciary Committee, Senator Patrick Leahy, tried hard to pin him down on abortion, to no avail. Here is the transcript of that exchange, as quoted in David Brock's book *The Real Anita Hill*:

"Judge, does a fetus have a constitutional status as a person?"

"Senator, I cannot think of any cases that have held that. I would have to go back and rethink that. I cannot think of any cases that have held that."

Leahy then asked whether he had discussed *Roe* v. *Wade* when the decision was handed down in 1973.

"I cannot remember personally engaging in those discussions."

"Have you ever had any discussion of *Roe* v. *Wade* other than in this room? In the seventeen or eighteen years it's been there?"

"Only, I guess, Senator, in the fact that in the most general sense that other individuals express concerns. One way or the other and you listen and you try to be thoughtful. If you're asking me whether I ever debated the contents of it, the answer to that is no, Senator."

Thomas's refusal to comment on the subject deeply angered and frustrated his opponents. But what made them angry in Thomas's case did not make them angry in others. Years later, Ruth Bader Ginsburg—President Bill Clinton's nominee—also declined to talk about abortion. The reaction of the women's groups and civil rights groups? They applauded lustily, offering garlands of congratulations and paeans of praise. Double standard? What double standard?

All of this opprobrium and ridicule was heaped upon the head of Clarence Thomas long before the world ever heard of Long Dong Silver and tainted cans of Coke. And yet the savage campaign against him did not appear destined to succeed. By late September, we were preparing to vote on the nomination. Despite the efforts of an unconscionably bitter and biased alliance of special interests, and despite the complicity of the press, it appeared that Thomas would be confirmed.

Then came Anita Hill.

The Senate Judiciary Committee became aware of Hill a few days before we were scheduled to vote. The FBI had interviewed both her and Judge Thomas. We were presented with the results of its investigation. Few people who followed the media coverage of that story would ever believe it now, but when Hill was first contacted by committee staff, she did not in any way allege that Clarence Thomas had harassed her sexually. She said she merely wanted the committee "to be aware of his behavior." It is important to understand that the FBI doesn't leave anything out of its investigative reports. The agents simply compile reams of unsubstantiated information—complaints from an ex-wife, rumors of an individual's sexual prowess, whatever—and put it all together in a folder for the committee to see. Despite this bizarre, catch-all method of investigation, in the case of Clarence Thomas, there was never a single accusation of sexual harassment lodged by Anita Hill or anyone else. With regard to Thomas's "behavior," the judge vehemently denied Hill's allegations. It was simply her word against his. Furthermore, and most important, we Senate committee members were informed that Anita Hill had not wanted her name to become public, and had not wanted Clarence Thomas to even know she was leveling these accusations.

Some would later claim that those of us on the Judiciary Committee "just didn't get it"—that we over-the-hill, bald-headed white guys somehow did not appreciate what Hill was saying. Believe me, we got it. Each member fully understood the sensitivity and gravity of the situation. Most of us had once practiced law for a living. But what were we to believe? On one hand we had Clarence Thomas, whom we knew. The U.S. Senate had confirmed Thomas for three jobs in the past, and not once had any one of us heard any of Anita Hill's allegations, or even her name. On the other hand, we had Anita Hill. She was a mystery witness who was trying desperately not to come forward publicly and who did not wish her name to be known to the accused. Senator Jack Danforth, Clarence Thomas's sponsor and good friend, was adamant that we go ahead with our confirmation vote. What would justify a delay? Some on our committee apparently thought more of Hill's revelations than I did; our vote wound up in a 7–7 tie, and the nomination was sent to the Senate with no recommendation.

We now know that certain activist women's rights advocates were also aware of the things Anita Hill was saying. One book on the subject revealed that in a phone call to a financial contributor, Kate Michelman of the National Abortion Rights League boasted that she had information that would certainly force Clarence Thomas to withdraw his nomination. The fond hope of the liberal lobby was that the information could be used to scare Thomas off—and that Anita Hill could remain forever anonymous. When it became clear that Hill would indeed have to go public if Thomas was to be properly done away with, the liberals relied on their old friends—and willing tools—in the media.

Somebody—a member of a Senate staff? a member of the Judiciary Committee?—decided that the public had a right to know about this woman's wholly unsubstantiated allegations. The informant, whoever he or she was, delivered Hill's confidential statements and even the FBI report to writer Tim Phelps of *Newsday* in New York and to Nina Totenberg of National Public Radio. Both reporters worked frantically and hysterically to get the story (indeed, to get Clarence Thomas), only to have Anita Hill at first refuse to cooperate. This numbed, saddened, utterly reluctant witness knew even then that her life could well be ruined if her name became public. That was no concern of Nina Totenberg, who told Hill at one point that the story was "out there" and that she planned to go with it even if Hill did not cooperate. Eventually, Hill broke down and gave the interview.

The leak of the FBI reports came as no surprise to anyone who knows Washington. It's unfortunate, but true: This town could not function without leaks. Sometimes, opponents of a certain idea float it in hopes that someone will shoot it down immediately. A clever bureaucrat may leak information to a special interest group as a way of preventing the implementation of a policy he or she has always resisted. Every presidential administration leaks idle thoughts and solid ideas in an effort to see how people respond before any official decision is made by the president. A lot of presidential insiders love this tactic because they know that the stinking bad idea—if it is judged to be that bad—will never be associated with their guy, the prez. All this talk about leaking reminds me of the guy who would go to church and renounce drink once a year, then go back to a life of sin, booze, women, and song. One year at the altar rail he cried, "Fill me up, Lord! Fill me up!" And a guy in the back hollered, "Don't do it. He leaks!" That's Washington.

Whatever the leakers' motivations, the media always lap up leaked information with real excitement. Leaked information has an air of mystery, and the ego-driven reporter who gets it cannot resist the sense that he or she has acquired something special. Holy, even. Media people should be more suspicious of those who try to pass off information quietly and anonymously, but in their clamoring desire to get a scoop, they rarely consider the motivations of their sources.

I don't think Nina Totenberg was very much concerned with the motivation of the person or people who leaked her the information about Clarence Thomas. If anything, she eagerly supported the leakers' agenda—to defeat the nomination of Clarence Thomas as associate justice of the United States Supreme Court. Which is precisely why they chose her. Surely no one with a lick of sense would argue with the notion that Thomas's liberal opponents believed that Totenberg would tell the story the way they wanted it told. Her reporting on that nomination, and on the Bork nomination before it, always had a clear liberal slant.

One night during the Thomas debacle, I attempted to make that very point on Ted Koppel's *Nightline* show. Nina Totenberg was also a guest that evening. During our debate, I said, "What politicians get tired of is bias in reporters. You've been beating the drums on this one almost every day since it started in the most extraordinary way. Let's not pretend that you're being objective here. That just would be absurd."

Nina said, "Senator, you've attacked me. May I respond? . . . I do not appreciate being blamed just because I do my job and report the news."

"I didn't ask you to appreciate it," I said.

Later, Nina and I got into quite a "conversation" out in the parking lot. I had my copy of the journalists' code of ethics with me, and I started pointing out sections she had violated. I told her, "I just wanted to tell you those things I said were not said lightly. I meant everything I said."

Nina Totenberg shouted, "[Sex act] you! You big [body part]! You are so full of [human by-product]!"

"Nina, you love to dish it out, but you sure don't like to take it," I said.

"[Sex act] you! I don't have to listen to this [human by-product]! You're a bitter, evil man!"

This was the journalist whom we were supposed to trust to tell us the truth about Anita Hill and Clarence Thomas.

Nina and I made up later. She called me and asked me to join her at the National Press Club dinner. Equally eager to bury the hatchet, I agreed. I bought her a corsage, picked her up at home, and strolled into the room with Nina on my arm. Folks just about dropped dead. It was all in good fun. I enjoyed it—and her. The irony was that Nina was given the big award of the night—for her coverage of the Thomas-Hill story.

But now, back to my point. Let's assume for a moment that the public did have a right to know the content of Anita Hill's original and revised statements—neither of which, incidentally, was given under oath. If that is true, did not the public also have a right to know who was making those statements public, and why? The nation received only one part of the story—the accusations. But the public was denied any information that might have put the accusations in their proper context. By making public only part of what they knew—the information but not who provided it—Nina Totenberg and Timothy Phelps produced lively, interesting, and profoundly biased reports.

Timothy Phelps called me the night before the story broke. All I remember about the call is that he was plenty damn excited. He knew he really had a big story. But neither he nor Nina paid any attention to what would happen to either of the principals—Thomas and Hill—as a result of what they reported. What reporter would ever think of such a sensitive thing?

Her identity now glaringly revealed and her accusations luridly published, Anita Hill gathered her forces—and the forces gathered Anita Hill—for press conferences, interviews, and other forms of media manipulation. The effect of her sensational allegations put a whole new spin on the nomination, making it now a purely media-driven event rather than a thoughtful Senate proceeding in which we were to give advice and consent. This was what the liberal interest groups had wanted all along. They knew that their best chance to defeat Thomas's nomination was to convene a kangaroo court, a wild, open, unstructured series of hearings with no rules of evidence, no right of cross-examination, and no due process. If they could but accuse Thomas of enough bizarre and outlandish things, and if they could make the charges sufficiently vague and puzzling that he could not truly defend himself, maybe, just maybe, they could get rid of him for good. And so the circus began.

Perhaps the saner approach for us would have been to conduct the hearings in executive session, thereby better protecting the rights of privacy of both the nominee and the accuser. Imagine the media reaction if the chairman of the Judiciary Committee had said, "We are now going to have closed executive hearings. The parties will have their lawyers present. The hearing will be conducted under the rules of evidence as defined in the federal code of civil procedure, with all rights of discovery, due process, and cross-examination." The media would have pulled the whole temple down around our ears.

Anita Hill soon appeared before the Judiciary Committee. I must say I was honestly shocked at her testimony—not because of what she was saying, but because she had never said it before. The FBI agents investigating the case had told Hill during her initial interview to be as frank, direct, and specific as possible. One of the agents was a man, the other a woman. They told her that the male agent would leave the room if she felt at all uncomfortable with him there. Hill told them that would not be necessary. And then she told her story. She made no mention of pubic hair on Coke cans or of the X-rated-movie character Long Dong Silver. But now here she was before us, giving us explicit detail about things she had not even mentioned to the FBI. How odd that she had forgotten those seemingly unforgettable dramatic details during her exhaustive interview with federal agents. How odd that she recalled them only now, under the bright television lights in our committee room.

Perhaps in her nervousness, she simply forgot to mention those things to the FBI. But even if she did, why didn't she come forward on any of the three previous occasions during which Clarence Thomas was confirmed by a Democratically controlled Senate? Where were Anita Hill and Long Dong Silver when Thomas was being considered for a position on the federal appellate bench? That was a time in Hill's life when she had absolutely no professional—and little personal—contact with Thomas, and thus presumably would have had nothing to lose professionally by coming forward.

But if Clarence Thomas had not talked to Anita Hill about Long Dong Silver, where did she hear about this generously endowed chap? Senator Orrin Hatch eventually offered a possible explanation: Long Dong Silver was mentioned in a federal sexual harassment case from her jurisdiction that Anita Hill might well have seen during her tenure as a law professor.

The media found their darling in Anita Hill, a symbol of all that was supposedly wrong with modern male America. She was portrayed as a tragic victim, then applauded for her courage in coming forward to tell the truth about this ogre. And yet the public did not quite see her in the same way the media did. According to various polls at the time, most Americans believed Anita Hill was not telling the truth. The media skewed reality so thoroughly that someone would ask me three years later if I was one of the senators involved in the "Anita Hill rape trial."

The media later portrayed an equally jaded and slanted picture of my able Senate colleague Arlen Specter. During the hearings, Specter asked a wholly rational, legal, and professional series of questions of Professor Hill. Among them, he asked whether she had ever been told that Clarence Thomas would withdraw as a nominee if she came forward with her story. At first she said she could not recall whether she had been told that. Later she said yes, she had been told that. Specter was right on target with his observation that Hill would have been guilty of perjury if she had not changed her story. But when a female candidate challenged Specter for his Pennsylvania Senate seat, the media were overly eager to portray it as the Year of the Woman. The implication was that Specter's hard questioning of Anita Hill was somehow not part of his duty and responsibility as a committee member—that, instead, he had questioned Professor Hill vigorously just to give her a rough time. What bullshit. The media did not mention that in this so-called Year of the Woman, Specter was supported in his campaign by thoughtful women of every creed, color, and philosophy—women who testified to his fundamental honesty and intellectual prowess and strength. Specter told the truth about Anita Hill, and for that he was poleaxed.

The only individual who even attempted to offer any corroboration of Anita Hill's testimony—in the true legal sense—was the redoubtable, stoic, and icy Judge Susan Hoerchner. But her testimony about the timing and substance of Anita Hill's conversations with her about Clarence Thomas was wholly inconsistent. She almost seemed to be making it up as she went. Hoerchner may also have committed perjury with regard to her own previous accusations of sexual harassment against a colleague in California. She said first that she had never made such an allegation, then backpedaled when confronted with documents, names, places, and events that fully contradicted her sworn testimony. Hoerchner was one tough, obsessed, driven woman, horrified by the idea that Thomas would surely be the swing vote to overturn *Roe* v. *Wade*.

Clarence Thomas came eloquently, fiercely, proudly, and passionately to his own defense, denying every detail of Hill's allegations. He could think of nothing in his relationship with his accuser—or with anyone else—that could possibly be construed as sexual harassment. His testimony was supported by numerous women who had worked closely with him over the years. If he had been the sort of man to sexually harass his employees, why had he harassed only one? If he were the kind of man who made wholly inappropriate remarks to one woman, would he not have made them to others?

Could it be that Clarence Thomas was telling the truth? I feel very much so. If the allegations against Judge Thomas had been aired in any court of law, he would have been fully exonerated, whether the standard was the preponderance of the evidence, as in a civil trial, or guilt beyond a reasonable doubt, as in a criminal one. And so, when his confirmation came before the full Senate, I cast my vote in his favor. Thomas was confirmed 52–48, and thus became a member of the United States Supreme Court. And yet he was found guilty in the court convened by the liberal media, who tried—and are still trying—to sentence him to a life of scorn and ridicule.

I thoroughly reject the notion that sixteen white, middle-aged (or older) males on the Senate Judiciary Committee were incapable of feeling any compassion for a victim of sexual harassment. To say such a thing is to engage in exactly the same kind of bigoted stereotyping of which we were accused, but were innocent of. I also reject the idea that the Judiciary Committee was incapable of conducting a bipartisan, thoughtful, thorough investigation of Anita Hill. Given a full opportunity, we would have found the true reason for her increasingly graphic and dramatic accusations. But the liberal groups and the sheeplike media were not interested in witnessing a thoughtful, reasoned, and honest investigation. They wanted a circus, and they made damn sure they got one.

After Thomas was confirmed, the media hung targets on all of us. Perhaps the largest target was posted on me—front and back! During those hearings, I made several remarks that made the liberal groups and the liberal press unhappy. At one point, I told Clarence Thomas: "You have been before us for 105 days. We have seen everything, known everything, heard every bit of 'dirt,' as you call it so well. And what do we know about Professor Hill? Not very much. I am waiting for 105 days of surveillance of Ms. Hill and then we will see, you know, who ate the cabbage, as we say out in the Wild West. This is an impossible thing.

"And now, I really am getting stuff over the transom about Professor Hill. I've got letters hanging out of my pockets. I've got faxes. I've got statements from her former law professors, statements from people that know her, statements from Tulsa, Oklahoma, saying, 'Watch out for this woman!' But nobody has got the guts to say that because it gets all tangled up in this sexual harassment crap!"

Yes, that is exactly what I said. I wouldn't take back a word of it.

I went on, "I believe sexual harassment is a terrible thing. I had a bill in a year ago, doubling the penalties on sexual harassment. I don't need any test. Don't need anybody to give me the saliva test on whether one believes more or less about sexual harassment. It is repugnant, it is disgusting in any form. And the stuff we listened to. I mean, you know, come on—from the moon."

I said a lot of other things, too—before and after. But those particular comments landed me in a large caldron of boiling hot oil. The champions of Anita Hill, in concert with many of those in the fawning media, zeroed in on two elements of that statement—the part about stuff coming in "over the transom" and the infamous and indelicate phrase "sexual harassment crap."

It would have been nice—and yes, even fair—if the media had used the same standard to judge Anita Hill that they had used to judge Clarence Thomas. Remember, Thomas's opponents had gone so far as to advertise for harmful information about the man. They literally ran full-page ads in America's newspapers asking people to grab a spade and shovel dirt on him. They distorted his religious beliefs, invaded his privacy with stories about his first marriage, even read the titles of the books in his garage. The media saw few problems with any of that. But when I said in exasperation that people were sending me unsolicited information about Anita Hill by fax, phone, and memo, the Fourth Estate said I was out of line. Why? If it was all right to sully the reputation of Clarence Thomas with absurd, unprovable, and half-sick allegations, why was it not all right to report what people were saying about Anita Hill?

No reason that I could think of. Finally, I went to the Senate floor and reported some of what I was hearing and reading, since reporters from the *Washington Post* and the Los Angeles *Times Mirror* refused to print the letters from the woman lawyer from Tulsa and the one from the law school dean and an affidavit from a member of her former law firm. So you will find my remarks and

those of others in the *Congressional Record* of October 15, 1991.
You can be sure that most of the material there painted a less than
dazzling portrait of one Professor Hill. The accusations I read into
the record did not prove her guilty of anything—any more than
her allegations proved Clarence Thomas guilty. I just wanted people to be "aware of her behavior." The stuff I read into the record
may have been no more credible than the stuff people were using
to discredit Clarence Thomas.

I knew the time would come when the press would come full-
bore after me; after all, I was not only a conservative Republican
senator, but one who constantly and loudly criticized the media.
My friend Bill Cohen had warned me years earlier that my road
down from the mountaintop would be rutty, steep, and bumpy as
hell. It sure was. In the weeks after the hearings, some of my oldest
"friends" in the journalism business did their damnedest to portray
me as a nasty, stooped, and stupid relic. The media took everything
I did—even the little things of life, things of the heart—grotesquely out of context, and sometimes printed things that were
simply lies.

Ann's sixtieth-birthday celebration is a vivid example. For her
big day, Ann planned a luncheon at the Capitol Building. Scheduled to attend were our daughter, Susan, Barbara Bush, Lynne
Cheney (wife of the secretary of defense), wives of senators, Ann's
business associates, and many old and new friends. Ann was excited
about it. A few nights before the luncheon, I asked genially, "Am
I invited?"

"No, you are not!" She smiled. "But you can drop by for
exactly two and a half minutes."

On the day of the party, I did just that. I stepped right over to
Ann's place at the table, stood behind her chair with my hands
gently on her shoulders, and raised a toast in her honor. I said it
had been a singularly marvelous thing for me to have shared thirty-
seven years of my life with her. I noted that she was born on the
tenth day of the tenth month, and that she was therefore a "ten"
in every way. I said she had been a magnificent mother to three
loving children, and that I never would have dreamed when I
married at twenty-two that I would ever sleep with such a beautiful

sixty-year-old woman. I remember Barbara Bush saying, "Oh, Al! You are a fright!" Lynne Cheney laughed and said, "I swear, Ann, what do you do with him?" Others said, "You'll never get him trained!"

After a few more minutes of banter Ann said, "Okay, Al, that's enough. Love you. Now you're out of here!" I said good-bye to everyone, kissed Ann, and sidled out the door. It was a fun time.

There was nothing fun about reading the *Washington Post*'s story about the event. No media people were present—none were invited—and yet the *Post* somehow strung together an account of what happened that day. You assess the fairness and accuracy (or lack thereof) in this story:

> It's been a rough couple of weeks for Alan Simpson, the tart tongued senator from Wyoming who has been slapped around by some pretty strong women of late. Now you can add Barbara Bush to the list.
>
> At a 60th birthday luncheon last Thursday for his wife, Anne (sic), the Republican senator stopped by the Capitol and wedged his foot firmly in his mouth.
>
> In his younger days, noted the senator, "I never imagined I'd be sleeping with a 60-year-old woman." There was, said two guests, a stilted ripple of laughter.
>
> "Well, that wasn't very funny!" jokingly shot back Mrs. Bush, one of 12 women invited to the party.
>
> "I guess I better leave now," said the man who is rarely at a loss for words.
>
> And he did.

Apparently somebody at the party casually told the anecdote to someone else, only to have the truth hideously gnarled and twisted in the newspaper. I had not wedged my foot in my mouth, nor had I been "slapped around" by Barbara Bush, who seemed to genuinely enjoy my joke. There was no "stilted ripple of laughter." To have my loving words for Ann portrayed as a crude, sexist rant simply stunned me; I felt I had been slugged in the gut. I know, I know. I'm not supposed to be that sensitive. But I am!

Then there was the coverage of a confrontation I had with Betty Friedan, the liberal feminist Democrat. Reading the stories, you would have thought I had provoked her. Hardly! Friedan was in one of the hallways of the Capitol Building one day. When I saw her, I walked forward and extended my hand, saying, "How are you? You've been a busy one!"

Betty Friedan refused to shake my hand. Instead, she sneered, swung her hand away, and pulled it behind her back. She told me I was an evil and foul man. Then she said—in a jocular way—that she and her feminist friends had hung my picture on the wall in their office and occasionally threw darts at it. I had a chuckle out of that. Then she told me that she and her friends would work hard to defeat me in the next election.

"Do you really and truly believe that you alone speak for all the women of America?"

"Yes, I do!" she said.

I told her she was full of it. I said that what hurt the feminist cause most was her and her supporters' arrogance and lack of civility. Anyone who cannot muster the decency to shake the hand of an ideological opponent cannot hope to inspire much confidence in the American public. She went off in a huff. Some media people overheard what happened—but they didn't report it quite the way it happened. The coverage of that encounter took on a decidedly nasty, mean-spirited, anti-Simpson slant. For example, the headline in the *Washington Post* said, "The Senator's Spat with the Feminist."

What spat? I offered to shake her hand and tried to begin a civil conversation, but Betty Friedan wasn't interested.

On another occasion, Molly Yard, president of the National Organization for Women, was being interviewed by a reporter and a cameraman in the hallway of the Dirksen Building. Molly is one snappish and tough woman who could make a stevedore blush when she starts spewing it out. I walked by, waved, and said, "How are you, Molly?" My greeting was met with a snarl and a quickly turned back. Molly Yard actually stalked away, rounding the corner into the next hallway. The camera was still cranking, so I stepped in front of it and said something like "How about that? I think that was about the rudest thing I've seen around this place. These people love to dish it out and then take everything personally and then just stomp around like that." I kept going for a while. I was saying what needed saying.

Within moments, one of Molly Yard's staff people appeared, almost dragging Molly, who said, "I didn't mean to be rude; it's just that we really can't stand you." Thanks for clearing that up! My hunch is that when the staff person saw me speaking glibly to the camera, she ran to her boss and said, "Molly, you'd better get out there. He's getting in his licks on you and all they have is the footage of you spinning on your heels and stalking off." So back she came. What a bunch!

By this time, I was feeling myself wearing thin. The media had really poured it to me. One day in October I shared lunch at the White House with the president and staff members Boyden Gray and John Sununu. I remember that I told a pretty good (and pretty shaggy) joke, but not with the usual enthusiasm. I felt beaten down by my scraps with the press—fights I brought on myself, and fights I had waged on behalf of my president. When I finished eating, I pushed back my chair, stood up, and told George Bush, "I find it harder to be able to really help you as I have before. Because I want so to defend you—and in defending you I finally get defensive. I'm not doing myself much good either. Because when I defend myself and am always on the prod, I'm getting testy as hell too."

The president placed his hand lightly on my arm and said, "Now, Al, I deeply appreciate what you did for me. Don't be down." We talked a while longer—I don't remember much more of what was said—and then I went back to my office.

Later in the afternoon I received a hand-delivered manila envelope from the White House marked "Personal and Confidential." Inside was a three-page, handwritten letter on White House stationery. The handwriting was unmistakably that of George Bush.

"After you left today I got to worrying," he wrote. "I don't like to see my friend burdened down by anything at all. You seemed a little low.

"The joke was vintage Simpson alright, but I am concerned that the press bashing may have been weighing on you.

"You were right on all this. You helped a decent man turn the tide.

"You walked where angels feared to tread by zapping some groups and some press; and in the process, they climbed all over your ass—but dammit you were right!

"Besides, even though some were sore at you, they won't stay sore. They like you. They respect you and they know you to be fair."

George went on to share some of his own intimate feelings about the burdens of the presidency. Then he concluded, "This President depends on you and believes in you and is grateful to you.

"Nothing you can do can change that. Abortion, immigration, deficits, Judiciary hearings, all those together pale in importance when up against friendship.

"George."

Should there ever be any wonder about how strongly I feel about George Bush, my friend?

I needed that lift, because the media kept hacking away. Another example was the reporting of an incident at the White House on the day of Clarence Thomas's swearing-in ceremony. That was one great day—sunny, fresh, the skies bright blue. Justice Byron White swore in his new colleague. I sat with members of Clarence's family. After the long ordeal they were grateful and relieved, but also deeply bruised. I visited with Clarence's mother, with his father (who had returned from a long absence to be with his son on this special day), with Clarence's son, Jamal, and finally with his wife, Ginni (whom I had known and admired long before I knew Clarence), and her proud parents. After a while, some of Clarence's closest friends surrounded me and began asking for my autograph. Don't think I didn't love that! Especially after all the crap I had been taking.

Mary McGrory, the syndicated columnist and experienced ace reporter, was standing nearby. Mary is bright, strong-willed, wise—and determined. But you can talk to her. She will hear you.

She will listen. She has never twisted or distorted anything I've ever told her. She could see that big smile playing on my face as I stood tall among Clarence's friends. She smiled and said, "You're loving this, aren't you?"

"Boy, I sure am—I needed this!" I said.

Then Barbara Bush did something that made me even happier. After the ceremony, she wagged a finger at me and said, "Come on over here, Al. Let's have our picture taken together. I'll tell them I love you instead of all that rubbish about Ann's birthday!" That's Barbara Bush. She gave me a big smacker and sent me on my way.

Soon it was time to go. I was bound for Wyoming that afternoon, and departure time was coming. I left by the northwest gate of the White House, walking through security to my car, which was waiting to take me to the airport. I was about to step in when I saw a man swiftly approaching me. He looked rather disheveled; he had a heavy beard, hair down over his shoulders, and flashing eyes. The fellow said, "You murderer. You put a man on the Court who is for abortion—who will kill babies." What? For five months, all we had heard was that Clarence Thomas was going to make abortion illegal forever. This guy was a loon. The light was on but nobody was home.

As I ducked into the car he shouted, "I curse you in the name of Jesus Christ!"

Well, I couldn't let that go. That's my failing; I always take 'em on. I told the guy, "What a terrible name to use to put a curse on someone." Then I waved him off—without using any digital gestures—and headed for the airport.

I remember turning to Eugene Barton, the driver, and sighing, "How about that? That's the way it goes in our line of work."

"I don't know how you people handle those kind," he said.

I didn't see any media people there, but sure enough, the *Washington Post* had a very brief story on the incident. And what did the story say? Here it is.

"Capping an active week in which he offended both Betty Friedan and Barbara Bush, Sen. Alan Simpson (R-Wyo.) yesterday mixed it up with a protester outside the White House. Leaving via the West Gate after the swearing-in ceremony of Supreme Court Justice Clarence Thomas, Simpson was seen leaning out of his chauffeured car, shaking his fist and trading epithets with a man carrying an anti-Thomas sign."

How wrong is this account? Let me count the ways. First, I did not offend Betty Friedan; she offended me. Second, I most surely did not offend Barbara Bush, who is my friend and who knows a joke when she hears one. Third, I did not shake my fist or use any epithets. Fourth, the guy who accosted me was not carrying a sign.

That's a lot of errors in a one-paragraph story. But the individual mistakes are not important. What matters is the unfairness of the whole story. I was portrayed as someone who goes around randomly offending people, and who then goes berserk when approached by a mild-mannered citizen exercising his right to protest. I was stunned to see how casually the *Post* went about casting me in this light. To the newspaper, the story was just a "cute" item on the Personalities page. To me, it was character assassination—part of a disconcerting pattern.

Ann and I headed for Wyoming for a weekend slate of activities. The criticism had been raining down on me hard in those days following the Senate vote. I was hurt and saddened. I knew there were damn sure some lessons I needed to learn, and some accusations about me that damn sure weren't fair, and never would be. I needed some time to sort out the difference.

Alas, I would not get it, at least not right away. In Laramie I was met by a group of protesters. Ann was there with me. When the protesters saw her, some of them looked embarrassed. Here I was, stepping out of the car with this bright, independent, modern woman. Some of the slogans on their protest signs didn't gibe much with reality.

On our second day in our home state, Annie and I went to Cheyenne for a "roast and toast" dinner in my honor. Sometimes those old roasts get out of hand, but I knew that this one would be good fun. It was planned by many wonderful friends and supporters, people who genuinely cared about me and Ann. I knew, too, that this would be an audience that would be willing to hear how I was really feeling. That afternoon before the dinner I told Annie, "I've just got to get some of this stuff off my chest. It's getting all clogged up down in there." As always, she patiently listened to what I wanted to say, then helped me to cast it in just the right way. While she talked, I scribbled, writing and rewriting.

The evening was all that I'd imagined it would be. I listened to a lot of great and goofy stories and kind words and good-natured ribbing. And then I stood up and said my piece.

"I see some of my previous life's behavior held up to a prism I had never noticed before, through different eyes," I said. "It has been personally uncomfortable to see your good name equated with McCarthy, sleaze, slime, smarmy, evil, ugly, mean-spirited, slasher, vindictive, menacing, and much more.

"I have been riding high, a bit too cocky, arrogant—and yeah—too smart by half sometimes. I do not blame the media for anything, nothing. They are blameless. I don't blame radical women's groups. The responsibility is mine and I shall handle it well."

I said more, too. I got it all out, and it felt good. I was pleased by the response. Heads nodded and eyes welled up. A few people looked puzzled, as if they were thinking, I wonder if the pressure is getting to Al. Well, they were right. It was.

A few newspaper reporters and TV people were present. The coverage said a lot about the way the media filter things. The early reports said I "expressed remorse" or "apologized" for my actions during the Anita Hill spectacle. But I didn't. What I did was to take responsibility for my own actions. I was not sorry at all that I had vigorously defended Clarence Thomas, who I believed deserved to be confirmed to the Supreme Court. I felt no remorse about having been skeptical—at times bitterly so—of Anita Hill's increasingly outlandish and weird statements. In my speech in Wyoming, I was merely acknowledging my personal role in bringing on whatever criticism I had received. Some reports suggested that I made my "apology" because of the chilly reception I had received in Laramie. And maybe that is partly true. But that was not the big "why."

The Hill-Thomas saga had taught me an important lesson about myself. When I keep an emotional distance from the work I am doing, I tend to do it calmly, and well. But when I internalize a problem—when I see someone else's battle and begin fighting it as if it were my own—I quickly can become ferocious. Often still effective, but definitely ferocious. When I see someone else being wronged and think, How would I feel if it were me?—well, that is when I need to lean back in my chair and just think for a bit, because I really fire up when I feel that. I had internalized Clarence Thomas's struggle, fought the good fight as if it were my own. And so I had done things that invited criticism. But even as I learned this lesson, I knew the Thomas case would not be the last time I internalized something in that way. I knew well I would eventually come to somebody's defense again. Damn betcha!

Several years have passed since Clarence Thomas was confirmed, and yet the radical women's groups and liberal media are still desperately trying to rewrite history. A *Wall Street Journal/ NBC News* poll taken during the Judiciary Committee hearings of October 1991 showed that Americans believed Clarence Thomas over Anita Hill by 47 percent to 24 percent. A year after the hearings, a new poll showed that the majority of people now believed Anita Hill, 44 percent to 34 percent. What had happened? Well, the media had written and broadcast a metric ton of slanted, ridiculous garbage in that year, and a lot of people had swallowed it—instead of believing their own eyes and ears.

The worst example of this media revisionism was the "review" in *The New Yorker* of David Brock's *The Real Anita Hill,* a book which had previously received rather positive notices in the *Washington Post,* the *New York Times*, and other major papers. The two reviewers for *The New Yorker* viciously trashed the book and its author; they smeared Brock as an unethical partisan and his book as an anti-Hill manifesto. This was not too surprising, for they themselves were working on a book on the same subject, except theirs was pro–Anita Hill. Apparently the only way they could justify their own shoddy, biased work was to tear down the conclusions of someone who disagreed with them. What's ethical about that? The new elite running *The New Yorker* should be ashamed. But don't count on it!

I learned some other lessons from the volatile confirmation hearings on Thomas, but I'm not sure the Fourth Estate did. The media continue to find the personal lives of public officials far more titillating, riveting, and marketable than their professional lives. The precious right to privacy which reporters are so quick to claim for themselves is brushed aside when the private life is somebody else's.

There were damn sure no winners in the Hill-Thomas story. Clarence Thomas will sit in judgment on the U.S. Supreme Court for many years to come, but will probably never shake off all the personal pain and suffering he had to endure. Anita Hill is touring the country giving speeches at a few grand a pop, and yet she will never cease to be regarded as a curiosity, revered by some and despised by others. Her privacy too is gone forever.

The U.S. Senate suffered an all-out assault on its integrity. The attack was launched in part by people who themselves were candidates for public office. In 1992, four more women members joined the Senate, and one—Diane Feinstein of California—joined the Judiciary Committee. She adds a positive dimension to the committee's workings. Still, it remains to be seen whether the "Anita Hill class" will make perceptible changes in the Senate. The Year of the Woman cannot yet be judged by history. (As a side note, it may be worth saying that 1990 was also a year of the woman. In that year, six women were running for the U.S. Senate. The press did not make too much of that though, because those women had what the press considers a serious political and personality flaw: They had an R next to their names instead of a D.)

The Hill-Thomas hearings changed the way I lived for a time. Certainly, I remained viscerally opposed to the tactics of those who tried to strip all sense of honor and respect from a decent and sensitive nominee. But I no longer trumpeted my feelings. Instead, I lay low for a while, canceling social engagements and staying away from some of those big Washington dinner parties. I felt good doing that, because that quiet time really gave me a chance to rethink. When I reflected on those hearings, I could say, "Simpson, just because you get a bellyful of something doesn't mean you have to do things the way you did them there."

I would hope all of us involved in that nomination process learned a similar lesson.

CHAPTER TEN

Pols, Polls, and the Press

L ong before Americans trudged to their polling places on November 3, 1992, they already pretty well knew that Bill Clinton had defeated George Bush and thus would become the next president. Indeed, the voters knew not only who would win, but also why he would win. They knew all this because the media told them so. The whole election was a done deal before the first ballot was even cast.

The media knew what would happen because they commissioned many a public opinion poll in an effort to find out. The practice of buying information in this way has become very fashionable in big-bucks journalism. The graphs and charts we see on our televisions and in our newspapers are all very attractive—and their effect is subtly manipulative. The media use polls not just to tell us what we think. They also use them to tell us what *to* think.

There are too numerous problems with the media's use of polls. Probably the most obvious is that the polls too often portray campaigns as mere horse races. (Know the difference between a horse race and a political race? In a horse race, the entire horse runs!

Enough.) The polls tell us whether a certain candidate is ahead or behind, but don't tell us much of what the candidate believes. How many times have you heard news reports about a presidential candidate who is losing crucial support in the South, is suffering an erosion of his backing in the West, is seeing the North rise up in arms against him, or whatever? Poll results such as these tell us what is happening, but don't say why. What is it that the candidate is saying or doing that is causing the erosion (or strengthening) of support? We are rarely told. Instead, we are told only who is going to win based on the opinions of a small sampling of voters. Such superficial reporting robs citizens of the basic right to cast a ballot based solely upon their own views of the candidates. And it surely diminishes people's sense that their votes make a difference. Ross Perot brilliantly capitalized on this phenomenon when he chirped, "Don't let 'em tell you what to do. Don't listen to the boobs on the banks of the Potomac. Don't listen to the elite. Don't listen to the media. Just vote your conscience." In other words, vote for him!

Years ago, public opinion polls were largely the province of the Gallop and Harris organizations. These companies would conduct fairly broad-based national polls on a variety of issues, with varying degrees of accuracy. Soon, politicians figured out that they could benefit handsomely from having some of this information, especially during campaigns. Today, the hiring of a reputable pollster is an important decision in any campaign, even a local one. I hired a pollster in all three of my U.S. Senate campaigns, but never had one on board in the interims. Understood properly, polls can help in establishing campaign tactics and strategy. But any good politician also knows that polls can be highly subjective, and are readily distorted.

Then the media got into the act. In the 1970s and 1980s, journalists began to see that political campaigns often had better information about what people were thinking than they did. You can imagine their feelings of surprise and vexation when they realized that the politicians had scooped them! And so the media began paying for polls too.

The media companies soon figured out what every beleaguered

politician has always known—that polling is damnably expensive. The big-time journalism outfits realized they could save money without giving up too much of their competitive advantage by joining up with other media outlets to commission polls. These days, you might see the *Washington Post* and ABC teaming up to conduct one poll, and the *New York Times* and CBS commissioning another. These relationships change frequently. The polling alliances may work nicely for the companies involved, but I don't think they do much to further the cause of good journalism. When two big companies—say, a television network and one of the major newspapers—gather and convey exactly the same information, with exactly the same emphasis on certain facts, the public gets a smaller serving of news than it might have received from two competing companies. When media outlets get together in this way, originality does suffer and the public gets the sense that there is only one sanctioned way to view the world. Never mind that any poll—even the most reputable—reflects only the views of a certain subset of us at a fleeting, flashing moment of time.

Perhaps worse, these same poll results eventually dictate which stories the major media cover, and how closely they cover them. Inevitably, the media will produce stories that confirm their poll results—especially when the poll results seem to favor a liberal rather than conservative candidate. The media also tend to focus on the few issues that were discussed in the polls. As a result, lots of worthwhile stories don't get done. The media commission poll after poll about abortion, the death penalty, gun control, and the deficit, and thus during campaigns we rarely read about anything else.

That great old journalism teacher, Miss Gertrude Smith, would be appalled at the way today's journalists use the information they glean from polls. The media use this material in a way that goes far beyond the trusty who, what, where, when, and why of good journalism. Indeed, they use this objective information to make wholly subjective—and highly debatable—pronouncements. We all have seen stories in which a certain candidate is said to be 10 percentage points behind his or her opponent just a short time before the election. Such a statistic is an objective fact, assuming that the poll was done well. But the media will often use that fact to make a great leap of reasoning. They will say, "Candidate Sturdly has little chance of catching up before election day." Now, wait a minute. If the voters decide they like what candidate Sturdly is saying, he'll damn sure catch up. But the media don't let that happen; their poll-based pronouncements become self-fulfilling prophecies. People reading the papers and watching the news simply assume that poor old Sturdly is going to be history, so why waste time going to the polls to vote for the guy?

The media misuse polls in other ways, too. When Los Angeles erupted in violence after five police officers who had been video-taped beating motorist Rodney King were found not guilty, the media covered the story in unprecedented detail. The media covered the rioting extensively, as I believe they were obligated to do. But extensive coverage wasn't enough for the mainstream media, which then crossed a thin ethical line by conducting an endless series of polls. One *New York Times* article breathlessly cited a *New York Times*/CBS News poll to support the statement that the public was "in a shaken, worried mood more likely to see the unrest as a symptom of festering social needs than as a simple issue of law and order."

Well, well. Given that you couldn't watch television or pick up a newspaper without seeing or reading of the rioting, looting, and mayhem in Los Angeles, the description of the public as shaken and worried is truly a no-brainer of huge proportions. The *Times* report continued, "There was no indication that Gov. Bill Clinton of Arkansas, the likely Democratic nominee, or Ross Perot, a likely independent candidate, was gaining much of an immediate advantage from the episode. Still, the poll suggested that the issues of race and poverty weigh heavily on the public's mind these days, and will doubtless figure in the campaign debate." Again, it was obvious that many Americans were thinking about race and poverty. But by commissioning a poll during such an emotional time, the media probably gave those issues far more prominence than they were really going to have in the election.

The *Times* story went on to handily fix the blame for what was happening: "President Bush, who pledged his commitment to the stricken neighborhoods of Los Angeles last week, was given poor marks by both blacks and whites for his response to the riots. Moreover, 53 percent of all whites and 76 percent of all blacks said they disapproved of the way Mr. Bush was handling race relations in general." Please. Anybody who turned on CNN was going to feel that race relations in America were being handled badly. The city was on fire! It seems to me incredibly unfair to reach conclusions about the quality of a presidency—any presidency—based on such loaded questions at such a volatile time.

In their effort to entertain their audiences—for surely the news business is known to most of us now as an entertainment business—the news media give us great dollops of distortion, hype, hyperventilation, and manipulation, all presented to us as objective reporting.

During election time, the media freely and blithely insert value judgments about candidates into their supposedly objective reports. Television people do this all the time. It is easy to see whether a network news reporter likes or dislikes a candidate; each story is either grossly positive or grossly negative. What matters to the network journalist is not laying out the five W's, but often only making a name for himself or herself. When reporting on polls, the networks always clearly identify one candidate as "winner" and the other as "loser." Why? Because the complex issues of a campaign are never as interesting as that good horse race.

As I've said, the Democrat is often the candidate who is portrayed as the winning horse, while the Republican is described as the horse's rump. The research supports what I'm saying. The Center for Media and Public Affairs is a nonprofit organization based in Washington, D.C., which does extensive studies on the media coverage of politics. From what I have been able to discern, it is completely nonpartisan. The center's August/September 1992 newsletter contained these conclusions about the Bush-Clinton presidential race:

Horse race evaluations include assessments of poll results, campaign organization and fund raising, crowd response, interest group support, etc. Since late June these reports

have been far kinder toward Clinton than Bush. During
the first three weeks after the primaries ended, Clinton's
horse race notices were 69 percent negative. Since then
they have been 83 percent positive. The perception that
he had enjoyed a successful convention, coupled with his
upward movement in the polls, triggered a wave of positive horse race evaluations for Clinton. On the Democrats'
post convention bus tour, for example, Richard Threlkeld
described the crowds as "big, vocal and enthusiastic" (CBS
7/18), while Garrick Utley said Clinton was "on a roll"
(NBC 7/18). Clinton's rise served to spotlight how far
Bush had fallen. Even during the week of the Republican
convention, nearly two out of three assessments of Bush's
prospects were negative, while three out of four judgments of Clinton's chances continued to be positive.

The same organization had earlier reported that George Bush
received extremely favorable treatment during the 1988 campaign, and that the coverage of Mike Dukakis was much less
complimentary. That was surely not right, either. Whether a news
story is about Republicans or Democrats, liberals or conservatives,
it should never be kinder to one side than it is to the other.
No news report should ever be easily seen as either positive or
negative.

In recent years, thoughtful members of the Fourth Estate—and
there are many—have given serious study to ways in which journalists could do a better job of covering elections. The topic has
been at the center of countless media forums and media corpora-
tion meetings. I think the media have learned from these discussions. For example, the Center for Media and Public Affairs
reported in the same newsletter cited above that the networks increased their coverage of policy issues during the 1992 campaign.
We are also seeing less dependence on sound bites, less emphasis
on horse races, less intrusion into people's private lives. But not
much less. The media may be inching in the right direction, but
I submit that they still have a long way to go.

I was pleased to see the media begin to focus more on issues and less on spectacle. In the 1988 campaign, the media were often blatantly used by flag-waving opportunists across the political spectrum. In 1992, the media resolved to pay more attention to the issues. Trouble was that the journalists then took it upon themselves to decide just what those issues would be. They began ignoring what the candidates, their handlers, and the pollsters were saying. They did not even listen to the stump speech of the day. Instead, they pursued their own agenda. And how did they decide which issues to pursue? Ah, this is where the dog really starts chasing its tail. The media had paid for the polls which told them what a few people considered the issues to be. Then they reported stories which gave increased attention to those issues. Seeing those issues more often trumpeted in the news, the voters then declared them to be vitally important. And the circle was complete! Did the media people ever look up long enough to find out where the hell they were going?

This convoluted process severely underestimates and undersells American voters. I honestly do believe in the plain, old-fashioned notion that the basic function of journalism is simply to report the news. Instead, the national media now create the news. This is a most serious and troubling difference.

If the media would simply report what Bill Clinton said—or what Bob Dole or Steve Forbes or any of the others said—the American people could discern which one had a real vision, which one was sincere, and which one was full of crap. They really could. The elitists of the press apparently have no faith in Americans' ability to think, but they should. Many Americans are every bit the experts that the media people are. Believe it!

Some years ago I was part of a National Press Club forum on politics and the media. The panelists that day included politicians, members of the media, and various other Washington "players." Among the members of the Fourth Estate was David Broder, the highly respected and justly revered political writer and columnist for the *Washington Post*. I greatly admire Broder. He lays it all out without becoming overly judgmental and preachy. He quotes his sources by name—shocking as that sounds—and always tries to arrive at a fair version of the truth. On this particular day, however,

Broder and I would part company. During that forum, the media people beat themselves up mercilessly over their own coverage of the 1988 presidential campaign. I think some were upset simply because the "wrong" candidate won. But others legitimately felt that the campaign could have been covered in more professional fashion—that they could have given the public more useful information and less flag-waving and hooey. I agreed.

Broder was among those lamenting the superficial way in which the media covered major political campaigns. I was with him to that point. But then he cited as an example the Illinois U.S. Senate campaign between incumbent Democrat Paul Simon and Republican challenger Lynn Martin. With impatience and a tinge of disgust, Broder recalled that one major focus of that campaign was not the economy or the budget deficit, but the University of Illinois mascot. That's right, the mascot, an American Indian in full headdress. Paul Simon believed that the mascot belittled Native Americans and therefore should be changed. Fans of the school disagreed—loudly! They liked The Chief. The whole discussion erupted into charges of racism, discrimination, bigotry, and political correctness. The press diligently covered the whole dustup. That was what bothered David Broder. He deeply felt that such an ancillary issue should not be a priority in any campaign. He said he wished the press had steered the coverage back toward the "major" issues.

Dave is entitled to that opinion. But I disagree. It is not up to me, Dave, or anybody else on the outside to tell the voters which issues are "major" and which are not. I would readily concur that school mascot selection or retention is not a priority task for a United States senator. But if Joe Voter happens to believe that a candidate's position on the school mascot best defines who the candidate is, then Joe Voter has every right to so judge.

Journalism must ever be on guard against paternalism, especially when deciding which issues are "legitimate" and which are not. When journalists set the agenda, they cannot help but manipulate the news.

Now, I can earnestly empathize with the difficulties journalists encounter as they attempt to cover elective politics. The world of politics is an enormous, steaming swamp bog in which distinctions between right and wrong can easily become blurred. Finding the truth in the morass is a daunting job. But I feel the media would be well advised to trust the voters just a little bit more—and to lower the level of sarcasm, cynicism, and plain old bias in their reporting.

The media could begin by focusing less—and relying less—on the consultants who have become so prominent in American politics. These days, the political consultants are often a bigger story than the candidates themselves. Instead of focusing on what the candidates think and say and do, we are subjected to story after story about the effectiveness (or lack of effectiveness) of James Carville, Mary Matalin, Ed Rollins, Roger Ailes, Bob Squires, and the rest. These stories leave the impression that the consultants are towering Machiavellian figures possessing massive brain power, savvy, skill, and cunning—and that the candidates are bumbling, mumbling, mouth-breathing boobs who can't form an idea without "the master" at their side. That is simply wrong.

The media loved to peddle the notion that Ronald Reagan could not have been successful in politics without Mike Deaver running a super-sophisticated media manipulation machine. Roger Ailes was said to be pulling the strings at George Bush and Dan Quayle's puppet show. James Carville, we were told, performed his Cajun hoodoo magic on Bill Clinton and Al Gore, who woodenly, soulfully, and dutifully did as they were told. Ridiculous. This view of politics undersells the person who actually has the courage and energy to run and oversells the role of the advisers. The political consultants I have named are bright, witty, and clever people—every one of them. But they are hardly the whole show.

So why do the media pay so much attention to them? Silly question. Because the consultants are often their best sources during a campaign. When you read a quotation from an "anonymous" or "well-informed" source "close to the campaign," you can bet you're hearing the voice of Carville or Rollins or Ailes or some other consultant. There is a tremendous ethical conflict here. First, the media use these manipulators as their best sources during the campaign—and then produce stories glorifying these same people.

James Carville and Mary Matalin might never have sold all those
copies of their book if the American media had not first glorified
them as geniuses—and then given them exhaustive coverage during their book tour. By making stars of the consultants, the media
misled the electorate. Instead of telling Americans about the two
candidates, journalists cast the campaign as a showdown between
hired political guns. Turning a political race into a game makes for
great copy inside the Beltway, but hardly helps to furnish the kind
of information voters need if they are to make good, solid decisions
about candidates.

Whenever the media glorify someone, they eventually get
around to attacking him or her, as I have found. Roger Ailes is an
example of a political consultant who eventually got his, too.
Among political masters, Ailes is one of the biggest of the big. As
I have said, Ailes gave me some of the best media advice I ever
received. "Speak to the mike in a conversational way. Let it come
to you," he told me, and from that day forward, I did. Ailes has
dispensed equally useful political advice to hundreds of candidates
for public office. He has solved many a campaign puzzle. And for
a long time, the media portrayed him as nothing less than a genius,
often making him appear much more important and skillful than
the candidates themselves. He was really riding high. But when
Roger became a vital cog in George Bush's victorious presidential
campaign, he also became Media Enemy No. 1. The very people
who had placed him on this tall pedestal were reaching up and
trying to claw him down from it. Why? Because they blamed him
for the infamous Willie Horton campaign ad of 1988. And blamed
him wrongly.

The distortion of that tawdry tale is simply amazing. The truth
is that it was not Roger Ailes or George Bush—or anyone connected with the Bush campaign—who first introduced the issue
of furloughed killers to that campaign. No indeed—the issue was
first raised by Democratic candidate Al Gore during an April 1988
debate held prior to the New York presidential primary. I'm
sure that will come as news to most Americans. On that day in
April, Senator Al Gore, the Rev. Jesse Jackson, and Governor
Michael Dukakis of Massachusetts were all in hot pursuit of the

Democratic presidential nomination. The debate format allowed the candidates to pose questions to one another. It was in a question directed to Mike Dukakis that Al Gore first raised the specter of furloughs for convicted murderers. I quote now from the debate transcript:

"We haven't discussed the issue of crime very much. Governor Dukakis, you've been the principal advocate and defender of a program in Massachusetts that has just been canceled over your objections by the legislature. [This program] provided for weekend passes for convicted criminals, including those convicted of first-degree murder who are serving life sentences without parole. Eleven of them decided their two-week passes were not long enough and left. Two of them committed other murders while they were on their passes. If you were elected president, would you advocate a similar program for federal penitentiaries?"

Dukakis's answer was as weak as nail soup.

Later in that campaign season, the Bush campaign used the very same information Al Gore had used. Again, the idea was to attack Dukakis. The only difference was that the Bush people apparently got their message across more clearly than Gore had done. The Bush campaign ran a series of advertisements carefully and dramatically documenting the Massachusetts program and Michael Dukakis's support for it. *These ads made no mention of Willie Horton.* None. They contained no scary pictures of criminals. Still, the voters were outraged that Michael Dukakis had been so soft on crime.

Certainly Willie Horton had benefited from Michael Dukakis's leniency: While on furlough, he had committed a tragic murder. But it is important to say clearly that the Bush-Quayle campaign never once produced an advertisement bearing a picture of Horton. A third-party group that supported Bush and opposed Dukakis then exercised its rights under the First Amendment (remember it?) to run a television ad featuring Horton's picture.

The intensity of the voter reaction to the furlough program caught the Dukakis campaign—and the media—by surprise. The

Democrats and their friends in the press could hardly argue that giving furloughs to dangerous criminals was a good idea. So they used the only weapon they had—they charged Bush and the Republicans with racism. Never mind that American voters would have been just as furious with Michael Dukakis if Willie Horton had been white. For many in the Democratic Party and the media, accusing Bush of racism was one way to duck the real issue— the furlough program. It didn't sell. *The Washington Post* stated crisply:

> Add to the charges the presidential campaigns are hurling back and forth the Dukakis campaign's new charge that the Bush campaign is making racist appeals. We think it's a phony, no more credible than those vicious and baseless charges that the Bush campaign had been making about Gov. Dukakis' patriotism. Lloyd Bentsen, asked whether there is a racial element to the Bush campaign's emphasis on furloughs, replied, "When you add it up, I think there is." Jesse Jackson, speaking in Boston, said "There have been a number of rather ugly race-conscious signals sent from that campaign." Some have gone so far as to charge that Mr. Bush's assertion that Mr. Dukakis is a liberal also has racist undertones. If that term is out of bounds, what form of discourse is not?
>
> The one serious question in this is whether the Bush campaign's attacks on the furlough program that freed prisoner Willie Horton, sentenced to life-without-parole, are an appeal to racism. You can believe that the importance of this topic was greatly overstated and that the "lessons" drawn from it were demagogic and extravagantly sinister without accepting its use as the basis for a charge of racism against Mr. Bush. To begin with, the Bush campaign wasn't the first to raise the furlough issue against Gov. Dukakis; Sen. Albert Gore was, in an April 1988 debate in New York. The Bush campaign has done some disgusting things in this campaign. But the facts are that

Massachusetts is the only state that furloughed prisoners
sentenced to life without parole, and that for 11 years Mr.
Dukakis supported that policy and resisted attempts to end
it. It may or may not be relevant to stress that, but it isn't
racist.

George Bush and Roger Ailes were not responsible for the
Willie Horton ad. But the media accused them so many times of
producing the ad that many people eventually believed it was true.
If you print and air something often enough, and if you repeat it
with sufficient gall, guile, and gravity, that is what happens. In the
media version of the truth, Roger Ailes orchestrated the race-
baiting campaign that turned the election for George Bush—while
Bush stood and eagerly watched it happen. What pure crap. This
form of distortion later became an issue in several other campaigns
in which Ailes served as consultant.

The role of campaign consultants was again absurdly empha-
sized in the 1993 gubernatorial election in New Jersey. The incumbent governor, Jim Florio, a Democrat, hired political whiz
James Carville to energize his lagging campaign effort. Intrepid
challenger Christine Whitman, a Republican, signed up the controversial but equally successful Ed Rollins to manage her campaign. The media—not the candidates or the public—billed the
race as a battle of the titans. They were talking about Carville and
Rollins, not Florio and Whitman. Hell, the media hardly paid
attention to the candidates—one of whom, after all, was going to
lead the Garden State when the whole thing was over. The real
news, in the press's view, was whether Carville or Rollins would
emerge victorious. Again, it was the old game of win or lose—
except this time the game was played by substitutes from the
bench.

Whitman won the race that really mattered, but you barely
would have known it by studying the news coverage. In the
media's presentation of this campaign, Rollins vanquished
Carville, thus becoming the toast of the Washington political
world.

Oh, how quickly things do change! After the campaign, Rollins was a guest at the weekly Washington breakfast hosted by Geoff "Budge" Sperling of the *Christian Science Monitor*. Now, Budge has a way of getting you to say more than you thought you ever would. I know! Rollins knows now, too. Rollins boldly—and incomprehensibly—boasted of his effort to give "walking-around money" to African-Americans in order to keep them from voting. The apparent idea was that black voters were unlikely to support Whitman and therefore it would be best to keep them away from the polls. The media were incensed—but not at Rollins. No, the person who got the blame was none other than Christine Whitman, the governor-elect. During the campaign, the media had portrayed Ed Rollins as being the true brains of the operation. But now that something had gone wrong—and gone wrong in a way that suggested racism—they quickly placed the blame on the candidate herself. Rollins, the journalists' longtime source—someone they had probably quoted without attribution for many a year—had given them a hook on which to hang the carcass of this fine, new, refreshing Republican governor-elect. Boy, what she went through! And of course, many of Rollins's "revelations" smacked of things often unfairly and sloppily associated with Republicans—elements of racism, buying elections with big money and unlimited contributions, and slick tricks. Rollins rather promptly recanted his extraordinary and dramatic claim, and not a single shred of evidence ever connected Whitman to any effort to limit minority turnout at the polls. As you can imagine, the story of her complete innocence received much less prominent play than the ones implicating her.

In the interest of real, honest-to-God objectivity, journalists must learn to approach stories without bias. Wouldn't that be encouraging? More and more these days, most stories are already half-written even before the reporter has conducted the first interview. This is especially true when the story is about someone in politics. Labels, value judgments, pegs, biases, and prejudices must be discarded before the hard work begins. That is the only honest way to serve the public's right to know the truth. What I am suggesting should not be all that complicated. The reporting of an election campaign should be a straightforward account of what a candidate said and did on any given day. The result would be pretty dry stuff, and I'm sure that journalists fear that such objective coverage would cause people to turn off the TV or cancel their newspaper subscriptions. What journalists must remember is that the purpose of their craft is not to provide entertainment. It is to share truthful news. Naive, I know.

The selective reporting of information can seriously warp the public's perception of an election campaign. A textbook example from the 1992 campaign was the great big fuss over Dan Quayle's remarks about the television character Murphy Brown. You will recall that the character, played by actress Candice Bergen, had decided to have a baby though she was not married and did not have a partner. In a speech in San Francisco, Quayle criticized the character for "mocking the importance of fathers by bearing a child alone, and calling it just another lifestyle choice."

Boy, were the media happy with that one. Journalists had been trying to get Dan Quayle since the day he stepped excitedly out of the crowd in New Orleans to accept George Bush's invitation to be his running mate. Whether reporting on his shopping trips in South America or his spelling of "potato," members of the Fourth Estate had always been patently unfair to him, and dismissive of him.

And then came the Murphy Brown comment. Well, that damn sure did it for Quayle! Never mind that Dan was making a perfectly valid comment about the way the entertainment business routinely plays down the importance of family and glorifies meaningless and glandular quickie relationships. The media came down on Quayle in full fury. The anti-Quayle news media and the liberal chiefs of the entertainment industry portrayed that simple, brief remark as antiwoman, anti-single-parent, anticompassion, anti-everything-decent. They also called it stupid and outright idiotic and laughable. If there ever was a distinction between the news business and the entertainment business, it disappeared right then.

But in this case, what the media didn't say was as important as what they did say. Only days earlier, my friend Carl Rowan, the syndicated columnist, had penned a responsible criticism of Hollywood glamorization of single parenting. He wrote:

> Let's face the truth. The births out of wedlock of a host of glamorous Hollywood personalities have removed the stigma from unmarried pregnancies.
>
> . . . When widely watched sitcoms bore in on a devastating social problem, the producers ought to ask what purpose they have in mind other than getting high ratings. They ought to ask what message they are sending to young women.
>
> Are we supposed to just laugh, or find something of enduring morality in a "pro-choice," slightly promiscuous newswoman refusing to have an abortion? Are we supposed to accept the implication that lectures about sexual morality are meant only for poor females, not those with bank accounts large enough to pay for the consequences of indiscretions?
>
> CBS must be free to air *Murphy Brown* or any other sitcom. Thoughtful people must exercise their freedom to say that this "baby" plot is a bummer that will project a lot of gullible girls into almost-fatal sexual encounters.

Now, Carl Rowan is not exactly an archconservative! On the contrary, he is one bright, tough, opinionated, powerful liberal advocate. Nobody remembered any of that in the heat of the moment. More recently, NBC reporter Betty Rollins, in a report aired on the *Nightly News,* brought forth legitimate criticism of Hollywood's treatment of single parenting and unwed mothers. Where was the anguished outcry when Carl Rowan criticized Hollywood? Where was the hostile reaction when Betty Rollins made the same point? There wasn't a whit, because the people making the comments in both instances were members of the media. Dan Quayle, on the other hand, was (in the media's skewed view) this easily stereotyped, banjo-eyed, feather-light, country-clubbing, draft-dodging, white elitist. Such unmitigated horseshit.

Later, people in the entertainment business gleefully joined in the Quayle-bashing. First, during an Emmy Awards program televised nationwide, one snide, cruel, and mocking entertainer after another stepped forward to ridicule the vice president. Hollywood producers took time from the festivities to describe the horrors of twelve years with Republican presidents. Later that year, the very smug producers of the TV show *Murphy Brown* allowed Murphy to get in her licks, too. "Perhaps it's time for the vice president to expand his definition [of the family] and recognize that whether by choice or circumstance, families come in all shapes and sizes," she said.

I have another idea. Perhaps it's time for the liberal media and entertainment business to stop ganging up on people and start thinking about the values they portray and emphasize in their reporting and programming.

Yes, I said "liberal media." Irritates some, doesn't it? Though I am a pretty darn tough partisan Republican, I never wanted to believe that the media could or would be deliberately unfair. But they are. Forget, for a moment, that I am a Republican, and a friend of George Bush. Is there anyone among us who did not detect a strong anti-Bush bias during the 1992 campaign? Oh, yes, I know as I say this that I risk being labeled a conspiracy nut or a media baiter. But before you start calling names, take note of the numerous surveys in which journalists have admitted that they identify more with the Democratic Party than with mine. If people choose to be Democrats, that's perfectly jake with me. My problem is with the subtle yet crucial way in which their liberal leanings affect their work. And don't tell me they check their biases at the door. Sure they should but could anyone seriously argue that the overwhelmingly liberal media would somehow magically omit their political beliefs from what they write and broadcast? Please. I may be an ornery, old-fashioned Republican, but I ain't stupid.

And yet the media insist that I am, and that you are too. What galls this author, and I think most Americans, is that journalists instantly and defensively dismiss any suggestion that they are biased. How arrogant. How absurd. We all have biases. And whether or not we're aware of them, they affect everything we do. When journalists finally acknowledge and learn to set aside their own prejudices, the coverage of the electoral process will advance and mature.

Let American voters see the candidates, not the reporters. After all, no one elected the media—and probably no one would if he could.

CHAPTER ELEVEN

Saddle Up!

In the winter of 1995, I made the decision to retire from the United States Senate after eighteen years. The reason was simple: The old fire in the belly was not there. I had enjoyed a great run, but it was time to move on. I was sixty-four when I made the decision. I would not have minded another three years in the Senate, but the voters don't elect senators to three-year terms. They expect six hard years of service. I was not prepared to make that commitment, so I bowed out. I announced my decision on December 2, 1995, at a Chamber of Commerce dinner in my hometown of Cody, Wyoming. I quoted from Ecclesiastes ("To every thing there is a season"), made lengthy loving remarks about my dear Ann and family, and spoke warmly of the many Wyoming people who supported me and my work through the years. About halfway through my talk, I said:

> The media have an awesome responsibility in our land—
> and that is the word, responsibility. And they do not meet
> it well. While they were everlastingly babbling of gridlock,

we were passing a bipartisan unfunded mandates bill, a bi-partisan gift reform bill, a bipartisan lobbying reform bill, bipartisan work on clean air, clean water, safe drinking water standards, the Americans with Disabilities Act, GATT, the 1992 and 1994 Elementary and Secondary Ed-ucation Act, job training legislation, the Transportation Act, National Highway System legislation. There are so many of them, all passed by large bipartisan votes. But would you know that out there in the land, or inside the Beltway? You sure wouldn't.

The media are the only unaccountable branch of soci-ety. All the rest of us are held accountable. Me to you. Professionals, laborers, teachers, students—all held ac-countable. Yet any challenge to or criticism of them is eternally met by their drawing of the now tattered cloak of the First Amendment about their hunched shoulders, or crying out into the wind about the chilling effect.

People are getting as damn sick and tired of the media as they are of us. And when you have the two great en-gines of any democratic society, the media and the politi-cians, held in such abjectly low esteem, you have trouble in River City! It is for those of us laboring in both of those fine crafts to improve ourselves. The public surely won't do it for either of us. We readers and viewers must much more carefully sift and sort. That is our own per-sonal civic duty—for they thrive better on conflict and controversy, not clarity for their fellows.

You have now read that evening's comments about the media in their entirety. I spent perhaps three minutes of my swan song on the subject. That wasn't much, in a speech that ran to sixteen single-spaced pages and wound me up for seventy minutes!

A few journalists were present for the speech. Their reports made little mention of my remarks about my life and legislating. Instead, the accounts of my speech focused on what I had said about—you guessed it—the media. Who should have been sur-prised? This is a group of people whose job is to snoop around in search of news, and yet the moment they see me, the only thing they want to talk about is themselves and their cause. Strange business, journalism.

I had even more evidence of that when I got back to Washington. I was at my Senate office when I received a call from the publisher of *The Hill,* a weekly newspaper covering Congress. I have known this able man for years. He congratulated me on my retirement and said, "Al, would you please take just a few minutes to talk with our reporter? We'd like to do a story." I said that would be fine, but I added that I had already said my piece in Wyoming. Did he have a copy of the speech? "Well, yes, but we need just two minutes more with you," he said. For him, I obliged. I gave the reporter, a woman who uses the byline A. B. Stoddard, a generous fifteen- or-twenty-minute interview on a range of subjects, including Robert Bork, Anita Hill, immigration, clean air, and abortion. Then the story appeared.

"Simpson leaves with blast at news media," the headline said. The subheadline said, "Sharp-tongued Wyoming Republican to write memoirs [sic]." The first half-dozen paragraphs were about my comments on the media.

Isn't that always the way? My comments about the press were hardly the most important part of my night in Cody, but the media could not resist focusing on that part of the story. The story in *The Hill* is yet another dandy example of journalists' fascination with themselves—and their love of conflict in any form. Forty years ago, the renowned and respected journalist Walter Lippmann worried aloud about precisely this brand of distortion. Lippmann wrote, "When distant and unfamiliar and complex things are communicated to great masses of people, the truth suffers a considerable and often a radical distortion. The complex is made over into the simple, the hypothetical into the dogmatic, and the relative into an absolute." I can't imagine a better description of the present work and worth of today's big-time media.

Those in the media often fret and worry aloud about anything that might have a chilling effect—there's that phrase again—on journalism. You can't attend a media conference or forum without hearing that lament. But truth is, it's the media doing most of the chilling these days. They freeze the flow of good information by censoring, editing, selectively reporting, and manipulating the day's events according to their own biases and beliefs. The American public can no longer expect an honest, straightforward, and complete account of the day's important news.

Now sometimes, Americans don't get any important news at all. Instead of telling us what we really need to know—instead of telling us how and why Medicare and Social Security will soon go broke—the media give us salacious stories about horny Joey Buttafuoco and his underage Lolita, or about the hard-drinking, abusive John Bobbitt and his frightened, turned-off spouse who bobbed "it." The media today will use more resources to follow Michael Jackson and his estranged wife, Lisa Marie, around the world than they will to help us explain a crime bill or a health-reform package to the public. Journalists give us voyeurism, vapidity, vacuousness, venality, vulgarity, and vanity, but they forget about the only V word that really matters—veracity.

As I was finishing the writing of this book, I began to see many of my ideas about the media supported by some surprising people. One was James Fallows, Washington editor of *Atlantic Monthly* magazine and a commentator for National Public Radio and a close follower of my work on immigration. Fallows's 1996 book, *Breaking the News,* derided the media for their cynicism and arrogance, traits that have troubled me for decades. He wrote:

> Americans have never been truly fond of their press. Through the last decade, however, their disdain for the media establishment has reached new levels. Americans believe that the news media have become too arrogant, cynical, scandal-minded, and destructive. Public hostility shows up in opinion polls, through comments on talk shows, in waning support for news organizations in their showdowns with government officials, and in many other ways. The most important sign of public unhappiness may be a quiet consumers' boycott of the press. Year by year, a smaller proportion of Americans goes to the trouble of reading newspapers or watching news broadcasts on TV.

This is a loss not only for the media but also for the public as a whole. Ignoring the news leaves people with no way to prepare for trends they don't happen to observe themselves, no sense of what is happening in other countries or even other parts of their own town, no tools with which to make decisions about public leaders or policies. Evidently many people feel that these losses represent a smaller sacrifice than being exposed to what the news offers.

In response to suggestions that the press has failed to meet its public responsibilities, the first instinct of many journalists is to cry "First Amendment!," which is like the military's reflexive use of "national security" to rebut outside criticism of how it does its work.

Criticize reporters or editors for their negativity, and you will be told that they are merely reflecting the world as it is. Objecting to news coverage, they say, is merely "blaming the messenger"; *the press claims no responsibility for the world that it displays.*

The emphasis there is all mine.

The *New York Times* op-ed columnist Frank Rich, surely one of the most liberal and often nasty critics and commentators in the popular press, went even further than Fallows. In a column published just before the publication of "Breaking the News," Rich wrote that "even Mr. Fallows's picture of this crisis, bleak as it is, understates the case." Rich continued:

By Mr. Fallows's own account, traditional print journalism may be a "sunset industry" and TV news is already, to most Americans, the only news. Even if every newspaper devoted itself to explanatory 10-part series on the health-care system—and could survive in the marketplace by doing so—the effect would be nil on the toxic excesses of the electronic media that dominate Mr. Fallows's indictment.

That's because TV journalism at its most insidious has

less to do with content per se than with the market forces of the culture it inhabits. As Mr. Fallows documents, the driving principles behind TV news magazines and contentious panel shows alike are the same that guide the rest of Tv entertainment, from sitcoms to *Jenny Jones*. Journalists like Eleanor Clift and Mike Wallace and Sam Donaldson become continuing characters, with exaggerated personality traits as rigid as the cartoon figures in *I Love Lucy* or *The Flintstones*. The shows' "plots," which emphasize confrontation and glib opinion-mongering, are similarly formulaic, whether the topic is O. J. or Bosnia. Journalism is not only shortchanged but completely irrelevant. As one panel-show performer, Margaret Carlson of *Time* magazine, says of her job: "The less you know about something, the better off you are."

Rich concluded with these devastating thoughts:

Journalism is not better off. If the press's most visible figures on TV, many of them also representing the most prestigious brand names in print journalism, are indistinguishable from the most buffoonish entertainers and celebrities, the whole industry suffers a credibility problem that inevitably drives away the audience for all news. When you factor in the rise of tabloid TV journalism, the vapidity of local TV news and the unknown future of ABC News, the network leader, in the synergistic kingdom of Disney, it's hard to be sanguine about the survival of journalism as we once knew it in the mass media.

Worse, the medium is the message: as goes the news, Mr. Fallows concludes, so goes the country. A public estranged from the press is also disengaged from the institutions and news makers that journalists cover—and will understandably look outside the system for both information and leadership, whether to a Rush Limbaugh or a Ross Perot or worse. You don't have to be a media-basher—indeed, you can be a press-card-carrying media bashee yourself—to appreciate that the media are missing the story of their own role in compounding the alienation and anger that define the destabilized political culture of our time.

Amen, brothers and sisters!

A public estranged from the press is also disengaged from the institutions and news makers that journalists cover. Couldn't have said it better myself! The nation cannot be well served by media people who think it is better to be famous than reliable, and who consider it better to say something pithy than something useful. As I wrote this book, I was sure that some would read my criticism of the media and conclude that I am hopelessly partisan. I imagined that they would point to my dogged defenses of George Bush and Robert Bork and say that I am merely grinding an old ax for a few defeated Republicans. I am partisan. But I deeply believe my feelings about the press go beyond partisanship, and Frank Rich's column helps make my point. As Rich said, you don't have to be a media basher to see that the media's shoddy work is harming the democracy; if you're a thoughtful member of the media, you damn well know it too.

Howard Kurtz certainly qualifies as a thoughtful member of the media. Kurtz recently published another of his books of media criticism, this one titled *Hot Air*. In it, Kurtz gave serious attention to that little activity I have described that has bothered me for many years—the practice, by some famous journalists, of accepting big bucks to make speeches and public appearances. He called the phenomenon "buckraking," and he quoted me in the book.

The *Washington Post Magazine,* to its credit, published an excerpt. One of the moments I savored was when Kurtz attempted to question some of America's big-name, big-bucks reporters about how much money they get to give those dazzling speeches. Here are the answers:

"I'm not an elected official," says Fred Barnes.
"I'm a totally private citizen," says Chris Wallace.

"I'm not an elected official," says Gloria Borger.

"I'm not going to disclose it," says Al Hunt.

"I don't exercise the power of the state," says George Will.

"A private matter," says Robert MacNeil.

"That's private," says Hugh Sidey.

"I didn't do it for years, but it became more socially acceptable," says Michael Kinsley.

As is sometimes the case, George Will is quite right—he doesn't exercise the power of the state. He exercises the power of the media, a fearsome power indeed, a force with the potential to transform the nation much more quickly and permanently than most legislators could ever hope to do. As Ben H. Bagdikian wrote in his well-researched book *The Media Monopoly,* "Media power is political power." Nobody elected George Will (or Cokie Roberts or Chris Wallace or any of the others), but to use that as an excuse for unethical behavior is inexcusable. Inexcusable, but all too common.

This is the sort of hypocrisy that really rankles the American people, many of whom are as fed up with the media as I am. I wonder what it must be like for steady, hardworking journalists to know that people on the subway or the bus—or in the car next to their chauffeured limousine—are thinking, "There goes one of those arrogant bastards now. You know 'em—they just love to take pictures of a father holding his dead child, distort and belittle what went on at the city council meeting, and continually tear an issue to shreds with their own twisted personal biases." How must that feel to them?

Actually, I don't have to wonder how it feels, because we politicians are being judged in the same harsh way. I'm sure that when people see us these days, they may think all politicians are bums and crooks, an immoral, obnoxious bunch of greedy bastards whose sole mission is to cheat, feather their own nest, make a ton of bucks off of the poor taxpayers, and head home with a lifetime federal pension that would bloat a draft horse. The level of cynicism is so high now that when strangers ask what I do for a living,

I'm sometimes reluctant to tell them. This state of affairs is not good. When the American public perceives our two fine professions as being lower than whale crap, you have serious problems. Real problems.

So what is it we can do—journalists and public officials alike— to lift ourselves up in the eyes of the public? I have a thought or two, and I think it may be a good thing to churn around on 'em a bit. (Or it might end up like eating bear meat—the more you chew it, the bigger it gets!)

First, reporters and politicians must lower the volume on our rhetoric. Journalists could start by giving news, not opinions. Pick up any paper today and read a news column. You will find that most of what's in it is the reporter's "analysis," which is but another word for his or her opinion. Miss Gertrude Smith must be tossing in her tomb. As for politicians, we must stop engaging in raw partisanship solely for its own sake. These days, any senator who reaches out to the other side is too often instantly labeled disloyal, untrustworthy, a patsy, a wimp, and a traitor. Those who can actually do good work on both sides of the aisle can often lead a harrowing existence in the Congress.

Both professions, journalism and politics, also must do a better job of doing our homework. Let those in both fields educate themselves about the tough issues at hand, thus becoming more substantive and less manipulative. We politicians love to manipulate the press, and they love to manipulate us. The public knows what's going on. People are smarter than we think, and often smarter than we are.

Both sides need to do a much better job of dealing with criticism. Let's all admit that we are thin-skinned as hell. Politicians show it by saying, "I wouldn't sit for an interview with that asshole of a reporter again for all the tea in China," or "That stupid boob ripped my head off once and he'll never get the chance again," or "Why should I take his call? He's never written one damn positive thing about me." The press exposes its own testiness by stepping up the attack. "We'll find that sumbitch!" journalists say. "Where is he? Turn the hounds loose!"

The media must begin to make amends for their obvious mistakes, or at least own up to them. Why did Larry King himself—a respected member of the profession—have to threaten to sue *Washingtonian* when the magazine published a damn bunch of lies about him? Why couldn't the magazine simply admit to its errors? People are damned sick and tired of hearing the media say they stick by their lousy, incorrect, or false stories. Politicians must also learn to admit their mistakes. Some have. A few years ago, Ted Kennedy owned up to the anguish, pain, and agony of the Chappaquiddick tragedy. So he did it in a campaign year; it still takes guts to own up. I know. I try to do the same. I owned up to my actions with regard to Peter Arnett and the Clarence Thomas hearings. That was hard for me. But I felt I had to do it because in my gut it was completely wrong to shirk the responsibility. And I must always recognize that I can get in the habit of apologizing and then doing the same damn thing again. A childish cycle.

Journalists must admit that personalities are not really the news, and that the news should not always be about personalities. Many readers of America's major newspapers begin their day by reading the personality and gossip sections instead of the editorial pages. Why? Because that is where journalists can—and often do—hammer their fellow man and woman flat. To the reporters who write that stuff, I say: Let 'em live. Get a life. Find work with the *National Enquirer* or the *Weekly World News*. And to you serious journalists, I say: News should be news. It may be dry as hell, boring as hell, unexciting as hell. But don't juice it up—no O. J. pun intended. Just report it.

Hey, here's one—stop hunting people. How would you like to be hunted? How would you—yes, you out there in the Fourth Estate—like to have some brain-dead politician standing outside the back door of your home some Saturday morning, asking your eight-year-old daughter: "What are your daddy and mother doing in there now? When did your daddy get home? How did he get in? Was your mother crying?" And on and on and on. How would you like to have some hack politician ambush you with a microphone as you clamber off a plane, or stake you out after you have just finished your highly paid half hour on your talk show? I hunch you would not care for that at all. So stop hunting. Which mythical grand game warden issued your hunting license, anyway? You really can't imagine how stupid you look with that bazooka perched on your shoulder.

And quit telling the American people what they think. They know what they think: They think most politicians are jerks, and they think most reporters are jerks. Why wouldn't they? These people are not dummies. These are thoughtful folks who come home, snuggle the kids, snap open a suds, and flip on the tube or pick up a paper or magazine. And they are more than able to discern the truth for themselves. Do TV anchor people really think that the American people need them to analyze a presidential speech that they just saw and heard for themselves? Do journalists really think that Americans actually listened to all those "experts" who constantly offered breathless commentary during the Gulf War? Well, they didn't. So please, good media people: Stop telling folks what they think. You only speak down to them in doing it. They know it. You know it. They don't like it.

I earnestly embrace a fine idea proposed by Sheldon Hackney, chairman of the National Endowment for the Humanities. He sees the great divisions among Americans and believes it would be useful to have a national conversation about things—about greed, politicians, Congress, business, the media, race, ethnicity, immigration, the flag, and much more. Some folks think such a discussion would be a big waste of time. I disagree. We need to talk about all those issues and more. Let us really explore our deepest feelings about civil rights, affirmative action, and political correctness. And what about education today? How much longer will American parents put up with tenure and the tedium and mediocrity so evident in the public—and private—schools? How can we make our fine country hum again—in unison? Let us talk. But let us listen too.

And while the rest of America is talking and listening, politicians and the media should be doing the same. We ought to have more forums where both sides consider the tough questions. I promise that I shall be participating. As I write, I have just accepted an invitation from Marvin Kalb, the crack journalist, to be a visiting professor at the John F. Kennedy School of Government at Harvard University. My areas of specialty: legislating, politics, and the media. The name of the course? "The Creating of Legislation: Congress and the Press." A plateful of good discussions will also be taking place at the Kennedy School's Joan Shorenstein Center, the heart of the press, politics, and public policy studies program. Unfortunately, opportunities to participate in such forums are available only to a small number of persons. We must broaden the conversation. Throughout my political life, I have held town meetings so people could raise hell with me—or cheer me. The point was, I listened. If your jaws are always swinging, you can't possibly be listening. Media people should be listening to the public, too. The media barons should send their overworked and underpaid staffs out into the land to hear what the people have to say. Yes, yes, I do know some newspapers do that. But damn few.

Journalism schools should focus more attention on the terrible, trying ethical dilemmas facing journalists. Too many of our fine young journalists want to be Woodward or Bernstein—with or without good sources. Remembering the work of those two *Washington Post* scribes, today's journalists want to make their own names just as big on the byline. That's fine. Trouble is, these are often the same overzealous people who feed the public the line that everyone in public life is absolutely and utterly corrupt, contemptible, and cavalier. That approach may well make good copy. But it is not healthy and can be the virus causing the weakened body of a free press or an anemic democracy.

The media have become so large, so wealthy, so powerful, and so influential that they are now truly feared. Yes, that is the word, feared—feared by anyone who might have the misfortune to be seen as newsworthy. No one is afforded any privacy anymore—not a celebrity at a wedding (even his or her own!), not members of the Kennedy family out for a visit with friends, not Microsoft billionaire Bill Gates at a baseball game, not Clarence Thomas, not Anita Hill. I think the public has grown disgusted and appalled at the media's lack of taste, civility, and sensitivity. I knew an old grizzled ranch foreman who used to say of people he didn't much like, "That bastard must have been shit on a post and hatched out by the sun!" Plenty of people think exactly that about the media. Believe it.

Journalists need to establish some sort of workable peer review system to address clear abuses within their own ranks. Be accountable for what you do. It is certainly not enough to say, "If you don't like what we do, quit buying the paper." All of us in life, from attorneys to zipper makers, have some degree of accountability to the public. Why shouldn't journalists also answer for what they do? For all of the intrusive checking up on others that reporters do, they do damn little checking up on themselves. That needs to change.

Journalists ought to spend more time talking informally with decision-makers, the way they used to. There was a time when a reporter and a politician could feel comfortable just having a meal, sharing a drink, shooting the breeze, knowing that nothing would be repeated by either side. Those close contacts once inspired a degree of mutual confidence and respect. We all need to do more just plain talking to each other. Many reporters will read this sincere statement and counter in horror, "That sure as hell is not my job," or "I'm not some brown-noser," or "I didn't come here to schmooze these guys." And on and on and on.

Hear me: I'm not saying reporters should be cheerleaders. I'm not asking them to sell their journalistic souls to curry favor. I'm not suggesting they surrender their independence. I'm simply saying that they ought to help show an increasingly cynical, saddened, and disappointed American public what's right about this magnificent country. Let's talk about it. None of us can build up America while all around us are tearing it down. By now, the media have trained their microscopes on every local blemish, picked every state pimple, and scratched the scab off every national sore, to the point where our beautiful country is barely recognizable. We all yearn to recall what is good about the nation, and about us. My friend Ben Wattenberg, a journalist who follows the issues, does his homework, and pays attention, wrote a book a few years ago called *The Good News Is the Bad News Is Wrong*. The title still fits. Stop tearing down. Start building up.

And let me submit one final shard of verse that my dear grand-mother, "Nana," Mary Brown Kooi, would read to us soothingly and with misty-eyed whimsy:

> *There is so much good in the worst of us,*
> *And so much bad in the best of us,*
> *That it ill behooves any of us,*
> *To judge the rest of us.*

Sounds naive as hell, doesn't it? But I think those words help to remind us of what we're supposed to be all about. We all should be about the future of our children in this fine country. We should be about honesty and about patriotism. Corny, I know.

So where do we go from here? What should we do? Let me answer with some words I often use at the end of town meetings and speeches in Wyoming.

"Remember, you're not members of the AARP *first*. You're not members of the NRA *first*. You're not members of the AFL-CIO *first*. You're not members of the Farm Bureau *first*. You're not journalists *first*. I'm not a politician *first*. We are each citizens of the United States of America *first*. And if we've forgotten that, we're in for a heap of trouble. I'm ready to help make this great country even greater. Who'll help? It might well be exciting—and even fun! And after all you've got nothing to lose—but your country."

It's pretty simple, really: Let's start patting ourselves on the back. Let's be proud of this rugged young country. Let us remember it is the finest and fairest and freest country on the face of our globe. And it's all right to say it is the only country on earth founded on a belief in God. The world knows it. The brightest and best of every other country try desperately to come here. The true story of America is well known around this planet. It's a crying shame we don't tell it more to ourselves—and to our children and grand-children.

There is still time. Saddle up! Start!

INDEX

Index 269

Squires, Bob, 21, 238
Stafford, Bob, 64
Stanford Daily, 57–58, 89
Stanford University Hospital, 57
Stevens, Ted, 94–95
Stoddard, A. B., 250
subpoenas, 58–59
Supreme Court, U.S., 9, 57–58, 104–106,
    171

tabloids, 103
taxes, 80–81, 156–158
television, 5, 25–27, 34, 180–181, 234, 244–
    246, 252–254
Temple, Joe, 34
Tennessee Tombigbee Waterway, 55
Thomas, Clarence, 204–229
    as African American, 205, 206
    family of, 109, 129
    Hill's accusations against, 9–10, 54, 207,
        208–219
    liberal observation to, 208, 211, 212, 213–
        214, 217, 218
    media coverage of, 54, 96, 109, 129, 173–
        174, 204–229
    privacy of, 109, 206, 207, 214, 218, 228,
        259
    Senate confirmation of, 205, 208–212,
        217, 228–229
    Simpson's views on, 146, 147, 212–213,
        216–217, 257
    swearing-in ceremony of, 223–225
Thomas, Ginni, 173–174, 223
Thomas, Jamal, 223
Thompson, Marilyn W., 152–155
Thomson, Keith, 24
Three Mile Island nuclear accident, 48–54,
    65, 185–186
Threlkeld, Richard, 235
Thurmond, Nancy Moore, 155
Thurmond, Strom, 64, 65, 66, 77, 151–
    155
Time, 130–131, 173, 187
Totenberg, Nina, 85, 211, 212–213
Tower, John, 202
"transient," 48
"trial balloons," 172–173
Trueheart, Charles, 200–201
Twain, Mark, 207

Union Pacific Depot, 36
Union Pacific Railroad, 35–38
United Farm Workers of America, 68–69
U.S. News & World Report, 117
Utley, Garrick, 235

veterans, 163, 165
Vietnam War, 123–124, 125, 126
Village Voice, 103

Wallace, Chris, 184, 254
Wallop, Malcolm, 40–41, 54, 151
Wall Street Journal, 71, 73–74, 108, 164
Walsh, Lawrence, 182
Warren, Earl, 208
Warren, Francis E., 68
Washingtonian, 257
Washington Post, 3–4, 5, 71, 84, 85, 88–96,
    100, 126–132, 136–138, 145, 147,
    151–152, 154, 157, 183, 196, 197,
    198, 200, 218, 220, 221, 224–225,
    232, 241
Washington Post Magazine, 254–255
Washington Press Club, 84
Watergate scandal, 182, 199
Watt, James G., 25
Wattenberg, Ben, 260
"W" Club, 18
Webster, David, 129
Westmoreland v. *CBS,* 106
White, Byron, 58, 171, 223
White House Correspondents Dinner, 142–
    143
Whitman, Christine, 242–243
Will, George, 255
Williams, Pete, 33, 123
Williams, Walter, xiii–xiv, 10
Wood, Kimba, 172–174
Woodward, Bob, 153, 199, 259
Wyoming:
    budget of, 33
    constitution of, 29
    media coverage in, 25–26, 30–34, 35, 37,
        109–110, 163–164, 225–226
    public lands in, 16
    railroad in, 35–38
    state legislature of, 28–29, 40
    Supreme Court of, 29
    trucking business in, 80–81
    voters of, 42
Wyoming, University of, 17, 18–21, 30,
    34, 107
Wyoming Press Association, 109–110,
    112
Wyoming State Tribune, 33
Wyoming Tribune-Eagle, 30, 117–118

Yard, Molly, 221–222
Yellowstone National Park, 96–100

Zeder, Fred and Martha, 138